Acclaim for the work of
William Esper and Damon DiMarco

▌▌▌▌

THE ACTOR'S GUIDE
TO CREATING A CHARACTER

"Anyone serious about acting ought to read this excellent book and then run to New York to study with Bill. He is the real deal—insightful, generous, uncompromising, and endlessly inspiring."
—Stephen Adly Guirgis, actor, playwright, and artistic codirector of Labyrinth Theater Company

"I read Bill Esper's first book with total glee because it reminded me of all the guidance he gave me not only as a beginning actor but as a person hungry to live a full artistic life. His words not only illuminate the Meisner technique brilliantly; they also serve as a beautiful rumination on how to live a creative life. He was and is my teacher and spirit guide. Bill Esper is a national treasure and he has generously shared his wisdom and effervescent soul through these books, and I am eternally grateful."
—Three-time Emmy Award winner Patricia Wettig

"I feel so lucky to have studied at Bill's studio. . . . His teaching of the Meisner technique is beautiful in its simplicity, clarity, and honesty. I think about his lessons days after day, in every role. Bill's teaching is a gift that every actor should have, and reading this book is like being back there in his studio again (minus the F train, two buses, and the questionable deli coffee)."
—Mary McCormack

THE ACTOR'S ART AND CRAFT

"A fantastic, long-overdue exploration of actor training. . . . Esper is one of the most accomplished and recognized acting teachers in the United States. . . . An amazing tool and resource without being dogmatic or hampering." *—Backstage*

"A must-read for aspiring and established actors of all stripes. . . . The book is a nimble read, yet DiMarco's engaging prose adds a textured layer to some of the everyday circumstances encountered by Esper's students." *—Show Business Weekly*

"Whether you're a fan, a novice actor, or a seasoned professional, you'll find something to like in this book. . . . You feel like you're the fly on the wall observing the work of the master with his students." *—Armchair Interviews*

"Esper's book provides the reader a front-row seat in the classroom of one of our most important contemporary master-acting teachers." *—Theatre Topics*

"A veritable magnum opus on acting from a master teacher."
—Olympia Dukakis

"Every serious actor who dreams of becoming a first-rate artist must read this book!" —Calista Flockhart

"It's the best book on the craft of acting that I have ever read." —Mary Steenburgen

"Bill Esper changed my life. . . . After studying with Bill, I had the tools and techniques to deliver great performances regardless of talent and inspiration, even if I wasn't in the mood. His method delivers consistent results." —Tonya Pinkins

"The time I spent studying under Bill has been invaluable. He helped me find a road map to my craft that has stayed with me along my journey as an actor. I am forever grateful to Bill for the wisdom and expertise he has shared." —Dulé Hill

"The essence of this book is like William Esper himself: kind/clear, caring/generous, passionate/graceful, brilliant/profound. Inspiring. Invaluable." —Jeff Goldblum

"This book is a wonderful journey into Bill's process. It gives the novice and even the veteran actor a vocabulary and guidelines on how to solve the acting problems that any text presents." —Sam Rockwell

THE ACTOR'S GUIDE TO CREATING A CHARACTER
▮▮▮▮

WILLIAM ESPER AND DAMON DiMARCO

WILLIAM ESPER is considered one of the world's foremost experts on the subject of Professional Actor Training. He is a graduate of Case Western Reserve University and the Neighborhood Playhouse School of the Theatre in New York City, where he worked closely with legendary teacher Sanford Meisner for seventeen years. Bill served as associate director of the Playhouse's Acting Department from 1973 to 1976. He founded the William Esper Studio in 1965 and the Professional Actor Training Program at Rutgers University's Mason Gross School of the Arts in 1977. These two schools are renowned for routinely contributing actors of the highest quality to the international stage and screen.

A short list of Bill's more visible former students includes Kim Basinger, Kathy Bates, Jennifer Beals, Larry David, Kristin Davis, Kim Delaney, Aaron Eckhart, Calista Flockhart, Peter Gallagher, Jeff Goldblum, Glenne Headly, Patricia Heaton, Dulé Hill, William Hurt, Christine Lahti, Wendie Malick, John Malkovich, Gretchen Mol, David Morse, Timothy Olyphant, Tonya Pinkins, Molly Price, Sam Rockwell, Tracee Ellis Ross, Richard Schiff, Michele Shay, Paul Sorvino, Mary Steenburgen, Patricia Wettig, and Dean Winters.

Bill was voted New York City's Best Acting Teacher in the *Backstage* poll for 2006, 2007, and 2008. (In 2009, *Backstage* dropped the Best Acting Teacher category, probably because the poll's results were a foregone conclusion.) He has served as a member of the National Board of the National Association of

Schools of Theatre and as a vice president and board member of the University Resident Theatre Association. The Screen Actors Guild Conservatory honored Bill with a Certificate of Achievement for his service to the profession. In 2011, he received the Association for Theatre in Higher Education (ATHE)'s Lifetime Achievement in Academic Theatre Award, and he has received many other awards and honors. In 2013, he was inducted into the College of Fellows of the American Theatre. Bill's first book, *The Actor's Art and Craft*, written with Damon DiMarco, was published by Anchor Books in 2008.

DAMON DIMARCO earned his master of fine arts degree from the Rutgers University Mason Gross School of the Arts under Bill Esper's tutelage. He has acted on stage, screen, and television, and he has taught acting and directing on the faculty of Drew University, as well as privately. Damon is the author of *Tower Stories: An Oral History of 9/11; Heart of War: Soldiers' Voices from the Front Lines of Iraq; My Two Chinas: The Memoir of a Chinese Counterrevolutionary*, with Baiqiao Tang; *The Actor's Art and Craft*, with William Esper; *Shock & Awe: A Play in Two Acts*; and many other projects. He teaches writing at Drew University's Caspersen School of Graduate Studies. For more information, visit www.damondimarco.com.

THE
ACTOR'S GUIDE
TO
CREATING
A
CHARACTER

▪▪▪▪

WILLIAM ESPER TEACHES
THE MEISNER TECHNIQUE

WILLIAM ESPER
AND DAMON DiMARCO

ANCHOR BOOKS

A DIVISION OF RANDOM HOUSE LLC

NEW YORK

AN ANCHOR BOOKS ORIGINAL, APRIL 2014

Library of Congress Cataloging-in-Publication Data
Esper, William.
The actor's guide to creating a character : William Esper teaches
the Meisner technique / by William Esper and Damon DiMarco.
pages cm
1. Acting. 2. Meisner, Sanford. I. DiMarco, Damon. II. Title.
PN2061.E88 2014   792.02'8—dc23   2013042480

Anchor Trade Paperback ISBN: 978-0-345-80568-3
eBook ISBN: 978-0-345-80569-0

Book design by Joy O'Meara

www.anchorbooks.com

Printed in the United States of America
10 9 8 7 6 5 4 3 2 1

For Suzanne,

Michael, and Shannon.

As always.

CONTENTS

INTRODUCTION

▌▐▐▌

PATRICIA HEATON

William Esper saved my life.

Having graduated (just) from Ohio State University with a very hasty BA in Theater and having no idea of how to "do" acting, I ventured off to New York to try to figure it out. I wasted time and money lurching from class to class, never finding a teacher who had a cohesive, reliable method that would give me the tools to harness what I thought I might be capable of.

I remember one class in particular, filled with a lot of models, where the goal was to work up some emotion. One very pretty young woman stood awkwardly onstage, twisting her fingers together, while the teacher kept asking her to think of something sad. Nothing. "Anything at all that was sad for you." Awkward giggle, then nothing. "Like maybe a boyfriend broke up with you?" Nothing. Then a (dim) lightbulb went on in her head. "I had a cat that died . . . that was saahd."

Hmm.

I now know the problem with this class. It wasn't just that there was no particular technique being taught; the greater sin was that the teacher was trying to get his students to go for a "result."

If you're new to acting, let me help you—never go for the "result." Working in this fashion produced a number of very embarrassing scene studies for me. I'd be in my seat waiting for my turn, trying to think of something "saahd" so that I would be sure to cry real tears when I got to that one particular point in the scene where some emotion was required. In one case, after I had huffed and puffed my way through a scene from *The Children's Hour,* the teacher shook his head and said, "What were you DOING?!" I yelled back, "Why didn't you STOP me?!" Disaster.

I was desperate. I didn't know what the hell I was doing. The very few auditions I managed to scare up were going badly. And the thought of moving back to Ohio with my tail between my legs was unacceptable. It was Act or Die—but who was going to help me?

When I heard about a class that was almost impossible to get into, I instinctively knew that I needed to be there. It was the William Esper Studio, and though I didn't know anything about the Meisner Technique, or Bill, something told me this was the answer to my problem.

I left a number of pestering messages until I got an interview. I sat in Bill's tiny office on the second floor of a building on Seventh Avenue that also housed the best slice-for-a-dollar in New York City. Bill's office was small and cramped, and he was disarmingly sweet and gentle. We bonded a bit over our shared Cleveland roots, and I expressed my frustration at not finding the right acting class. He told me his class was full, but that I could study with his assistants and sit in on his class until someone dropped out. He gently assured me that someone always drops out. Hmm . . . a little scary . . .

I was a bit disappointed to have to be an alternate, but I soon realized that being a safe distance from the proceedings allowed me to learn the rules by observing them, not breaking them. One of Bill's rules was that there was no legitimate excuse for missing his class. None. If your parent died, you better go directly to class from the funeral, and bring the death certificate with you just to prove it was legit. Bill wasn't there to fool around, or waste his enormous gifts on students who weren't one hundred percent committed, because he knew how hard our business is and that only total dedication would do.

One day, we saw how serious Bill was about attendance. In class, we all sat in chairs on risers at the end of the room. Bill's office was at the other end, and a student asked Bill if he could speak to him privately before we started. We watched them both walk into Bill's office, and a few minutes later our eyes widened as we heard the normally soft-spoken teacher thunder from behind the closed door. *"Get out! Get out of my class! And don't come back!"*

The student, a tall, handsome, well-muscled specimen, was beet red in the face, and he hurriedly left the building. Bill was red-faced, too, breathing heavily as he walked into the studio and sat at his desk. He turned to us, spitting out his words: "His *manager* got him *theater* tickets . . . told him it was important to be there tonight because he was going to meet the *producers* . . . said he had to skip class because these guys were going to be *good* for his career . . . . His *career*?! Maybe he should learn to *act*!!!! *That* would help his *career*!!!!"

As we sat in tense silence, Bill stayed quiet for a few minutes, shaking his head in disbelief while waiting for his blood pressure to return to normal. Then he turned back to the class and said, "Okay, who wants to go first?" *Gulp*.

Another rule was that you never justified what you were doing if Bill questioned it. This rule was unspoken, but I learned it because I saw so many students break it. As I was an alternate, I got to sit and watch classmates defend their bad choices after Bill pointed them out. A few people seemed to think they knew better than Bill what they should be doing, and more than once

I wanted to shake a fellow thesp and say, "Shut up! You're paying him to find out what *he* knows, not to tell him what *you* think!" This is always a good rule to observe when studying with Bill, or any Meisner teacher, for that matter.

I did finally get a spot in Bill's class, and was well prepared, having spent a year working with his wonderful associates. I had great scene partners with whom I enjoyed exciting, invigorating improvisations. But in those two years of soaking in and trying to absorb everything that Bill was saying, there was one definitive moment that hit me like a ton of bricks. It was the moment that I heard Bill say, "You know, you don't have to DO anything. Just LISTEN."

Pow. This was the problem I had been trying to overcome for so long. I was never really listening to the other person. I was always a ball of pent-up emotion, waiting for the other actor to stop talking so I could do my thing.

Now, I'm sure some of you reading this must think I was a complete idiot, but that's where I was. After years of carrying the weight of being responsible for results, being given the permission to relax, trust, and listen was lifesaving.

Right there in class, I started to quietly weep. (Everything was dramatically magnified when I was in my early twenties. Thankfully I've grown out of it. You should, too, if you haven't by now. Save it for the stage.)

It was all finally falling into place. I didn't have to force anything to happen. I didn't have to dredge up some emotion and then hang on to it until the script indicated I should explode. I didn't have to go for a result. I could know my character, listen to the other character, and then respond truthfully and authentically. Because I had trusted Bill for two years, I could now trust myself.

▮▮▮▮

If you are lucky enough to get anywhere near William Esper's class, if you sit there and pay attention, if you carefully observe and attentively listen to everything he says and does, you will (assuming you also have talent) find that you have been given a gift that is priceless. You will be able to walk into any situation—a multi-camera sitcom with four days of rehearsal or a movie with no rehearsal at all—and be able to execute your craft.

It can take a while to internalize all the knowledge you gain during those two years, and the only way to really master your craft is to continually practice it whenever and wherever you can, making mistakes, suffering failures, and conquering your personal issues that might be getting in the way. Once you start making a living as an actor, you will find yourself in situations. Auditions where no one seems to be paying attention to you. Sixteen-hour shooting days where you finally get your coverage at four a.m.— with a stand-in! Doing a scene in 90-degree weather wearing a winter coat and a wool hat. And in all of these situations, the only thing you will have to hold on to is what you learned in those two years at Bill's studio.

I would not have been able to navigate any of those difficult waters without Bill's incredible tutelage.

William Esper is eloquent and elegant, graceful and gracious, thoughtful and thorough. His profound care and concern for his students, along with his dedication to developing actors of depth, intelligence, and authenticity, is a gift to the world, and to me personally.

I consider myself blessed—and always will—to count William Esper as my teacher, my mentor, and my friend.

THE
ACTOR'S GUIDE
TO
CREATING
A
CHARACTER

PROLOGUE

"Ars est celare artem."
(Art lies in concealing art.)

—Maxim, of ancient origins, often
attributed to Ovid

I hit the switch on my voice recorder and perch it atop Bill Esper's desk. "I just realized there's something about the work that doesn't make sense to me."

Bill glances up from the page he was reading. "What's that?"

"Last year, we said that acting is living truthfully under imaginary circumstances."

"Actually, that was Sandy Meisner's definition. We used that as a starting point but defined acting a bit more specifically."

"Right. We drilled deeper into the term 'living' and realized that living people *do* things. They walk down the street. They read romance novels. They sing in the shower. They tell bad jokes. They go on blind dates, pay utility bills, bake birthday cakes, and so on. Which led us to adjust the definition of acting and say that 'acting is *doing things* truthfully under imaginary circumstances.'"

"I like that better," says Bill.

"So do I, but therein lies my problem." For a moment, I grope for the proper phrasing. "Let's talk about this 'truthful' part. It goes without saying that good actors must be truthful in their work."

Bill nods. "Nobody ever left a theater or cinema and said, 'The actors in that show were great! I didn't believe *anything* they said or did!'"

"Exactly. Truthfulness is so important to an actor's work, you spend the whole first year of an actor's training drilling truthfulness into him or her. Your exercises teach actors to always create from a truthful place, sourcing their performances from what is honest, real, and unique about them."

"That's right," Bill says.

"But that's the part where I'm getting confused. Suppose you're a pacifist by nature, but you get cast in the role of a warmonger. Or you're a shy woman playing an extrovert. Or a bon vivant playing somebody dour. What I'm asking you, Bill, is: *How can you play a character whose reactions are totally alien to your normal behavior, yet still remain truthful?*"

Bill's eyes begin to sparkle in a way I've grown very familiar with. This always happens when he discusses his greatest passion: the actor's art and craft. "That's a very advanced question," he says. "The answer lies in character acting, the very pinnacle of our art. *A character performance is one where an actor alters his or her native behavior so as to become unrecognizable from his or her normal persona, yet still be one hundred percent truthful.*"

"That sounds like a paradox. How is it done?"

"There's no way to tell you outright. Answering this subject becomes the entire second year's work. As it turns out, the class you followed through the first year will be starting their second-year classes soon."

"I'd like to tag along on those."

Bill grins. "I had a feeling you would."

"Who knows? It might make a really good book. Maybe a follow-up to *The Actor's Art and Craft.*" I aim my recorder's microphone so it points more precisely toward Bill. "Give me some background on what the second-year work is like."

Bill steeples his fingers. "Sandy used to say the first year of training an actor is like putting money in the bank. The second year is about learning to spend that money wisely. In other words, the first-year work lays a solid foundation of basic skills the actor will use throughout his or her professional career. These include how to listen and respond from your own sense of truth. How to generate a rich and compelling inner life. How to work unerringly off the other person. How to do nothing unless someone or something causes you to do it. How to source your work from your own experience. How to pin down the requirements of a role so you can freely improvise within a framework you've created."

"I remember," I say.

"But perhaps you noticed something peculiar about the first-year work: It was all about straight acting. *The actor used his or her true-life responses in the imaginary world of the exercise, so, technically, the actor was the character in those exercises.* There's good reason for this. We needed the students to explore their true-life reactions so they would trust those responses and work from them without fail. But make no mistake, they were playing themselves, and this is a limitation.

"Playing yourself—straight acting—can lead to great commercial success," Bill says. "Armed with the first-year work alone, many of my students have gone on to enjoy exciting and lucrative careers, particularly when they're handsome or beautiful or unique in some other way the business recognizes and rewards. Many movie stars have had great careers playing themselves over and over again, or giving the illusion they're playing themselves."

"What do you mean, 'illusion'?" I say.

"One might be tempted to think that actors like Cary Grant and Marilyn Monroe played themselves in all of their films. The truth is, they were playing screen personas that were carefully crafted to appeal to large audiences. Cary Grant always came across as heterosexual, when, reportedly, he lived with a male partner for many years. Marilyn Monroe's persona of sexy blond bombshell hid the much more real and fragile psyche of a woman named Norma Jean Mortenson."

"So they *were* playing characters," I say. "But they played the same character over and over throughout their entire career." I ponder this some. "You're right, that's sort of limiting, isn't it?"

Bill nods. "Actors who nurture a vision of themselves as true theater artists will want to push their talents further. They'll know that they won't be able to bring the greatest roles ever written to life using the first-year work alone. Stella Adler once said, 'The ideas of the great playwrights are almost always larger than the experiences of even the best actors.' *The greatest writers our culture has ever produced did not and do not write plays about you being yourself.* They write roles that define the human condition in specific and marvelous ways—and they ask actors to fill them."

"So that's the art of creating a character, and that's what actors learn in their second year at Esper Studio."

"Yes," Bill says. "Without an understanding of how to play characters, you can never tackle Stanley Kowalski or Blanche DuBois. You won't have the foggiest notion of how to approach Uncle Vanya, Arkadina, Hedda Gabler, or Willy Loman. And while we're at it, say good-bye to Shakespeare's wonderful gallery: Falstaff. Hamlet. Viola. Rosalind. Beatrice. Benedick. Great heroes like Henry V or great villains like Richard III, Iago, and Lady Macbeth. Some of these roles are centuries old, but they continue to resonate across epochs and national boundaries. I would argue that some of them have intertwined with the very fabric of human culture—and they're all character roles."

"I never thought of it like that."

"Few people do. But the truth is, if you want to be at your best as an actor, you have to challenge yourself with excellent material.

Rich ideas. Vibrant themes. Exceptional circumstances. Heightened language. Inimitable characters. These are what you'll find in the works of Shaw, Ibsen, Pinter, O'Neill, Mamet, Molière, Albee, and so on. Each of these writers demands that an actor collaborate fully in the creation of a living, three-dimensional person up on the stage. To do this, the actor must possess an abundant imagination, plus a set of powerful, honed techniques. Nothing less will allow him or her to rise to the challenge presented by great material."

"That reminds me of something you once told me the great pianist Vladimir Horowitz said. There are three things a musical artist needs. First, a disciplined, clear-thinking mind with an abundant and rich imagination. Second, a wide and feeling heart. And third, total technical command of his instrument. Would you say the same about character acting?"

"Absolutely," Bill says. "The principles are the same."

"In our first book, we talked a lot about how imagination and the wide, feeling heart are essential to the actor's work. You could say they're the focus of the first year of training here at Esper Studio. But Horowitz's third point—technical command of the instrument—that's really what your second year's work is about, isn't it? Techniques that allow the actor to create inimitable characters."

Bill frowns. "I want to be clear on this point, so I'll repeat it. *None of last year's work required skill at character acting.* The students worked on plot-driven scenes where they used themselves as the character. But the people in O'Neill, Pinter, and Williams behave quite differently. The things that happen to them in these plays are not a function of plot, but of their character. Take Stanley Kowalski. He finds himself in the situation he's in for no other reason than that he's Stanley Kowalski. It's in his personality. It's in his nature. Or take Macbeth. His character is utterly driven by ambition. Therefore, if you don't have any ambition or can't relate to ambition in some other way, you're better off leaving that part for somebody who's better suited to play it."

"Name a good character actor," I say.

Bill doesn't hesitate. "Marlon Brando. He was unquestionably talented, but his talent has often been misunderstood. Yes, he became an icon playing Stanley Kowalski in *A Streetcar Named Desire* and Terry Malloy in *On the Waterfront,* but those were two very different characters. Watch him do Emiliano Zapata in *Viva Zapata!* Compare that to the man you see playing Don Corleone in *The Godfather* or Weldon Penderton in *Reflections in a Golden Eye.* Brando was a chameleon. In every film he ever did, he was utterly different from the film he did before, and yet he was one hundred percent authentic. You believed what he did. You had to, because he believed it. I think it's fitting that he's still revered as one of the world's greatest actors."

"So when it comes to technical command of the actor's instrument, what skills are we talking about?"

"A great facility with language," Bill says. "Imagine doing a Tom Stoppard play without being literate and witty. That's like playing Beethoven on a kazoo; something would get lost in the translation, don't you think?"

I grin. "What else?"

"A good character actor must have a sophisticated command of his or her own physicality. I see this omission more often than not in so-called period plays. The curtain comes up and the actors walk onstage using twenty-first-century posture and body language. Yet they expect us to believe that we're in the late-seventeenth-century London of a Restoration comedy. Or how many times have I seen an actor playing Caliban with no ability to manifest his deformities, let alone appreciate how they might shape the essence of his character? Good character actors must have a chameleon-like ability to shift their shape, and it goes without saying that the same thing applies to their vocal range."

"Speech. Physicality. Voice," I say. "What else?"

"Good character actors have a deep curiosity regarding all matters artistic," Bill says. "They must be cultured. They should possess an interest in art, dance, music, sculpture, poetry, and literature."

"Why is that important?"

"Because art inspires art," Bill says. "This is a powerful notion Oscar Wilde espoused when he championed the Aesthetic Movement. I uphold it as well. *The more we study different mediums, the greater our depth of command in our own.* For instance, my son was cast in a play one time. During the first rehearsal, his director said, 'This play is like a David Hockney painting.' Well, if you don't know what that is, you have to find out. Moreover, you have to possess a capacity to appreciate what David Hockney says in his work."

"You're saying that character actors need to be educated," I say.

Bill frowns. "Not educated. Cultured. You don't need to go to college to be a good actor. Academia is not conducive to artistic development, because moving works of art are never generated from the intellect; they spring from another set of faculties. As I understand it, Picasso couldn't remember the alphabet in its proper order—but why should he? It had no importance to his work with paint, canvas, wood, and ceramics. If formal education is study, memorization, and intellect, then culture has more to do with curiosity, feeling, and imagination. Do you see the difference?"

"I do, and isn't it interesting? You mentioned imagination again. That word seems to walk hand in hand with acting."

"Actors are very special people," Bill says. "Think of an ordinary person walking through the woods at night. He'll hear something

scurry in the brush and he'll say, 'Aha. That's a small animal bur-
rowing down for the night.' He'll hear a spooky, creaking noise
and say, 'Huh. That must be the wind picking up. And that hoot I
just heard? Must be some kind of owl.' A normal person will exit
the woods in the same condition he entered them, whereas an
actor would come out in hysterics."

"The imagination is that powerful," I say.

"It is to an artist." Bill pauses. "Now that we're talking about it,
probably the most important thing a character actor possesses is
the sense of freedom he finds when playing other people. Good
character actors can't play straight roles; they become too self-
conscious. It's as if they can't find themselves interesting enough
or confident enough; they have to don some kind of mask in order
to present themselves to an audience. Sandy was like that. He
freely admitted he could never play a role without hiding behind
some character element."

"It reminds me of a poem by Emily Dickinson," I say. "'Tell all
the Truth but tell it slant.' The character actor is being himself,
but in a way that feels comfortable, within the behaviors of a different personality. What else will you cover this year?"

"The ability to make choices," Bill says. "This is an important
concept, and one of the biggest shifts students encounter when
they move into second-year work. In the first-year exercises, the
actors set meanings, time limits, and standards of perfection for
their activities. They knocked at the door with an objective and
answered the door with an expectation. They crafted relationships with their partners and created Emotional Preparations.
These were all conscious choices the actors made to provide a
framework for their unconscious responses. The exercises tricked
them into telling the truth by distracting them from interfering in
their own process.

"But now we must move deeper than that. To produce the deepest work an actor is capable of, the unconscious must be made conscious. The actor must make choices that create his interpretation of the role." Bill spreads his hands. "Making choices is the essence of character work, perhaps the essence of all great art. *Higher levels of creative expression can arise only from interpretation, and interpretation can be rendered only when the artist makes conscious choices.* When painters say 'I'm going to paint a sunset,' what they're really saying is that they will ultimately paint *their version* of that sunset. To pursue their vision, they choose which colors they will use, the angle and perspective from which they will approach the work, the degree of light they want to portray, and so on."

"So interpreting a character is really about choosing responses, many of which run against the actor's natural inclinations. The second year's work sounds like a very full plate," I say. "Also potentially more rewarding than the first year's work."

"It is," Bill says. "We'll also tackle the question of acting for different mediums. An actor might say, 'I want to spend my life acting in the theater.' Sadly, the theater doesn't pay very well these days. So we'll apply what the actor learns about playing onstage to working in film and television. The goal, of course, is to help the actor take on a sitcom as readily as he takes on Shakespeare, to feel as comfortable in his technique onstage as he does in front of a camera. I'm thinking of actors like John Lithgow, Philip Seymour Hoffman, and Kathy Bates. In my opinion, every actor should aspire to such incredible versatility. The wherewithal to apply your talents to several mediums dictates your ability to survive in the business."

"So how do we get started?" I say.

Bill nods at my recorder and smiles. "I think we already have."

∎∎∎∎

That is how my next journey with Bill began—our exploration into the challenges of creating a character.

Bill trained me as an actor, and I've been auditing his classes on and off for seven years, ever since our writing collaboration began. The narrative you're about to read combines my observations with Bill's decades of teaching experience.

If you've already read our first book, you'll recognize most of the students you're about to meet. By and large, they're the same group who completed the first year's work in *The Actor's Art and Craft,* and again it must be stated: These students are not based on actual persons; they're composites of students and issues that both Bill and I have encountered over the years.

And now for another disclaimer. It's challenging to write about acting. Bill and I selected this format because we think it's effective for conveying certain essential principles. We did not intend these chapters to work as a syllabus—more like a guide or companion to accompany work with a qualified, talented instructor.

The only real way to study acting is to practice, reach, fail, reach again. Learn. Laugh. Cry. Rejoice. Repeat the process. Go deeper. Repeat.

In acting, as in any art, the journey is what's important.

BILL'S CLASS FOR
THE SECOND YEAR
8 MEN / 8 WOMEN

1. **RAY**—A new addition to this class. Ray is a compact, powerfully built man, about forty years old, with a handsome face, thinning hair, and piercing blue eyes. There's something about his manner that suggests a man of the earth, someone who works long hours with his hands, like a farmer, a rancher, a carpenter, or a cabinetmaker.
2. **TREVOR**—A wiry young man with a contagious grin and a shock of coarse black hair.
3. **AMBER**—A pretty, blond English woman with a sense for the ironic and the absurd.
4. **VANESSA**—A petite African-American woman with a spirit that defies her diminutive size.
5. **JOYCE**—An older woman who worked for years as an actor in regional theater before taking time off from the business to raise a family. She has a direct gaze and an ironic twist to her lips that makes her at once endearing and formidable.
6. **DOM**—A slim, ascetic-looking guy with thick black hair and an open expression that is both alarmingly direct and vulnerable. He has large, dark, liquid eyes.
7. **QUID**—A lanky young African-American man with a perpetual pout.
8. **REG**—An African-American man built like Zero Mostel, with a pencil-thin mustache and a soft Southern lilt to his vowels.

9. MIMI—A television star from a 1980s sitcom.

10. TYRONE—A muscular Latino with a gravelly bass voice. Tyrone must sleep with a dumbbell in each hand. His arms are as thick as peanut-fed hams.

11. JON—A short, balding man with a round build, from Denmark. "My family," he says, "thinks that I'm dreaming. They tell me all the time, 'You'll never be an actor. Grow up. Get a real job. Wake up and smell the coffee.'"

12. CHERYL—A young woman from a rural part of Illinois. Very wide-eyed and sweet.

13. MELISSA—A tall, lithe woman with a dancer's physique and bright eyes that sparkle in a face that holds many secrets. She has a tendency to withhold her emotions.

14. DONNA—A woman in her late twenties, with dark hair and eyes. She left a high-paying job as a financial consultant to return to her first love: acting.

15. UMA—Think Kathy Bates in her thirties. Perhaps she is of Eastern European descent. Uma comes across as shy but fiercely intelligent. Her eyes are glistening flints beneath her black bangs, and she listens constantly, rarely speaking but always taking in.

16. ADAM—Has the stocky build of a lumberjack. Due to his whitish-blond hair and clear blue eyes, he appears to be of Scandinavian descent. But his name is Italian and he is, in fact, Sicilian.

ONE

WELCOME BACK—AND BACK TO WORK

"As you reach your goals, set new ones. That is how you grow and become a more powerful person."

—LES BROWN

Bill walks into the studio and the class falls silent. I let my eyes roam over the sixteen faces I see in the bleachers. Everyone looks excited to begin working again. It's been only four months since the end of the first year's work, but these students have changed. The effect is subtle, hard to put a finger on. Suffice it to say that these students seem like *clearer* versions of the people they were before. They laugh a little louder, and more readily. They smile a lot. And they listen well. They really listen.

Each time I look into a student's eyes, I see something new—or perhaps that's not right. Perhaps it's really something old, an original part of him or her that was there all along, but pushed to the back and hidden. Now that part has stepped to the fore. It was always ready. All it needed was permission to come forth and shine.

But there's one face I don't recognize.

Bill takes a seat at his table, which, like the student bleachers, looks out on the studio's playing space: two beds, some chairs, a table, and shelves full of odds and ends that the students can use in rehearsal. Bill opens his roll book and thumbs to a page. "Ray?" he says. "Where are you?"

The man with the face I don't recognize holds up a hand, and all eyes turn that way. He appears to be about forty. He has a compact build, thinning hair, and a plain, handsome face with eyes the color of winter skies that shift from blue to gray. There's something about his manner that suggests a man of the earth, someone who works long hours with his hands. A farmer or a rancher. Maybe a cabinetmaker or carpenter.

Bill turns to the rest of the class. "Everyone, this is Ray. He did the first year's work in another class here at the Studio. He'll join us now for the second year's work."

Everyone waves to Ray and says hi. Ray, who seems shy, waves back.

"So," says Bill. He closes his roll book and looks around the room. "Before we begin, I want to tell you a story from my distant, ignoble past."

The class laughs, and Bill smiles.

"I went to college at Case Western Reserve, which is in Cleveland," Bill says. "I had always wanted to study acting, so I enrolled in the program there, but my first year was disastrous. I was very young and, when I acted, I didn't have a truthful bone in my body.

"Fortunately, a woman named Nadine Miles was my acting teacher. She had once played on Broadway with Sandy Meisner in a production of Eugene O'Neill's *Marco Millions*. This woman was merciless with me. She kicked my butt, metaphorically speaking, up and down campus. It took me a while, but eventually I figured out that I didn't know much of anything about acting. That was the beginning of my education."

One glance around the room and I can tell that Bill has struck a chord with this group. All eyes are on him, the students rapt.

"So this is what I did," Bill says. "I went to the main branch of the Cleveland downtown library where they had a small collection of theater books. The titles all looked the same to me. I didn't know which were considered seminal works, which would make an impact on me, which were regarded as must-reads—I was like a babe in the woods. So I picked up the first book on the shelf and I started to read. When I finished that book, I read the next one, and the next, and the next, until I'd read right through the shelf. Doing that turned my work around. I can't say I became a great artist overnight, but I can say I began to appreciate what important art is about.

"It's funny how life works. Years later, I was studying at the Neighborhood Playhouse. Sandy Meisner assigned us oral reports on famous figures in the theater. Sandy felt then the way I do now: most actors don't have enough knowledge about the great artists who have preceded them. He assigned me to report on Edward Gordon Craig, and I already knew all about him. I had read Craig's books during my spree in the Cleveland library.

"Among other things, Craig was a set designer. He designed a very famous production of *Hamlet* that Stanislavsky directed featuring giant screens that shifted continuously in the background. It was a brilliant idea, but it wasn't practical. The screens were big and cumbersome. Every time somebody tried to move them, they fell over. After endless attempts to keep them upright, Stanislavsky, in despair, ordered them nailed to the floor of the stage.

"I confess, my report disparaged Craig somewhat. I compared him to another designer of the time, Adolphe Appia, who is credited with breaking away from the two-dimensional painted set pieces that dominated the late nineteenth century and constructing the first three-dimensional sets. Appia built environments that worked with light and shadow in ways that were more natural to life. His constructions were always practical; Appia never built a set that fell down. And by crafting a three-dimensional set, he was, in fact, granting actors the license to behave in three-dimensional ways. Actors could walk on Appia's sets. Climb on them. Sit on them. Really live.

"In my report I said that, in my opinion, Edward Gordon Craig was a dreamer, while Adolphe Appia was more practical-minded. But Sandy took issue with this. 'Aren't dreamers important?' he asked. 'Don't we need people who dream?' He had a point, of course. Ultimately, Craig fell short of presenting his vision of *Hamlet*. But as with all visionaries, his true gift was the ability to change our perceptions of what is possible, to push our horizons further into what we consider the unknown.

"I admitted to Sandy that the relationship between dreamer and pragmatist is often closer than we first imagine it to be. Dreamers contribute something essential to society and especially to art. In fact, I said, dreamers are more important than pragmatists; you can't obtain any far-reaching goal until you've conceived of it in the first place. Sandy seemed impressed by that. In fact, I think that was the moment that sparked our long collaboration. Years later, he would say to me, 'Do you remember the talk we had about Craig and Appia?' Of course I did! And—just so I'm being clear on this point—the whole thing started from reading those books!"

The class laughs. Bill grins, but then his face grows sober again. "Why do I mention this story? Because I have always hated dilettantes. I simply don't understand people who don't have passions, who aren't insatiably curious, and who don't want to know absolutely everything about their chosen profession. And of course this applies to you, right now. Because whether you know it or not, you find yourself at a crossroads."

Now the class grows sober as well.

"Not everyone is a character actor," Bill says. "The talent some actors possess lies in straight acting. They may be marvelous at it. Certainly, for many it's sufficient to get them work and allow them to have a career. Even if you're *not* a character actor, there's a great deal to get from this second year's work. Though I warn you all: The second-year work will push you to the very limits of your talent. Will that be a problem for anyone here?"

None of the students move. None so much as flinch. Bill appears satisfied.

"Good," he says. "Then let's review what you learned last year."

Amber answers. "The reality of doing."

Bill nods. "Practice the reality of doing when you work and you almost *can't* go wrong. What else?"

"Acting is really an improvisation." This is Adam speaking. "You learn your lines mechanically, without interpretation. You pin down certain meanings, then you set about rehearsing. Your scene won't happen the same way twice if you're working from moment to moment."

Bill smiles. "That was a mouthful, but it's all correct. Acting is most exciting to watch when it's a ping-pong game of impulses between you and your partner. If you lose the moment-to-moment work, it's like you've missed a swing with your paddle. The ping-pong ball flies off the table and the game comes to a screeching halt. Let me ask you: Where should your attention always be placed when you act?"

Melissa says, "On your partner. Or on your activity."

"Very good," Bill says. "God forbid that you keep your attention on yourself. There's nothing more uninteresting to watch. Trevor? Can you add something?"

"I think so." Trevor holds up one of his famous notebooks. Last year, he was always taking notes. He went through five whole notebooks before Christmas. "I wrote this down, like, a hundred times last year: *Don't do anything unless someone or something else makes you do it.*"

Bill nods. "I'm glad you wrote that down so often. It's one of the most important concepts in acting, and yes, it'll certainly come up this year as well. Yes, Dom? What is it?"

Dom tilts his head thoughtfully. "Everything has to be personal," he says.

Bill nods. "Could you more specific?"

"You can only work from things that really and truly motivate you. Like with daydreams, for instance. A fantasy that sparks behavior in me might not bring Melissa or Reg to life. Their fantasies probably won't inspire me. Crafting has to be personal. It has to be unique to you, based on the things that activate you and you alone."

"Very good," Bill says. "By drawing your work from the well of yourself, you create a performance which is not only truthful, but inimitable. We've all seen actors with no inner life. They're awful to watch, cardboard cutouts of human beings. You and you alone know the things that make you tick. Last year, you spent a lot of time using Independent Activities and Emotional Preparations to create an emotional life."

Trevor has started leafing through another notebook. He raises his hand again. "Bill? I also wrote this down a lot: *Be specific. Never be general.*"

"Yes," Bill says. "But what does that mean?"

"Things that are specific have meaning," says Donna. "Whereas general things do not."

"That's true," Bill said. "Most people walk through their lives without closely examining anything. They don't dig down to the heart of things, they stay on the barren crust. An actor can't afford to do that. In truth, nothing general happens in nature, so nothing general should happen in your acting."

Each student in class brings up a point that struck him or her from last year's work. Cheryl says she often thinks about coming to the door in the early phases of the exercise. She talks about entering the room and letting yourself stand there, open and ready to be affected by your partner.

"Vulnerability," she says. "It's everything when you're acting."

"Yes," Bill says. "No one wants to watch an actor who's wearing a Kevlar vest over his emotions. The actor's job is not to fancy himself superhuman. We must open ourselves to every moment and live it out fully in a way that audiences only dream about doing. Invulnerability has as much place in acting as a sledge-hammer has in the art of glassblowing. When you come to act, you must tear down your walls. Allow yourself to be free."

"Like a feather in the breeze," Reg says. "That was how you described it last year. Or a cork bobbing on ocean waves. Allow yourself to go in any direction the current takes you."

"Yes," Bill says. "Exactly."

Joyce recalls the proper way to play an objective. "You have to leave your objective alone. That made an impact on me. When I was a younger actor, I used to go after everything with such a terrible intensity. I thought I was being good. I wasn't. Intensity hurt my work, overall."

"Remember the story I told about driving to Chicago?" Bill says. "Nobody gets in their car and starts muttering, 'I'm going to Chicago! I'm going to Chicago!' You can't keep your focus so rigid. Just know what you want, then let it go. Once you do, you'll have all the energy in the world to concentrate on the highway signs and check your map and deal with the traffic and do all the little things that have to be done to *really* get to Chicago."

"It's funny," Joyce says. "That kind of approach works in life as well as in acting."

After some more discussion, Bill draws this conversation to a close. "Well," he says. "We could talk like this all afternoon, but there's work to be done." He pauses, regarding the class for a moment. "Everything you recall from last year's work is still valid. None of it gets thrown away as we continue. If anything, the skills you learned last year will be put to use more than ever in charac-ter acting. I'll give you an example."

Bill looks at Quid. "Suppose you're doing a period piece. You're playing a Christian who's being persecuted because of your reli-gious beliefs. Do you consider yourself a Christian, Quid?"

Quid snorts. "Not hardly."

"Huh. Well, in one of the scenes you've been given, the lead villain walks right up to you and slaps you in the face. I wonder, Quid. How would you react if someone slapped you in the face?"

Quid snorts again. "I'd slap him back, and ten times harder than he slapped me!"

Bill seems amused. "Why harder?"

"To make sure he won't slap me again," says Quid.

"What if he spits in your face?"

"I'd spit in *his* face," says Quid.

Bill shakes his head. "I see. But as I said, you're playing a Christian. What if the script won't *let* you strike back? What if the script says you turn the other cheek? That you do so cheerfully, even ecstatically?"

Quid looks confused. "I would never do that."

Bill shrugs. "No problem. I'm sure they'll find someone else to do the part."

The class laughs. Quid pouts, but then he collects himself. "But that's my honest reaction," he says. "And that's what we learned last year."

"Then you should thank your lucky stars there's a second year," says Bill.

Again everyone laughs, and Quid falls silent. He's thinking the matter over as Bill turns back to the rest of the class.

"This is the issue, you see?" Bill says. "How would you play a character whose values, reactions, and behaviors are grossly different from your own? Clearly, Quid has very strong feelings about getting slapped. But how could he work with himself so that he'd willingly, *gladly* turn his cheek to show the strength of his faith? How would he make turning his cheek his authentic, spontaneous, true response?"

Quid's still thinking about it. He finally shakes his head. "I don't know."

"Good," says Bill. "That's a good place to start." He turns back to the class. "We're going to take this slowly, using a version of the exercises you learned last year. By the end of last year, you were creating deeply personal circumstances that resulted in highly volatile behavior. But these first exercises will be simpler than that. I'm asking you to restrict yourselves to simple objectives when you come to the door. Maybe your TV blew out and you want to see the Knicks game, or you're going away next week and need your neighbors to take care of your cat."

Adam raises his hand. "Bill, should we craft a relationship for these exercises?"

"Yes. The partners can be friends, lovers, roommates, complete strangers, whatever you like. But again, keep it simple. And remember: If the relationship you craft doesn't involve cohabitation, what do you need?"

"A knock," says Vanessa. "Which means the person inside the room should have an expectation."

"Yes," Bill says. "But again—can I say this enough?—keep it simple. Maybe the expectation you're working with is that you've ordered a book online and you're expecting the UPS man to drop by and deliver it. Or a friend told you she'd drop by with the twenty dollars she owes you. You see? Very simple. When the two partners come together, the improvisation begins, and we'll see what happens." Bill pauses and looks at the class for a moment. "Why am I keeping these early exercises simple? So you can focus your full attention on a new and very important element I'm going to add right now: I would like each partner to come to the exercise with a Physical Impediment."

Jon blinks. "A what?"

"A Physical Impediment is a concrete, specific addition to your straight behavior. As the name implies, this addition should be purely physical—something you do with your body."

"Like a limp?" Adam says.

Bill nods. "A limp would work well, so long as you pin it down. By which I mean that every Physical Impediment must be carefully researched. So you must ask yourself: Why am I limping? Is it because I stepped on a thumbtack while walking around my apartment barefoot last night?"

"Ouch," says Adam.

"Ouch is right. But that's a different kind of limp than one you might get from pulling a hamstring at basketball practice. Or the kind you get when your sciatica acts up."

"Okay," Adam says. "I get it. This goes back to being specific instead of general."

Bill nods. "There is no such thing as a generalized Physical Impediment. You have to create the Impediment through careful study. Then you must rehearse your Impediment until you can do it at the drop of a hat and sustain it without any effort. Why is this last part important?"

Vanessa says, "Because effort would obstruct your ability to play out the improvisation with your partner."

Bill nods. "You'll find this is not so easily done, but yes, that's what you're working for." He calls on Melissa, who looks at her notebook.

"I just wrote down some ideas," she says. "Will any of these work as Physical Impediments? A strained back. A lisp. Tennis elbow. A hip replacement. Being deaf. Being blind."

"Those could all work," Bill says. "And I'm glad that you mentioned being blind, since I think that's an Impediment every actor should try. You can learn a lot about your physical instrument, specifically the power of your other senses, by exploring blindness."

Dom says, "What about accents, Bill? Could we consider an accent a Physical Impediment?"

"Accents and dialects could work," Bill says. "But with one

condition: The accent or dialect you choose should be done to a professional level of quality. By which I mean a level where you wouldn't feel embarrassed using this accent or dialect in a Broadway play, at a major regional theater, or in a film."

Dom scribbles something in his notebook and grins. "Got it," he says.

"Good," Bill says. "In a moment, I'll assign new partners. Go home and research your Impediments. Make sure you practice them separately, outside the work you do here in class and outside rehearsals you have with your partner. And welcome back. It's good to see everyone here again."

TWO

GIMPS, LIMPS, AND LISPS:
PHYSICAL IMPEDIMENTS

"The body never lies."

—MARTHA GRAHAM

The new student, Ray, sits at a table in the center of the playing space. He wears a bright yellow polo shirt with bright blue Chinese characters stenciled across the left breast. Ray has covered the tabletop with a plastic tarp to protect its surface and has set down a large bowl of water to which he's added flour. The result is a paste with the consistency of heavy cream. A black plastic garbage bag overflowing with shredded newspaper bulges on the floor by his feet.

Next, Ray pulls a handful of balloons from his pocket, the kind that professional clowns inflate and twist into animal shapes for bank openings and children's birthday parties. Ray puts a balloon to his lips, puffs his cheeks, and blows. A thin tube extends until it is three feet long. It is bright red, the color of cherry Kool-Aid. Ray ties off the open end and holds the balloon in front of his face, examining it with a practiced eye. Then he folds it and twists it to form a loop. Picking up a green balloon, he blows it long, ties it off, and twists it around the red one. A blue balloon follows. A pink one. Then another red one.

Ray quickly creates a cartoon chain of swollen balloon links. By the time he adds the seventh link, the chain is more than six feet long. Ray begins to tremble with rage. His blue-gray eyes flash with anger and his face deepens in shade, from bright red to purple. He starts to shout obscenities. I do not know at whom.

At this point, I'm certain of only two things. One: Ray seems to be furious. Two: I'm back in Bill Esper's Studio, the only place on earth where you'd expect a person to work himself into an emotional fit while playing with balloons.

Ray adds three more links to the chain before setting it down on the table. Cursing louder, he starts to pull strips of shredded newspaper from the black plastic bag at his feet. He dips each strip in the bowl of starch paste and slaps it on a balloon. Ray works quickly, quivering with rage. He covers one entire link with wet newspaper and is about to start on another, but a series of slow, measured knocks at the door interrupts him. Ray stops what he's doing and stares at the door.

"Go away!" he yells. *"Talk to my lawyer!"*

There's a pause, then a muffled sound from outside the door. The sound could be a person's voice. In fact, I think that it probably is. But it's garbled. Unintelligible.

Ray shakes his head, exasperated. He soaks more strips of paper in the bowl and holds them up. Paste drips all over the tabletop. "What did I tell you? What did I *tell* you?" he shouts. "Go away! I'll sue! I mean it!"

Again there's the soft sound of someone speaking. We still can't make out the words. Evidently, neither can Ray, because, furious, he slams down the dripping strips of newspaper and lurches to his feet. Grabbing a towel, he wipes his hands. "That's it!" he yells. "That's it, you son of a bitch! I'm gonna flatten you! *You hear me?!*"

With that, Ray leaps from the table, taking his towel, which he swings like a bullwhip. Livid, he charges the door. "I called the city housing department! Know what they told me? They told me to—"

He yanks open the door—and freezes. Quid is standing there, eerily still. He wears dark glasses and holds a white cane.

"Mister," Quid says softly. "I think you got me confused with somebody else."

"Who the hell are you, Ray Charles?"

With that, Ray slams the door in Quid's face.

This outburst is so sudden, so blunt, and so dismissive that several students jump in their seats in the bleachers. Ray wheels back toward his worktable. Muttering something to himself, he tosses his towel on the back of the chair and picks up his balloon chain. There's another tentative knock on the door.

Ray slams his fists on the tabletop, but this time he makes no outburst. Instead he hangs his head. Outside the door, Quid knocks again. Harder this time.

Ray's anger begins to fade. The color drains from his face and is replaced by a complex mix of emotions. He stares at the watch on his wrist. Then he stares at the door. His expression says, *I can't believe I just did that.* He's clearly wondering what he should do when Quid knocks again, and that does it. Ray's back on his feet, his fury rising once more, but something's different this time. This time he keeps his emotions in check, jerking them back like a dog on a leash. And this time, Ray is limping as he approaches the door with a curious crablike walk.

I glance at Bill, who's watching all this, frowning.

Ray grabs the doorknob and twists, opening the door. Quid is revealed once again. This time his hand is raised in mid-knock. He pauses like that, waiting. His head pans back and forth, positioning his ears to catch sound.

Ray doesn't seem to know what to do. He pauses, too. The two men stand there, frozen, on either side of the threshold.

"Mister?" Quid says finally.

"Yeah?" Ray sighs. "Look, I—"

"You are one mean son of a bitch, you know that? Anybody tell you that?"

Ray huffs and stares at his shoes. "Yeah," he says. "Look, I'm real sorry. See, you caught me at a real bad time and—"

"Real bad," Quid repeats. Slowly, he lowers his hand. "Uh-huh. You okay?"

"What?" The question takes Ray off guard. He looks up at Quid but quickly averts his gaze. "No. Yeah. I mean, look, I'm sorry, okay? I didn't mean—I'm just— How can I help you?"

"Don't call me Ray Charles."

Ray slaps a hand to his forehead and moans. "Yeah, look. Like I said, I'm real sorry about that—"

"You're white," says Quid.

Ray goes taut. "Excuse me?"

"You *gotta* be white," Quid says. "Call a blind man Ray Charles just because he's African-American?"

Ray fumes. "Hey, look. It wasn't like that."

"You're white," Quid says. He turns his head toward Ray. "You *gotta* be white. You got a white voice."

"Hey, why don't you go to hell!" Ray says.

"I'm already in it," Quid says. "This has gotta be hell if I'm standing here talking to a racist asshole like you!"

Ray sputters. "Hey, man! Who the hell do you think you are—"

"My name is Quid—"

"—coming in here talking like that—"

"In?" Quid says. "I'm not *in*! I'm sure as hell not *in*!"

"Well, I don't care what your name is—"

Quid is furious. "You see me *in*? I'm standing here in the *hall*, you asshole. That's not in, that's *out*—"

"—I want to know who the hell you think you are."

"You haven't invited me *in*—"

"What, I'm supposed to—"

"Your manners are shit. Were you raised in a barn?"

Ray's hands ball into fists by his sides. He looks like he's ready to strike Quid down. "You think I'm gonna invite you in when you insult me like that?"

Quid's head swings toward Ray again. "Insult?" Quid says. "Because I said you were white? That wasn't an insult, that's my *opinion.* Turned out to be correct, though, right?"

They argue like this for the next few minutes—a lively exchange that moves from funny to lacerating, then from obnoxious to outright appalling, and finally back to funny again. Ray becomes a ball of energy, flailing his arms and gnashing his teeth. At three separate points, he moves to throw Quid out, but restrains himself at the very last possible moment. The fact that Quid is blind seems to dampen Ray's ferocity. He steps back, fuming, each time, while Quid just stands there, still as a statue. There's something triumphant in his look. He seems to savor how Ray's come undone.

Finally Bill stops the exercise.

"Okay," he says. "Let's talk about this."

■ ■ ■ ■

Bill turns to Ray and says, *"Papier-mâché?"*

Ray shakes his head and looks to where his balloon chain rests, partially covered in wet strips of newspaper, on the tabletop. "Technically it's *carton pierre,* or it's going to be." He motions to a canvas bag that sits on the floor, next to the black plastic bag. "I brought some jars of prop makers' latex. As soon as the chain gets dry, I'll treat it and paint it to look like metal."

"Why?" asks Bill.

Ray sighs. "Falun Gong."

"I don't know what that is."

"It's a spiritual practice China has outlawed." Eight words into his explanation, Ray is getting agitated. "I went to China a few years back and made a few friends over there. You wouldn't *believe* what they do in China! The Communist government throws you in jail for practicing spiritual discipline! They even *kill* some people! Falun Gong is like meditation. Sort of like yoga or something. I don't know, I don't practice it myself. But it was like—I couldn't *believe* that, you know? To *kill* someone for meditating? I can't *believe* that!"

Bill nods. Once more, Ray is very upset. He is clearly a passionate man. Just as clearly, he's capable of putting that passion into his work.

"So you're making this chain to do what?" Bill asks.

"Tomorrow morning, there's a protest outside the Chinese consulate. The Falun Gong Society here in New York are going to demonstrate. A report just came out from Amnesty International. The Chinese Communist government arrested two hundred people in Beijing and beat them with batons for practicing Falun Gong. It's a crime! They beat them with *batons!*"

"So you're making a prop chain for a protest," Bill says. "That's good. That brought you to a full emotional life, but what's your Impediment?"

"I was working with shin splints."

Bill just looks at him. Ray begins to explain.

"It's what you get when you start running after a long time. Little micro fractures. They feel like your shins are being broken into tiny bits—"

"I know what they are," Bill says. "But you didn't have that behavior."

"I know," Ray says. "I sort of forgot. I was so into my activity, you know? Then I thought my landlord was at the door. He threatened to evict me because I haven't paid rent, but my shower's been busted for over a month and he won't fix it. So I got up to go to the door and give him a piece of my mind and I was so—I don't know. Upset. I forgot all about the shin splints."

"You can't forget," Bill says.

"I know." Ray hangs his head. "I was just so *into* what I was doing."

Bill shakes his head. "I'm sorry, I don't accept that. It's one of the reasons I asked you to keep these exercises simple. What if you were in a show? Would you get so *into* what you were doing that you'd forget your exits and entrances? Or your lines, for that matter? What if you had a stage combat sequence? Would you get so *into* what you're doing that you'd forget all the choreography and safety measures you'd worked out with the fight master?"

Ray gets it. He shakes his head, embarrassed.

Bill turns to the class. "Working with Physical Impediments *seems* simple. I asked you to come into class with a sore leg. A busted hand. A nasty case of rheumatism in your hips. Simple, right? Be careful. You have to practice Physical Impediments fiercely and diligently. Working with your Impediment must become like second nature to you."

Donna raises her hand. "Bill, I had shin splints once. It was funny. The pain came and went. That happens with injuries sometimes and I thought maybe that's what Ray was playing: intermittent pain. Could that be part of our crafting?"

Bill shakes his head. "You have to ask yourself, as an actor: What would create the best performance? Shin splints that come and go with no explanation at all? Or a case that's nearly crippling, so bad you can barely get up from the table?"

Bill turns to the rest of the class. "Remember this and remember it well: There's truth, and then there's what's theatrical. Never confuse the two. Andy Warhol once shot a film called *Sleep*. It showed a man sleeping for almost five and a half hours. Truth?

Sure. Theatrical? Hardly. We don't go to the theater to watch reality. Why on earth would we do that? Reality can be boring. We go to the theater to watch *heightened* reality. Drama. Unusual circumstances. Performing the truth for the sake of truth doesn't always belong onstage."

Cheryl raises her hand. "Then why did we work so hard last year to ground ourselves in truthfulness?"

"Because," Bill says, "like I said: There's room onstage for what's theatrical. But there's *never* room onstage for that which isn't grounded in truth."

I turn and look into the bleachers. The students are all taking notes.

Bill thinks for a moment, then turns to Quid, who's still wearing his dark glasses.

"You're blind?" Bill says.

Quid nods. "I am."

Bill sighs. "Everybody has trouble with the blind Impediment. The problem is, you're trying too hard to see, so it isn't working. You understand?"

Quid thinks about it. "No. Not really."

"How do you create the illusion of being blind?" Bill asks.

"I thought I could do it with just the dark glasses. Lots of blind people wear them."

"That's true," Bill says. "And just so I'm clear: It's not your glasses I have a problem with. It's your sensory work."

"My what?"

Bill turns to the class. "Last class, did I mention that being blind is something that every actor should work with?"

Amber checks her notes. "You did."

"There's a number of reasons for this," Bill says. "First of all, it's very common for actors to force their visual contact. Many actors will look right at you because they want the world to look right at them. It's a very bad habit, a false intensity. It makes the actor look strained. Playing blind nips that condition right in the bud. Or at least it usually does."

He turns back to Quid. "You were looking right at Ray during your exercise, did you know that? Tilting your head toward him."

Quid takes off the glasses and blinks. "I had my eyes closed behind the glasses."

"But you still didn't have a blind person's sensuality. A blind person wouldn't tilt his head toward someone he's speaking to, wouldn't face the person head on. Do you know who Stevie Wonder is?"

Quid grins. "Of course I do."

"Did you ever see Stevie Wonder accept a music award? It's very interesting. Pay attention the next time it happens. They lead Stevie Wonder up to the podium. They put the award in his hands. Does he look at the award? Not at all. Not once. He doesn't even bow his head toward it. Why should he? He's blind, and has been since shortly after birth. He could hold the award up in front of his nose, it wouldn't mean a thing to him. But watch how he touches it. Hefts it. Fondles it. He wants to know how the award *feels* in his hands. He reads every curve and every notch with the tips of his fingers. That's the way a blind man interacts with the world, through his sense of touch, his hearing, his sense of smell.

"Blind people rely on their other senses more than you and I do. This isn't some old wives' tale. They've done studies on people who've lost their sight. Scientists have scanned their brains and mapped them using advanced technology. You know what they've found? The part of the brain that handles vision starts to shrink when a person loses his or her sight. At the same time, the parts of the brain that handle hearing and smell and taste and touch will actually start to enlarge. The brain begins to compensate. A blind person's hearing is literally more acute than that of a sighted person."

Bill turns back to the class. "That's why I say that playing blind is a very good thing for actors. It demands that you find a new level of sensuality in your work. Working with blindness will bring a new life to your contact with other actors. Being blind also demands that you be vulnerable. You have to give up. You have to surrender to the fact that you can't see what goes on around you, that you're physically defenseless. Most actors resist that kind of absolute surrender. Of course they do. Absolute surrender can be scary, but playing blind demands it. It's not something you can dabble in, it requires total commitment."

The class is writing steadily now.

Bill turns back to Quid.

"I think I mentioned this last year when Adam and Amber did a scene from *Butterflies Are Free*. It bears repeating. There's many ways to play blind. For today's scene, you put on a pair of dark glasses and closed your eyes. That's accurate. As you said, some blind people wear dark glasses. Therefore, your audience will get what you're doing. They'll get the convention.

"But a more interesting way to play blind is to keep your eyes open and focus your vision on the middle distance. That's what Keir Dullea did when he played Don in the original Broadway production of *Butterflies Are Free*. He also had the extra advantage of being onstage. That way, whenever he wanted, he could look up into the lighting grid. You won't see a thing when you look directly up into stage lights. It helps the actor who's playing blind create the reality of his Impediment."

Bill scratches his beard. "I'm told that Al Pacino chose a different technique when he filmed *Scent of a Woman*. Obviously, he kept his eyes open. But I hear he concentrated on his peripheral vision. The effect was very truthful, I thought, and I like the idea of this technique because it gives the actor something concrete to *do*. But I wonder. It seems to me that concentrating on your

peripheral vision might distract you from listening with the keen-
ness that blind people have. I also wonder if you could sustain this
peripheral vision technique throughout a full-length play onstage.
It's easier to do in film, where a scene lasts just a few seconds. You
let the editors work things out, to distill a final product.

"I've also seen actors roll their eyes up inside their heads as a
way of producing the blind effect. Personally, I've never tried that
one. One of these days I'll have to experiment with it. By the way,"
he says suddenly, and turns back to Quid, "you brought a white
cane. That's nice. Do you know how to use it?"

Quid holds up the cane and nods. "I tried it out in my
apartment."

Bill shakes his head. "You wouldn't use it in your apartment. A
blind person knows every inch of his living space, every millime-
ter. Blind people have mapped out everything in their minds. They
can go to the bathroom as well as a sighted person. They know
which drawer has the kitchen knives, how many steps it takes to
get to the ottoman. Where they left their house keys. Where the
postage stamps are. They can tell how much money they've got
in their pockets because they fold each bill a certain way to indicate the denomination. They can walk out their front door and
down the steps of their building and find the subway and get on
a train and ride it to Times Square and transfer to another train,
just like you and me."

"I've seen that," Quid says. "Blind people on the subway. I
always think, 'Man, that takes guts.'"

"But you can't play guts," Bill says. "To do what I've just
described takes a system, and that's what you play as an actor: the
system. The *doing*.

"Do what a blind person does. Count your steps to the street
corner. Turn right ninety degrees. Count steps again until you get
to the subway entrance. Feel for the handrail. Grab it. Start down

the stairs, counting steps as you go—there should be five. You know there are five. Turn left at the landing, ninety degrees, and grab the next handrail. Go down another flight of steps; this time it's longer—there's ten. Pull out your fare card. You always keep it in your right front pants pocket. Feel for the side with the magnetic strip. You can tell which side is correct because, in New York City, a MetroCard comes with one corner cut off, apparently for this very purpose. Swipe the card at one of the turnstiles. Walk through the turnstile, but follow this pattern: three steps straight, turn right. Now listen. Do you hear the train coming? No? Then wait. It's coming; you know it will be along soon. When it comes, you can feel the air change; the train pulls to a stop right in front of you. Climb aboard, but mind the gap where the car meets the platform. Be sure to step over it. Use your hands and steady yourself against the car as you do so. Step inside. You hear the doors close behind you. You feel the train start moving again. It's six stops to Times Square, count each one as you come to it. When you get to Times Square, you will start up a whole new routine, different from the one you just did. This next one is for changing trains."

I look around. The class has stopped writing. They're staring at Bill, a bit spellbound. What he says makes sense. The methodical, almost inexorable precision he's outlined has deeply impressed the class.

Bill checks his watch.

"We'll talk more about this later. For now, I'm going to insist that everyone try a blind Impediment before we move on to our next section. Understood?" When everyone nods, Bill looks down at his roll book. It seems like he's about to call the next pair of partners, but he stops and looks back up at Quid. "By the way. Why did you come to the door?"

Quid shrugs. "I just moved in down the hall and someone's been playing their music too loud. It happens every night, and

I thought he might be the guy doing it." He points at Ray. "So I wanted to drop by, ask him if he's the culprit, and get him to agree to keep the music down."

Bill nods. "I like that. It's a simple objective, that's just what I asked for." He turns to the class. "No earth-shattering objectives, please. For now, at any rate." He looks back down at his roll book. "Who's next?"

■ ■ ■ ■

Amber and Vanessa have just finished working together.

"I'm sorry," Bill says. "You just didn't catch it."

He's speaking to Amber. She was working with being deaf as an Impediment.

"It's so difficult!" Amber says. She throws up her hands. "No matter how hard I pretend, I still hear things."

Bill appears stricken. "Pretend?" he says. "*Pretend?* There's no technique in *pretend.* What were you doing the whole first year, twiddling your thumbs in the back row? You can't pretend that you're deaf any more than you can fake falling asleep. Playing deaf, playing blind, playing anything—it's all the same. *You have to use the reality of doing and give yourself something concrete to work on. Something that's active and real.* Something you can pursue that provides the *illusion* of deafness for the audience."

Amber looks disconsolate. "But I don't—I mean—I don't even know where to begin with that. It's like— Wait. What are you doing?"

All eyes turn toward Bill, who's still looking at Amber, though his face has gone slack. His mouth droops open, ever so slightly. At first I think his eyes have fixed themselves on Amber's face. But then I see that no, that's wrong. He's not watching her face. He's watching her mouth.

Amber gets it. "Oh," she says. "You're trying to read my lips."

"Nyats wight," Bill says. Reg is sitting next to him; the portly actor jumps a little in his seat. Without any warning, Bill's speech has gone gummy around the consonants. His voice has fallen into an oddly toneless cadence. He nods at Amber a little too emphatically. "I'm weading myoor lips."

The class has gone completely silent. Bill has perfectly caught a deaf person's speech.

"How long haf nyoo been deaf?" Bill says.

For a moment, Amber says nothing. She stares at Bill. I understand her reaction. It's a little eerie hearing Bill talk like this.

"How long?" Amber asks. I stifle a chuckle. The reality of this exchange is suddenly so awkward, so fragile, it is—in my experience—exactly what talking to a deaf person can be like. "I'm sorry, did you say how long?"

"Nyes," Bill says. He's a little irritated that Amber can't understand him. "Dats what I said. How *long* haf nyoo been *deaf*?"

Amber laughs. She can't help it. Bill's behavior has made her uncomfortable. She turns her face away from him, hoping to hide her nervous chuckle. Bill turns his head and tracks her mouth with his eyes.

Of course, I think. That's just what someone who reads lips would do: He would focus on the mouth. Unless Bill is able to see Amber's lips, he can't know what she's saying.

"I guess I never figured out how—"

"Mwhat?" Bill says.

Amber turns to face him again and forces a smile that is slightly defiant. "I *said*, I guess I never figured out how long I've been deaf."

"Well," Bill says. He throws up his hands. "Nyoo haf to. Bekaws dat tells you how yore speech will be."

"I don't understand."

Bill sighs, exasperated. Then he begins to explain. "Peepuh who

haf been deaf for a long toyme . . . deir thpeech thtarts to erode."
In the next breath, he switches back to his normal voice. The
effect is abrupt. "Deaf people can't hear themselves talk. This
becomes an interesting dilemma. Physically, they can produce
the sounds of speech, but they can't hear whether they're hitting
the consonants right, or the vowels, for that matter. If they've
been deaf since birth, they might not even try to talk. But if you're
playing someone who lost her hearing a month ago, say, or even
a year, your speech will probably stay intact, though it may have
begun to slip."

Amber nods. "So you're saying I should research all that. How
long I've been deaf. Whether I can read lips or not. What kind of
impact being deaf has had on my speech."

"Of course," Bill says. "I told you, it's a lot of work. But look at
what that work will do. The more you research, the more choices
you make, the less mythological your job becomes. Give yourself
concrete things to do, things that—if you focus on them and do
them, *really* do them—make your job that much easier, and your
acting that much more clear and convincing.

"As a point of technique, remember that deaf people focus on
what they see the same way blind people focus on what they hear.
So that's what you have to play. Put every ounce of your focus
into what your eyes can take in. Maintain the contact with your
partner like that."

Amber seems unsatisfied. "But I'll still hear things," she says.

Bill spreads his hands. "You might, but I bet you'll be surprised.
The more concentration you put into what you see, the less you'll
pay attention to what you hear. When that happens, you've gotten
the hang of it. You've created the illusion of deafness, or part of
it anyway."

Bill turns to the class. *"The quality of your performance with
any Physical Impediment always boils down to how specific your*

crafting is. What questions have you answered for yourself about your condition? In Amber's case, she needs to pin down how long she's been deaf. Can she read lips? How well? And remember how I mentioned the tremendous vulnerability you must have to play someone blind? The same thing applies here. Let's say Amber recently lost her hearing in an accident. Well. Think of all the questions that spring from that single, given circumstance. What's it like to live in a world that suddenly has no sound? Is she disoriented? Nervous? Scared? How has the sudden lack of sound affected her balance? Does she raise her voice, or shout when she talks, trying to make herself heard? And so on. The more of these questions you ask and answer, the better your performance will be."

Dom has a question. "Bill, you mentioned that using a technique will take the mythology out of the actor's job. What do you mean by that?"

Bill chuckles. "People see a great actor perform and think that it's some kind of magic. It's not. A fine actor's talent should be respected, but let's not go overboard. This is a craft, like being a blacksmith, a tailor, or a plumber. You size up the job. You plan an approach to getting it done, then work your plan with all the commitment you can muster. It's no good to stand there gawking at the challenge. Pick a point of entry and get to work. Frankly, I believe this system can be used to approach nearly any endeavor. Business. The arts. Building a house. Planning a trip. The list goes on and on. Who's next?"

■ ■ ■ ■

A few classes later, Bill brings an exercise between Joyce and Tyrone to a halt. The improvisation was lively. The impulses flew. No moment was missed. Tyrone had a rich activity that brought him fully to life. Joyce came to the door with an objective that was never realized, but so much the better. She let go of what she wanted and worked moment to moment, the way she was trained. On top of all this, Tyrone had a bilateral lisp and Joyce had a facial tic. The two partners had their Impediments down pat. And this part is very important: They were so adept at producing their Impediments that they were able to work *through* them and concentrate on the exercise.

Bill is satisfied. He's about to call up the next set of partners when Tyrone asks a question.

"Bill, is it me? Or . . . When I worked with the lisp, I . . ."

He trails off, confused about what to say next. Bill waits, listening.

"I just want to make sure I say this correctly," Tyrone continues. He struggles with his words. "It's as if . . . It's as if my Impediment *fed back* on me and affected me internally. Like it began to bring out a whole different side of me. . . . I'm sorry, I'm not saying this right."

"No, no," Bill says. He's smiling, excited. "You're onto something, but let me help you. You're discovering that, *if you stay relaxed and keep yourself open, a simple addition to your normal behavior—something like a Physical Impediment—can begin to create a new and separate life within you.* Is that what you're trying to say?"

Tyrone nods gratefully. Bill nods back and turns to the class.

"Any adjustment that interferes with the actor's ability to communicate can trigger intense reactions. This is why working with Physical Impediments is so important, why you use them as a way of sticking your toes into the very deep pool that we call character acting. We're easing away from your straight behavior, taking it slow, but the change can already be felt. Tyrone just felt it now. He began to discover that *by adopting only one specific addition to your normal behavior and playing straight, focusing on what's happening in the contact between partners, a complete character can begin to emerge, if you allow it to happen.*

"But make no mistake," Bill says. "You must still remain open to the contact you share with your partner. Whatever Physical Impediment you adopt can never close that contact down. If anything, the Impediment should suggest new ways of keeping the contact open and rich—ways that are foreign to you, yes, but completely truthful nonetheless."

"Like the way being blind makes you listen more acutely," Quid says.

"Or being deaf makes you concentrate on what you see," Amber says.

"Or having a clubfoot makes you walk a little slower and work your hips more to move your legs," says Adam, referring to the Impediment he worked with.

"That's right," Bill says. "And on and on. It's still *you* that's doing all that, still *you* that's doing the improvisation. But a character is what begins to emerge when you and a Physical Impediment mix. It's an actor's first step toward deeper and richer playing of characters whose behavior patterns are different from yours."

■ ■ ■ ■

Later, Bill and I repair to his office.

"I noticed you spend a lot of time pointing out where the first-year work has atrophied."

"Whenever you add something new to the work, everything else seems to fall apart until the actors have had time to assimilate it. It's early days yet, and they're dealing with a lot. Impediments are new to them, so they're striving to play them with accuracy and commitment. While striving, they might come to class with an

Impediment they haven't fully pinned down. You saw that with Ray and Amber. They weren't able to maintain the illusion of their Impediments while keeping the simple reality of listening and responding that the improvisation demands."

"So in that case," I say, "the students know how to play the Impediment, but they focus too much attention on their arthritic hip, their lockjaw, or their Ménière's syndrome. Which leaves them too little attention to give to their partner."

"Exactly," Bill says. "One of the ways that we judge any art is by the ease the artist exhibits in his or her execution. Think of trapeze artists. They work for years to condition their bodies, honing their strength and agility to incredible levels of mastery. But have you ever seen a trapeze artist who isn't smiling? Never. They make it look easy. That's another level of craft."

"How long will you spend on Physical Impediments?" I ask.

"Each set of partners will get a few rounds. I want everyone to get these right before we move on to the next set of exercises, where we'll cause the students serious pain."

I look up from the notes I'm taking. "Sorry? What did you say?"

"Pain," Bill says, and he grins. "We'll be working with how to play the effects of intense physical pain."

THREE

HOW BEING IN INTENSE PAIN
CAN ACTUALLY HELP YOUR WORK

"Given the choice between the experience of pain and nothing, I would choose pain."

—WILLIAM FAULKNER

"Your pain is the breaking of the shell that encloses your understanding."

—KAHLIL GIBRAN

"Playing intense pain takes us into a new area of acting," Bill says. *"This area is concerned with the illusion of a reality rather than the reality itself.* In this area, you need only concern yourselves with how believable the audience finds your behavior."

Trevor snorts. "Are you saying we shouldn't injure ourselves before we come to class? You know, just to research our pain?"

Bill smiles. "Actors suffer for their art, but let's not go overboard. Imagine how high the Studio's insurance premiums would be if my students came to class with broken arms, sprained ankles, and nasty bouts of carpal tunnel syndrome." Everyone laughs, and then Bill gets serious. "A lot of inexperienced actors have very misguided notions about this. They think you have to feel actual pain in order to play it well. That's completely ridiculous."

"So how should we do it?" asks Trevor. "Obviously, we won't do anything that will cause us actual pain."

"Right. Don't bang your head against the wall to give yourself a headache."

"So what should we do instead?"

"Use your skills as a mimic to create the symptoms indicative of a particular condition," Bill says.

The class has begun to take notes. Jon raises his left hand while scribbling with his right. "Can you be more specific?"

"I mentioned a headache," Bill says. "So let's start with that. How would you play a headache?"

Jon thinks it over. "There's many different types of headache. I guess I'd first have to figure out which kind I was suffering from."

Bill grins. "Very astute. It all goes back to specifics, you see? The more specific your crafting is, the easier the work becomes. Let's try a migraine headache. Does anyone here know about migraines?"

"I do," says Amber. "I get them now and again. They're nasty, awful, horrible things."

"Perfect," Bill says. "Tell us what they feel like."

"Well," says Amber. "The way I get them, it's always on my right side, here at my temple. The pain comes on like a deep, dull throb. It feels like my brain is swelling inside my skull like a loaf of bread rising in a very tight oven."

Dom, sitting next to Amber, winces at the thought.

"What else?" says Bill.

"I get very dizzy," says Amber. "Sometimes the dizziness gets so bad that I can't stand up. I have to lie down. Also, lights and sound become incredibly irritating. A lot of times, I pull the shades and turn out the lights and put earplugs in and stay in bed for a day. Sometimes two."

"I'm sorry to hear that you suffer like that," Bill says. "But this could prove very useful to our work." He turns to the class. "Can someone list her symptoms again?"

Adam ticks them off. "A dull throb in her right temple. Dizziness. Sensitivity to light. Sensitivity to sound."

Bill nods. "That sounds like a migraine to me. So tell me this: If you create the illusion of these symptoms, what will an audience think you have?"

Ray grunts. "A migraine headache."

Bill spreads his hands. It's as simple as that.

Uma is thinking it over. "Bill, are you saying that *an actor can combine more than one Physical Impediment to play a condition of pain?*"

"That's exactly what I'm saying," Bill answers. "Let's try another example. How about a hangover? What are the symptoms of a hangover?"

"A headache," says Adam.

Bill nods. "A headache, sure. But again, let's be specific. What *kind* of headache?"

"A throb," says Adam. "As though your head is a time bomb that's about to explode."

"I like that a lot because what you said is a lot more descriptive, more *active,* than simply saying 'a headache.' Do you see how the more specific description can be more useful to your acting?"

Adam nods. "It gives me something more stimulating to work with."

"Indeed it does," Bill says. "What are some other hangover symptoms?"

"Hangovers leave you lethargic," says Trevor. "The alcohol leaches vitality from your body so you can barely stand up."

"Good," says Bill. "More symptoms, please."

"Dry mouth," says Joyce.

"Acid stomach," says Jon.

"Crankiness," says Quid.

"Bright lights hurt your eyes," says Mimi.

"Loud noises cause your ears to bleed," says Melissa.

"I agree," says Bill. "These are all classic symptoms of a hang-over. So these are symptoms we can enact that, if they're executed with some skill, will produce the *illusion* of a hangover."

Donna raises her hand. "Bill, isn't it true that everyone's body is different? Personally, I never get hangovers with dry mouth. Should I play that anyway?"

Bill shrugs. "An audience doesn't care about what kind of hang-over you get in real life. They only care about your performance. When you are playing pain, your work will be judged by two cri-teria: whether or not the audience can recognize the condition you're creating, and whether or not they believe the way you've portrayed it."

Donna arches an eyebrow. "You're saying that our goal should be to create a hangover the audience will believe. And to do that, I should use classic symptoms that people will recognize."

"That's it exactly," says Bill. He turns to the class. "Here are some other things to keep in mind when playing pain. Point num-ber one: *Keep the number of symptoms to three or four at most.* This will help you to focus, to play each symptom well. When you try to play too many symptoms, your behavior starts to get muddy. So keep it simple.

"Point number two: *Though you may be playing three or four Impediments at once, you must nonetheless act each one specifically.* It's no good to say, 'Gosh, it's so tough to concentrate on all this at once!' I'm sorry, but that's the challenge.

"Point number three: *Remember to stay relaxed.* Most actors tense their bodies when playing pain because, in real life, pain tends to cause physical tension. You must let go of that habit and keep your body loose. A loose body is essential for listening and responding to your partner, as well as for letting your emotions flow freely." Bill looks at the class. "We'll probably have some trouble with this part, but that's what we're here to work on. Staying relaxed at this stage of the game is a very advanced acting challenge."

Vanessa raises her hand. "Bill, how intense should our circumstances be?"

"For now, I still want you to steer away from highly charged emotional setups. In other words, don't enter a room preparing to go to your mother's funeral while your partner's husband just got hit by a bus and the dog is running around on fire. Imagine trying to improvise that with a sucking chest wound or an abscessed tooth." The class laughs. "For these exercises, both partners should choose a condition that would, in life, put them in severe physical pain. Craft a simple relationship. The partner in the room should have a simple activity. The partner who comes to the door should arrive with a simple objective. 'I want to borrow twenty dollars.' Something like that. The partner out in the hallway will knock on the door. That begins the interaction. After that, whatever happens, happens."

Bill checks his roster. "For next time, I want to see your migraines, your toothaches, your shingles, and all the crumbling discs in your lower back."

▌▌▌▌

Reg and Cheryl are the first to work. Reg starts the exercise inside the room. His right arm is bandaged and hangs in a sling. He sits at the table and takes out a sheet of high-bond stationery. Then he picks up a pen and begins to write a letter—or tries to. He's having a great deal of trouble; he's right-handed, but that hand's useless in the sling. He tries writing with his left hand instead, but it looks like an awful challenge. He frowns. The tip of his tongue pokes between his lips as he fights to keep the pen under control.

There's a sharp, perfunctory knock at the door. Reg sighs,

heaves his portly frame off the chair, saunters to the door, and opens it. Cheryl stands at the threshold. The two spend a few minutes trading impulses as though nothing at all were the matter, but Bill shakes his head and stops them.

"What's wrong with you?" he says to Reg.

"Huh?" says Reg. He holds up the arm in the sling. "I broke my arm. See?"

Bill raises his eyebrows. "So?"

Reg is confused. "Slings keep a broken arm immobile."

"I know," says Bill. "But that's not good enough. The assignment was to craft intense pain."

Reg gets a bit defensive. "It hurts to have a broken arm. I broke mine twice. In the same place, in fact."

"I'm sorry to hear it," Bill says. "But we're not talking about your personal medical history, we're talking about this exercise. And right now, all I see is an actor whose arm is in a sling. I'm not buying your condition."

"Well . . . ," says Reg. His voice trails off. "I just thought that . . . See, when I broke my arm, you know, they put it in a sling."

Bill shakes his head. "You're not acting. Putting your arm in a sling is a costume note. The sling forces you to do things with your other hand, but it doesn't require any real shift in your behavior. Do you see the difference?"

"I guess."

Bill turns to Cheryl. "What about you?"

"I have a broken toe," she says.

"Really?" Bill says. "I wonder how we'd ever know that."

"Well, the truth is, there's not much you can do for a broken toe. Doctors usually tape the toe that's broken to one that isn't and send you on your way. Most of the time, you can still walk around. It's irritating, but—"

"My point exactly," Bill says. "I asked you to play *intense* physical pain. You're light-years away from that. Next time, choose something more demanding, a condition where the pain adjustment dominates the exercise and creates real behavior. For instance, suppose I just had a tooth extracted." Bill's eyes droop halfway closed. Gingerly he strokes his cheek. He seems to be barely keeping his head upright. Each of his breaths seems like an exquisite effort. "You see?" he says quietly. *"The experience of the pain functions like an Independent Activity in that it involves your attention and affects the contact you maintain with your partner.* If you're really playing intense pain, everything the other actor gives you comes in through the filter of that pain, then bubbles back out of you—again through the filter of that pain."

Bill resumes his normal behavior and turns back to Reg. "By putting your arm in a sling, you didn't have to research the condition. You didn't have to practice how you'd play the specific symptoms. You didn't have to work until your performance was second nature. And you certainly didn't have to risk anything. Instead, all you had to do was tie your arm up in a sling. That's why your work here suffered. You chose the low road, the one that robbed you of any dramatic potential."

Reg thinks. "What would the high road be?"

Bill's eyes begin to sparkle. "Suppose you give yourself that you just fell down and broke your arm *five minutes ago.* You've just called your friend, who said he'd bring the car around to take you to the hospital—that could also serve as your expectation. Would that make for a much more interesting exercise?"

Reg's eyes start to sparkle as well. "It sure would," he says. "Can I bring this back in?"

"Of course," Bill says. He motions to Cheryl. "Go for broke. You can't come in and say, 'Oh well. Gee. Today I've got a little headache.' What would be the point of that? How many great scripts have you read where a character gets a little headache?

On the other hand, how many great scripts have you read where the character has a severe headache? A hangover? A heart attack? A slipped disc?"

Cheryl smiles. "I get it. You want me to really challenge myself and create something that will generate vivid behavior."

Bill nods and turns back to the class. "There's no point bringing work into class unless it's stageworthy. Encourage yourselves to go further. No one ever wrote a great script about a broken toe."

■ ■ ■ ■

Uma and Dom get up next to work. Dom starts the exercise inside the room. He is clearly ill. He's wrapped a blanket around his shoulders and stuffed a ski cap onto his head. He coughs. He sniffles. He winces whenever he moves. At a glance, I'd say he must be experiencing a horrible bout of the flu.

Dom's activity is to make himself a packet of instant noodle soup using a hot plate and some water. Normally, this would be a simple chore. In his present condition, however, Dom finds making soup as complex a task as disarming a bomb.

He sits at the table while his kettle heats up on the hot plate. For agonizing minutes, he tries to open a little foil packet of flavoring powder. He tries and he tries, but he just can't do it. His fingers are numb. His eyes keep closing. He can't seem to control his own body. There's a thundering knock at the door.

Dom turns his head toward the sudden hammering sound, wincing. He coughs and sniffles and blinks at the door. Another knock! This time it sounds as if someone's trying to break down the door with a battering ram. Dom moans a little and presses his hands to the crown of his head, which must be throbbing. Slowly—very slowly—he levers his body up from the chair and shuffles toward the door.

The knocks come harder. Each blow makes Dom cry out in

pain and clamp his hands to his ears. He reaches a trembling hand for the knob and twists it. Uma barrels inside, her face a mask of agony.

"Damn you, what took you so—" She puts weight on her left foot. "AAAARGH!"

"Aaaargh," says Dom. Uma's scream hurts his head. He covers his ears and moans and buckles a little, backing away.

Uma steps farther into the room. "What the hell are you—" Again, she puts weight on her left foot and screams.

"Stop," Dom pleads. "Please stop it, you're hurting my head."

Uma doesn't register this. She takes another step. "I don't— AAAAARGH! OW! AAAAAARGH!"

"Okay, let's stop," Bill says.

A silence falls over the studio.

Bill thinks for a moment and looks at Dom. "You've got the flu?" he says.

Dom nods. "Really bad."

"I get that." Bill turns to the rest of the class. "How many people thought he had the flu?"

They all raise their hands.

"Why?" Bill asks.

"The headache," says Joyce. "The sniffles. The coughing."

"He moves like he's in agony." Tyrone looks sympathetic. "Like all the joints and muscles in his body are on fire."

Bill looks at Dom and gestures toward the class. "Congratulations. That's the best and only test. If your audience can identify what you've crafted without being told, you've succeeded. Your work was simple and very specific. That's why it worked."

He turns to Uma. "Let's talk about you. What's going on?"

"I have a sprained ankle," she says.

"Really?" Bill says. "That was a sprain? You were yelling so loud, I thought someone was trying to cut off your leg."

The class laughs. Uma looks very embarrassed.

"But I thought . . . You told Reg and Cheryl to be more vivid in their choices."

"I did indeed," Bill says. "But did I ask them to lose all sense of proportion? I think not."

"I don't understand," Uma says.

"Proportion," says Bill. "It's an intrinsic part of any actor's talent. You have to know what's over the top. How much is too much and how much is too little. Proportion comes from your sense of truth. In fact, the two go hand in hand. Violate one, you'll destroy the other. After that, your performance is doomed."

Bill turns to the class. "Once, when I was at the Neighborhood Playhouse, some actors were doing a scene from Thornton Wilder's *The Skin of Our Teeth*. You know the play? It's the scene where the father comes onstage to confront his rebellious bastard of a son. The father has a gun and he's going to shoot his own kid. This is close to the end of the play, so the father has aged quite a bit.

"Well. When the actor playing the father came on, he wasn't old, he was ancient! His whole body quaked head to foot. He was so decrepit, he could barely make it across the stage. He gripped the gun with both hands, but it was so heavy, he could barely raise it. He took forever to get into position. By the time he made it, you sort of lost track of what was going on in the play.

"Sandy and I were sitting together in the audience. He turned to me and said, 'That man is *too old* to act.'"

The class laughs. Uma does, too. Bill turns back to her, smiling. "You see my point? You're laying it on too thick. Stanislavsky once said that you can cut out ninety percent of any performance and still have plenty left. Heed his advice in this instance."

Uma smiles. "I got it."

"But there's something else that went awry," Bill says. "You violated the truth by indulging in the drama of your injury. In reality, people in pain do everything they can to alleviate it. Remember how I said you have to work *through* a Physical Impediment? The same principle applies here." Bill gets up from his chair while talking. "For instance, a person with a badly sprained ankle tries *not to put any pressure on that leg.* A single ounce of your weight on that joint can send you through the roof. So you focus on that part of your body and treat it with the utmost care."

Gingerly, Bill moves around his desk. Holding the edge of the table, he takes a few tentative steps. He moves like a klutz who's about to step out on a tightrope hanging seventy feet above the ground. Each little movement makes him wince. It's clear that his foot is throbbing.

"You see?" he says. "Even the smallest motion feels like your foot is made of crystal. Any contact whatsoever will shatter it into a million pieces. So your whole life becomes about looking for a chair to sit down on. Or figuring out how to cross the room without falling. Or making sure you don't bump your foot on people passing by."

The room has grown quiet, respectful of Bill's agony. The slightest motion could rock his whole world. "And think how good it feels to relieve yourself from this pain," he says. "Every time you find a seat, you sink into it, luxuriating in comfort the way a man who's dying of thirst would enjoy a glass of cold water." Settling into his chair, he exhales deeply. "Then you look around and try to find ways to elevate the leg so the throbbing will stop." Carefully, using his hands to help, Bill raises his leg and places it on the desktop. Again he exhales, exhausted. "You see?" Smiling, he pulls his leg off the desk and resumes his normal posture.

Trevor blinks. "You shook that right off."

"Of course I did." Bill shrugs. "I told you, it's just an illusion."

"For a second there, I really thought you'd hurt your leg," Tyrone says.

"Thank you," says Bill. "What a kind thing to say."

The class laughs.

Bill spreads his hands. "Illusions can be powerful things. Just think of Charlie Chaplin. Do it now. Picture him in your head. How many of you see that little fellow with the black bowler, black mustache, black jacket, and cane?"

Everyone raises a hand.

Bill shrugs. "When people see old Chaplin films, they think that's who the man was. They think he really walked that way, behaved that way. They forget that the Tramp was Chaplin's alter ego, a role he could instantly assume. The real man, the artist behind the Tramp—now *he* was an interesting person. Let's do another one. Who's up next?"

▌▐▌▐

Mimi and Tyrone's exercise goes well. Tyrone has thrown his back out. Mimi comes to the door suffering from an awful case of arthritis in her hips. They work their improvisation for a good long while. Finally, Bill brings the exercise to a close.

"Very nice." He smiles. "I especially liked how you both stayed relaxed despite the afflictions you prepared."

"It was tough to do at first," Tyrone says.

During the exercise, he hobbled around, bent over as though his spine were broken. His legs barely worked. He winced at each minor movement. His face became a canvas painted with every gruesome hue of agony. But then the exercise stopped. Tyrone straightened right up, and now he's grinning like a bandit.

"I was tense the first couple of times I tried rehearsing it at home," he says. "Then I remembered something you told us last year. Something you keep saying this year, too."

"Which is what?" Bill asks.

"You say that tension will ruin our ability to act. It closes us down and blocks the audience from relating to what we're experiencing."

"I'm pleased to hear you say that," Bill says. "In real life, when we experience pain—and cold, for that matter—it tends to make us tense. But you can never play tension with tension." Bill eyes Tyrone critically. "You've really taken that lesson to heart. Last year, you were stiff as a piece of pressure-treated wood. Don't get me wrong; you did the work and you did it well, but you tended to muscularize your emotions. Now I see you opening up and allowing yourself to experience life. You've come a long way, Tyrone."

Tyrone looks pleased and embarrassed at the same time. His bodybuilder frame is trimmer than it was last year, but he's still a very big man. Coquettishness seems incongruous for a man who looks like a pit bull.

Bill turns to Mimi. "You've also come a long way. I liked your arthritis just now."

Mimi nods. "Thank you. I remembered how arthritis used to affect my mother. She once described it to me as having bits of ground glass infused in her joints. Whenever she moved, the joints rubbed the glass shards into her muscles, tissues, and bones."

"How did your mom deal with that?"

"She moved a little slower. Walked a certain way to favor her left side, which was afflicted more than her right. She was one tough lady."

"I bet." Bill calls on Amber, who's raised her hand.

"I'm a little confused," she says. "I know you said we can't tense up when playing pain. But I have to tell you, in real life, when I get a migraine, I often get very tense."

"So what's the problem?" Bill says.

"Well, if tension is part of the real condition, shouldn't tension be part of my performance?"

Bill shakes his head. "What happens when your migraine makes you tense?"

"In real life?" Amber says. "I get irritated and snippy. I hurt so much, my patience wears thin. I snap at people a lot."

"Fine," says Bill. "Snippy. Irritated. Snaps at people a lot. Can you add those symptoms to your performance and still be relaxed?"

Amber thinks about it and nods.

"Remember," says Bill, "for this part of the work, you create the illusion of a specific reality, not the reality itself."

Jon raises his hand. "Bill, last year we learned to put all our attention on the other person. But I found that close to impossible while creating the illusion of an appendicitis attack. Is that okay?"

"Yes," Bill says. "In life, pain tends to divide a person's concentration. In the exercise, whenever you work with physical pain, your attention will seem to fall back on yourself because, just as with playing a Physical Impediment, playing pain works like an Independent Activity. *You must concentrate on the symptoms you've given yourself to enact, and interact with your partner through the obstacle that pain creates. Your moment-to-moment reality will get filtered through your condition and enriched by it.*" Bill looks at the class. "If it's done well, dealing with severe pain can become your entire performance."

"How?" asks Cheryl.

"Creating intense pain can produce a lovely and moving death scene. Or think of the timeless characters for whom physical pain is essential. John Merrick in *The Elephant Man*. Julius Caesar, stabbed to death by a group of senators. Titus Andronicus, who loses a hand. Oedipus, who stabs out his own eyes."

Bill checks his roster. "We'll have everyone run through some rounds of pain. After that, we'll work with extreme temperatures.

Then we can start to work on the effects of drugs and alcohol." Eyeing the class, Bill adjusts his glasses. "Are you starting to see how this work will eventually help you to play a character? Each of the symptoms we've added has altered your straight behavior. But it's still you with the headache, the sprained ankle, the abscessed tooth. *This is the core of character work: No matter how far you get from your straight behavior, it's still always you that's doing it.*"

FOUR

HOW TO EXPLORE DRUGS AND ALCOHOL WITHOUT REHAB, PRISON, OR DEATH

"I hate to advocate drugs, alcohol, violence, or insanity to anyone, but they've always worked for me."

—HUNTER S. THOMPSON

"I've never had a problem with drugs. I've had problems with the police."

—KEITH RICHARDS

Bill tells the class: "The technical approach to creating the effects of drugs and alcohol is similar to the one we use to create pain. Once again, we're dealing with purely physical acting. *We are not dealing with the reality of drug use, only the illusion of it.* You will need to specify the symptoms that the drug you're working with would create if you took it in real life. The trick, as when creating pain, will be to maintain contact with your partner *through* the obstacles the drug would create."

I glance at the class. Everyone's furiously taking notes.

"We'll start with alcohol," Bill says. "Drunks come up a lot in both contemporary and classic scripts. You'll find them in plenty of Shakespeare's plays. Some of his greatest roles were drunks: Sir Toby Belch in *Twelfth Night,* Falstaff in *Henry IV,* Barnardine in *Measure for Measure,* Trinculo the jester in *The Tempest,* and on and on. From the modern canon, we have Honey in *Who's Afraid of Virginia Woolf?* Brick in *Cat on a Hot Tin Roof.* Reverend Shannon in *The Night of the Iguana.* Again, the list goes on.

"There used to be actors who made their living playing drunks. Watch a lot of old movies. If you look very closely, you'll probably notice the same character actors playing the drunk parts over and over again. Some actors are great at playing drunk, and some are downright awful. When you're good, you're good for a simple reason: you're allowing your state of drunkenness to illuminate truths about human nature for everyone who's watching. When you're bad, it's because you've fallen back on stock routines and gestures that make an audience cringe. I'm sure we've all seen that."

The class nods and murmurs. It seems that they have.

"Playing the effects of alcohol creates a particular set of problems for actors. First, you have the drunk's physical life. The actor has to understand the specific impact alcohol has on the human nervous system. Let's go into detail here. What are some of the physical symptoms of being drunk?"

"Your balance is off," says Uma.

"That's right," says Bill. "A person can get so drunk, they literally can't walk a straight line. The beauty of that test is that *the drunk is really trying to walk the straight line*! But no matter how hard he tries, it simply can't be done. What else?"

"Alcohol can affect your eyesight," says Dom. "Everything becomes blurry."

"That's a good one," says Bill. "If you're in a bar sometime, you might see a drunk sitting on a stool, sort of staring at the men's room door. Why? Well, in the first place, he's seeing more than one door. In the second place, each of the doors he sees is slowly spinning around. The drunk is trying to time the rotations so he can launch himself off his bar stool and make a beeline for the door and hopefully hit it in one straight shot."

Bill lets his face go slack. He stares at the door to the studio as though he's viewing it through a kaleidoscopic lens. His jaw hangs down. He tucks his chin and squints. His skull swivels gently back and forth as though his neck were a well-oiled hinge, his expression hilariously serious. The class laughs. Bill lets go of this adjustment and grins.

"Let's not forget impaired speech," he says. "Remember that alcohol is a depressant. It slows down the central nervous system, and as a result, it mangles a person's ability to articulate words." Bill lets his face go slack again. He turns to Ray, who's sitting close by, and says, quite seriously, "It's snot dat yer tryin to get the words zong. They just sorma commow tha-way."

The class laughs again, and Bill sobers up fast.

"So much for the drunk's physical life. *The actor also has to nail the drunk's emotional life.* You'll start to figure this part out when you delve into *why your character started drinking in the first place.*"

Reg raises his hand. "I'm not sure what you mean."

"*In vino veritas*—in wine, there is truth. People reveal their true nature while drinking. Some people drink to loosen up and have a good time. As Ovid once put it, 'Wine gives courage and makes men more apt for passion.' Some do it to recess into themselves. And on and on. *Whatever the reason a person starts drinking, the alcohol tends to reinforce and amplify it.* That's why there's so many types of drunks. Some drunks are sloppy and some are ecstatic. Some are brooding, while others are mischievous. Some are very dignified—the more they drink, the more august and superior they become."

Bill picks up the cup of decaf on his desk and holds it before him as though it's a martini glass. His body seems to stiffen, his nose floats up in the air. He gazes down at everyone as though his spine has lost its flexibility. The class snickers. Bill has become the very picture of an intellectual bore, a stuffed shirt stoned beyond reason at a hoity-toity cocktail party. Then, as quickly as he donned the adjustment, Bill slips out of it and picks up where he left off.

"Some drunks are morose. Some drunks burst into tears at the slightest provocation because everything, simply everything in life, is so awful. Then there are people who take one drink and they're suddenly having the time of their lives. They're up on the bar! They're dancing the limbo! They're forming a conga line! Some drunks are hostile. They'll pick a fight with the person on the next stool because they've lost the ability to foresee consequences for their actions. At its core, being drunk is about having a false sense of freedom.

"This notion of amplifying emotional tones holds true for practically every drug, and there's such an assortment to choose from. Modern scripts make use of what I call the classic drugs: alcohol, marijuana, cocaine, heroin, and crack. But you may also be called on to play a part involving hallucinogens like Ecstasy, LSD, or mescaline. Seems like every time you turn around, a new drug has risen to prominence and writers are writing about it. Look at how *Breaking Bad* treated the crystal meth epidemic. Or how *House* treated Vicodin abuse. Or how the title character in *Nurse Jackie* abuses, well, practically everything.

"In class," Bill says. "I want you to stick with the more time-honored drugs. I have a good reason for this. The whole point of crafting drug behavior is to make sure an audience will believe your performance. The symptoms for alcohol, cocaine, marijuana, and heroin use are pretty widely known. In fact, they're so widely known that none of us should have any trouble recognizing them, if you're successful at capturing their reality. Once you've mastered the basics, you shouldn't have any problem acting out the symptoms of any drug you choose.

"We'll set these exercises up the same way we did when you played pain. Partners will begin with a simple relationship. The actor who starts off inside the room will have a simple activity. The actor who comes to the door will have a simple objective. And of course it goes without saying that each actor will be under the influence. Choose a drug to explore, research it, and add its symptoms to your straight behavior. Does anyone have any questions?"

Ray claps his hands together. "This is going to be fun!"

Bill shoots him a look. "Be careful," he says. "Playing the effects of drugs and alcohol can certainly be fun. It can also be very tricky, full of traps for the actor."

▪ ▪ ▪ ▪

Ray falls into one of these traps almost immediately. He starts an exercise inside the room, sitting in a chair with a pile of knitting in his lap. His face has gone slack. He stares at the tangles of yarn. Lifting one of his knitting needles, he flicks it with a fingernail. The needle gives a metallic *ping* and Ray bursts into giggles. The sound of his voice is strangled and high. It appears to disturb Ray as much as it disturbs the rest of us, who are watching him, confused. Has Ray taken a hallucinogen? Is he drunk? What is he on?

Abruptly, Ray clamps his mouth shut and pulls at the tangles of yarn—a bird's nest if ever there was one. His movements are weak, almost fey. The motion of his limbs can best be described as flouncy. He giggles and tries to untangle his skein. This goes on for several minutes, during which I ask myself again: What kind of drug is Ray on? His symptoms don't correlate to those produced by any substance I'm aware of. Just when I think he's been smoking marijuana, I change my mind and become convinced he's been huffing glue, even though Bill specifically asked the actors to stick to traditional drugs for the first round of exercises.

There's a knock at the door. Ray gets up to answer it. He slides across the floor, pausing to do the Watusi, and presses himself against the wall like a coat of paint trying to apply itself. This behavior is strange, to say the least.

Whoever's outside in the hallway knocks again, more insistently. Ray doesn't answer. Instead he stands there, giggling softly. His eyes have slid halfway closed. His lips are pursed. He sucks at the air like a sea bass that's been hooked through the gills, yanked from the ocean, and placed on ice.

"Ray?"

Now I recognize the voice. It belongs to Melissa, Ray's scene partner. She's outside the door, but she sounds a bit fuzzy, like her voice has been wrapped in a mohair sweater. I wonder why that is.

Ray does nothing. His eyes go wide. He waits. Another knock at the door.

"Ray? Hey. Come on. Open up."

Ray mutters under his breath. He reaches a hand toward the doorknob—and stops. He pulls the hand back and mutters again. Stops. His face wrinkles into a mask of abject fear. Again he tries for the knob.

"Ray? Ray! Come on, I know you're in there."

He freezes with his fingers poised to turn the knob, but he doesn't do it. Instead he places his cheek against the wall and sighs as though his face were on fire and the wall were as cool as a cake of ice.

"Yo," he says. A groan of pleasure.

There's a pause. Melissa says, "Ray?"

He giggles. "Yo-yo-yo." He giggles again. "Yo-yo."

"Ray, come on! Will you please open up?"

Ray makes a pouty face. "Ray's not here," he croons.

This goes on for several minutes more, during which Melissa never gains access to the room. Bill wears a strange expression as he brings the exercise to a halt. When Melissa enters the room, he turns to her. "What were you working with?"

"I was stoned," she said. "I came over to see if Ray had any food."

"You got the munchies?" says Bill.

Melissa smiles and shrugs.

"That's good," Bill says. "That's a valid symptom of marijuana use. Unfortunately, we didn't really get a chance to see the behaviors you crafted, since you never got in the room. But tell us what symptoms you were working with."

"Well," says Melissa. "Marijuana's a pretty common drug, a mild hallucinogen. People have different reactions to it. Some get very sweet and dreamy when they use it. Some get kind of paranoid— that's what I was playing with. I let myself get hyperalert and tried to focus on little details to the point of utter distraction."

"Like what?"

Melissa laughs. "The paint job on the outside of this door." She motions toward the door that Ray never let her get through. "I've never noticed it before, but the paint has the exact same texture as a fresh-cut slice of seven-grain bread."

Someone in the class snickers. I think it's Tyrone, but I can't be sure. Then they're all laughing in spite of themselves. Including Melissa.

"So." Bill smiles. "You had the munchies. You were paranoid. You allowed yourself to obsess over details. That sounds pretty good for being stoned."

Melissa cocks her head to one side. "I thought about wearing a tie-dyed shirt."

"Let's not go overboard." Bill glances at Ray and turns to the class. "What kind of drug was Ray on?"

A brief poll is taken. Approximately a third of the students think Ray was stoned. Another third think that he might have been on Ecstasy. Vanessa thinks he might have been drunk, but she doesn't sound very convinced. Uma suggests that Ray might have been abusing lithium.

"Or maybe he *belongs* on lithium?" She frowns and shakes her head.

"LSD?" says Adam. "That's the only thing I could think of."

Bill turns back to Ray. "What were you working with?"

Ray frowns, chastened. "Heroin."

No one says a word.

Bill shakes his head. "I think you missed the boat on this one. What were the symptoms you researched?"

"Well . . ." Ray clears his throat. "I watched *Trainspotting*."

"If that's true, you must have been on crack cocaine when you watched it."

The class laughs.

"You were lazy," Bill says. "It's not hard to research the effects of heroin. The information is available on the Internet. Heroin belongs to the opiate family. It's very addictive. It was first synthesized back in the late nineteenth century and marketed by Bayer as a cure for morphine addiction, which was prevalent at the time. Treating a morphine addiction with heroin is sort of like treating a headache by blowing your brains out with a shotgun. Eventually, Bayer discovered its error. Heroin was banned soon after that, around 1914, I think."

"Oh," says Ray. "I didn't know that."

Bill shrugs as though he's not surprised. "You don't have to know the history of it, but it helps sometimes. This would be more useful: A classic symptom of heroin use is the intense sensuality felt by its users. Their insides feel all warm and gooey. The drug puts them in such a blissful state, they'll often fall into a deep and rapturous slumber. They'll come to—very suddenly, just for a moment. And then they'll nod off again.

"Heroin makes you feel so good, it takes a great deal of effort to accomplish practically anything. You're so out of it that getting up from your chair becomes more complicated than calculus. A person using heroin could be sitting on top of a pile of garbage and, to him, it would be a paradise. Like God came down from heaven above and kissed him on the forehead. He whispers the secrets of life in your ear and then He makes you pancakes."

Ray begins to shuffle a bit. He's started to realize his work was subpar. He'd clearly rather sit down again, but Bill doesn't seem to notice—or care.

"Years ago, the Studio was down on Third Avenue. Three junkies were out on the street in front of a delicatessen. All three of them were on the nod, and they had a little baby in a stroller. One junkie clung to the stroller. The second one held the baby's bottle. The third one held a carton of milk and was trying"—Bill demonstrates what he saw—"to . . . pour it . . . into . . . the bottle. It looked like the most complicated thing he'd ever done in his life, more complicated than brain surgery. Meanwhile, the baby just sat there, crying."

Amber's face has gone pale. "I would have killed them," she says. "All three of them."

Bill looks at her. "Let's stick to the acting lesson this offers." He turns back to Ray. "That yarn you were playing with could have been your whole performance. But a person on heroin probably wouldn't bother trying to untangle yarn, as you did. He'd sit there, staring at all the beautiful patterns. That would give you the preternatural focus heroin users have. A second symptom you could have explored might have been how wonderful it felt just to sit there, languishing in your own skin. There's an unmistakable dreaminess heroin users have, especially if they've just shot up. A third symptom? You could explore the nodding. Here we're assuming, of course, that you're used to getting high. If this had been your first time using, you could have worked with nausea and vomiting, which first-time users frequently experience."

"People on heroin get sick?" Ray says.

I wince. It's painful to see how poorly Ray has done his research.

"So you see, there were options you could have pursued." Bill lets this statement hang there.

Vanessa raises her hand. "Bill? You mentioned that there are some really good movies we can use to research drug abuse. Can you name a few?"

"If you're researching alcohol abuse, rent John Cassavetes's *A Woman under the Influence,* or *Julia* with Tilda Swinton. For cocaine abuse, *Boogie Nights* and *GoodFellas* can be helpful. For heroin abuse, *Trainspotting, High Art,* and *Candy.* I'm only scratching the surface here, and again: You must only use films in conjunction with your research, not in place of it."

Ray takes this small jab directly to heart. His cheeks start to burn. He bows his head and stares at the tips of his shoes.

"Can I bring my exercise back in?" he asks.

Bill looks at him. "Are you going to do some real work on it?"

"Yeah. I want to nail it this time."

"Then the answer is yes," Bill says. "But for now, sit down. We've got other actors who want to work."

▪▪▪▪

Donna and Trevor do a stunning exercise where Trevor is obviously drunk and Donna (everyone in the class agrees) is high as a kite on cocaine.

Bill brings their exercise to a close. Smiling, he turns to the class. "How did you know she was on cocaine?"

"She had so much energy!" Amber gasps.

"Yeah, but even with that," says Quid, "she couldn't focus on anything."

"But she still thought she was being crystal clear," says Cheryl. "The behavior Donna had was the same kind my cousin had, the same behavior that eventually tipped us off. He would be a ball of fire for three or four days straight. He barely ate. He wouldn't sleep. He'd spout the wildest theories. Then he would crash. It was . . ." She shakes her head. "It was not good."

Bill nods. "Did you notice how Donna also played with her nose and sniffed a lot? It's almost a stereotype, but that's what happens with serious cocaine addicts. They'll snort so much powder that the membranes in their noses dry up. They'll crackle like parchment, then burst."

Trevor frowns. "Why did you get so mad when I asked to borrow thirty bucks?"

He's referring to a moment in their exercise.

Donna shrugs. "I didn't have it. And if I did, I wouldn't give it to you. I'd give it to my dealer."

The class laughs.

"I gave myself that I was a longtime user who's started to run out of cash."

Bill nods and turns to Trevor. "I like what you did, but you must be careful. From time to time, you were laying it on a bit too thick."

Trevor nods. "I felt that."

"Well, the next time you feel that, let it be a warning. The biggest trap of drugs and alcohol is that, as an actor, you'll get so caught up in their behaviors that they will block the contact with the other person. It takes a lot of concentration to try to maintain that contact, but this can actually enhance your experience of the other person and enrich it.

"Remember Uma's sprained ankle? She fell in a trap when she played the Impairment rather than playing the effort to surmount that Impairment. The same holds true when playing the effects of drugs and alcohol. A staggering drunk isn't trying to stagger, he's trying his best to walk that straight line. Just like a slurring drunk isn't trying to slur, she's trying to speak very clearly. I'm saying that, to capture the reality of being on drugs and alcohol, you should often try to pass as sober. I cannot say this enough, nor emphasize it enough. Rehearse the impairment, then work on moving *through* it. When you're making an effort to appear normal, that's when your drunk will come to life."

Bill turns to the class. "This also bears repeating: It's still you doing all this work. If acting is doing, then character acting is *how* you do what you do. So you might do it drunk. You might do it stoned. You might do it with a Lithuanian accent. You might do it as though you're blind or deaf or with a bilateral lisp, but it's always you. *You* are the character. Or perhaps we could say, the character is a very particular aspect of you. Therefore, *even the wildest parts you play, the ones that bear no resemblance to your everyday behavior—they're always you at the core. You must simply turn up the volume on parts of yourself that are normally quiet.*"

Bill glances at his roster. "We have a few more rounds of these, but I think we'll get through by the beginning of next week. I want to introduce the next piece of work so some of you can start on it.

"For this next exercise, I want you to pick a real person. This should be someone you know, someone you've had an opportunity to observe. Come in and do a perfect imitation of that person. Not a lampoon or caricature: I want you to fully re-create that person's behavior and bring the person into the room. We have a simple name for these exercises; we call them Imitations. Some wonderful things emerge from this work. It may not happen in every exercise, but I think it's safe to say that we're bound to see some very interesting performances."

Reg raises his hand. "Can we imitate famous movie stars? Or politicians, maybe?"

"No, and while we're on the subject, don't imitate anyone here at the Studio. It would make everyone self-conscious if they came to class thinking that someone in here might dissect them in front of everyone else. Again: Imitate someone you know, someone you've had a great deal of opportunity to observe, but don't make it anyone *we* can identify."

"Then I'm confused," Reg says. "If you don't know who I'm imitating, how will you know if I've portrayed them accurately?"

"That's not why we're doing it," Bill says. "Don't think of it as a contest. We're not handing out ribbons for Best Mimic. We just want to see you alter your straight behavior in a truthful way using an actual person as inspiration."

Reg still isn't clear. "But if you don't know the person I'm imitating, how can you know if I'm doing the Imitation in a truthful way?"

"If the person we watch has humanity, we'll know that you're being truthful," Bill says.

"How about a friend?" Dom says. "A roommate. Can we imitate them?"

Bill nods. "Yes, so long as no one here at the Studio knows them. Cheryl?"

"You want us to work out our Imitations, then continue with the improvisation, same as usual?"

"That's right," Bill says. "I'll give you an example. Suppose you see someone on the street who has a walk that interests you. Be careful. Don't get *caught* imitating them. That would be bad." The class laughs, and Bill smiles. "But really: Try to get the person's walk down precisely. If you do, a funny thing may begin to happen; it's something that Tyrone touched on earlier. Remember when he said that his Impediment *fed back* on him and began to affect him internally? Well, just from exploring that person's walk, you may feel a personality begin to emerge, and I want you to encourage its growth. At the same time, let your fantasies start to spin out. Ask yourself: Where is Mr. Funny Walk going? What does he do for a living? Does he have a family? How did he vote in the last election? What are his beliefs? Who are his friends? What kind of music does he like? What else does he like? What does he *not* like?

"You may be surprised to find that there's a whole other person living inside you, waiting for you to let them take over. And when that starts to happen, you'll know that you're on the right track."

■■■■

I have things to discuss with Bill when class breaks up that afternoon, but I have to wait. As students filter out of the studio, Ray quietly approaches Bill's table. The two spend a few minutes talking. I hang back to give them privacy.

When their conversation ends, Bill claps a hand on Ray's shoulder. Ray smiles. He looks embarrassed. I hear him say "Thanks." He turns and walks away.

He nods when he passes me. I nod back. I like Ray. Apart from the strange experience we had with his heroin exercise, he usually does good work.

Bill motions for me to follow him and we walk upstairs toward his office. My curiosity must be written all over my face, because Bill says, "He wanted to apologize."

"What did you tell him?"

"I told him he didn't need to do that—not to me, at any rate. Then I reiterated something I mentioned when we started class this year. I hate people who are unprofessional. People who are dilettantes. People who don't focus."

"I remember," I say.

Nor do I think these are idle words. Last year, Bill asked a student named Kenny to leave the program. Kenny was a first-year student. Anyone could see that Bill's work and Kenny's attitude weren't a good fit for each other.

"I cannot stand it," Bill continues, "when someone doesn't commit to his work, when someone comes to class expecting that his mere presence here will make him a better actor. I've been privileged to be acquainted with many successful people in my life, and the one thing they had in common was that they were all fanatics about their work. To be a professional demands consistency."

"Ray has talent," I say. "He also understands the craft."

"That's true." Bill shakes his head. "It's always disappointing when a talented artist throws away his most priceless gift."

"Which is what?" I wonder. "His work ethic?"

"No," he says. "Though that's a good answer. I meant his curiosity."

We enter Bill's office. He takes a seat behind his desk and I pull up a chair.

"For some reason, Ray didn't allow himself to get *interested* in what heroin addiction can be. An actor who's afraid or doesn't bother to research a condition he's playing is like a blindfolded painter doing a still life."

"Or a violinist playing Ravel with his hands cuffed behind his back."

"Impossible," Bill snorts.

"Ludicrous," I say.

Again, Bill shakes his head. "This was Ray's first major gaffe, but now it's over. I'm sure he'll get back on track."

I pull out my notebook. "These Imitations you mentioned. It seems like they encourage actors to work *from the outside in* as well as *from the inside out.*"

Bill grins. "I'm glad you noticed that. Yes, that's exactly what I'm trying to do."

"That doesn't seem like classic Meisner Technique. Most people think Sandy worked from the inside out."

"That's not entirely true. Sandy focused less on external work than, say, Michael Chekhov or a British stage actor. But he often acknowledged and applied external techniques to his acting. Imitations are a classic example."

"This is New York City," I say. "I bet when these students look around, they'll find plenty of interesting behaviors to inspire them."

Bill laughs. "That's what I'm counting on."

FIVE

IMITATION AND POINT OF VIEW

"Men often applaud an imitation and hiss the real thing."

—AESOP

"Luke, you're going to find that many of the truths we cling to depend greatly on our own point of view."

—GHOST OF OBI-WAN KENOBI TO LUKE SKYWALKER
IN *RETURN OF THE JEDI*

Bill has assigned new partners. Dom and Joyce are first up to work with the Imitation exercises.

Joyce starts off in the room. She sits at the table and boots up a laptop and starts to type. Very soon, her fingers are pounding the keyboard. Her body stiffens. *Rat-a-tat-tat!* Her fingers beat a steady, savage tattoo. *Tat-a-tat-rat! Tat-tat-tat-rat!*

"Bastard!" she snarls. "You son of a bitch!"

Without warning, Joyce bursts into sobs. Her head falls forward and she buries her face in her hands. She weeps for a moment, then straightens back up. Forcing herself to regain her composure, she wipes tears from her eyes with the backs of her fingers and addresses the keyboard again. *Rat-a-tat! Tat-a-rat! Tat!* Tears stream down her cheeks. *Tat! Tat-a-rat! Tat-tat!*

"I'll teach you," Joyce mutters. "Oh, I'll teach you, you son of a bitch . . ."

In the audience, Trevor and I turn our heads at precisely the same moment. We catch each other's gaze and grin. I can tell we're thinking the same thing. Everyone's heard of a poison pen. I've used one myself on occasion. Joyce is using the modern equivalent: a caustic keyboard. No one in the audience has any clue who she's writing to or what she's writing about, but one thing is certain: Whoever receives this composition is in for a very bad day.

Again Joyce bursts into tears. There's a knock at the door.

The change in Joyce's demeanor is instant. Gasping with joy, she leaps to her feet and dances across the room.

"Coming!" she yodels. "Here! Wait! I'm coming!"

Skipping to an end table, she picks up a white envelope, which she holds over her head and waves like a winning lottery ticket. She capers back to the door and seizes the knob and gives it a twist. The door flies open. Dom is standing at the threshold. The sudden jolt to the door has scared him. Blinking owlishly, he steps back, throwing up both hands in a gesture that's somehow protective and suppliant at the same time.

"Aaaah!" cries Dom. "I didn't—I—oh!"

Joyce's elation dissolves at once. The hand that holds the white envelope sinks to her side and hangs there, the envelope forgotten. Clearly, Dom is not the person she expected to see.

"I startled you," she says.

"You certainly did!" Dom spouts the words, indignant. His fingers interlace themselves and he begins to rub his palms together, back and forth, back and forth, in front of his chest—a curious gesture, to say the least.

Joyce hasn't backed away from the door. She holds it open with one hand and cocks her hips to the left. At the same time, she flexes her legs as though she's preparing to launch herself off the ground, straight at Dom. This is the portrait of an aggravated, aggressive woman.

"Yeah," says Joyce. She cocks her hips to the right and raises her chin defiantly. "Yeah, well. I'm real sorry about that."

Dom appears to relax a bit, but his hands continue to knead each other in front of his chest. "It wasn't very nice," he says.

Joyce reacts as if insulted. "Oh no?"

Watch out, I think. Joyce cocks her hips to the left again. I've never seen her like this before. Normally, Joyce is warm and gracious, a friendly, ironic woman, wise and effortlessly maternal. But the person I see before me is different. This version of Joyce is volatile, even fierce: a bull getting ready to charge.

Dom seems to sense this. He takes another shuffle-step back. His hands separate and drop to his sides.

"No," he says. "Not nice at all. You should—you know."

"I should what?" Joyce demands.

"You should be nicer to people."

Such un-Dom-like behavior! I've never heard Dom whine before, but that's what he's doing. Though he's always impressed me as a sensitive man, Dom is no pushover. The students in this class gravitate toward him. But the person I see before me now shows none of Dom's worthy qualities. He's a wimp. A cream puff trying to project dimensions of substance and failing miserably.

Joyce detects this right away. She has nothing but contempt for Dom. "Oh yeah?" she snarls. "Is that a fact? I should be nicer to people?"

"Yes," Dom squeaks. "You really should." He starts to say more but stops himself as Joyce cocks her hips again. Without any warning, she slams the door in his face, spins around in a whirl of skirts, and stalks back toward her computer. But a knock at the door stops her cold. Five swift blows, like whacks from a hammer—*BAM! BAM! BAM! BAM! BAM!*

"Hey!" The door's thickness has muffled Dom's voice, but his indignation is clear. "Open up! Open *up!*"

Joyce wheels around. Two quick leaps put her back at the door, and she yanks it open.

In the hallway outside, Dom throws his hands up in front of his face. "Wait!" he says. "Just wait a minute! Please—"

"Who the hell do you think you are!" Joyce screams.

She bulldozes her way across the threshold and into the hallway beyond. The students in the bleachers gasp and snicker as Dom falls back out of our view and Joyce pursues him. We can no longer see the actors, but we hear their exercise continue in the hallway outside.

Dom sputters, "Look! I don't think that—"

"Just who the hell do you think you are?!?"

Dom sputters again. "Wait, just— Stop, okay? I—"

"Don't you ever touch my door!! Ever!!! You hear me???"

"Sorry! Look, I don't—I mean I'm—!"

"Ever!!!"

The whole class is laughing.

"Okay." Bill chuckles. "Okay. Can you hear me? Come on back inside and let's talk about this."

■■■■

Joyce and Dom reenter the room. Both are grinning and panting as though they've just run a very fast mile.

"'Imitation' has evolved into a derogatory term among artists," Bill says. "This is because most artists don't know how to use Imitation properly. I'm reminded of a story I once heard about two composers, George Gershwin and Maurice Ravel. In the mid-to-late 1920s, Gershwin was making a name for himself as a talented jazz musician. But he'd always been a great admirer of Ravel's, so one day he asked Ravel if he would accept him as his pupil. Ravel replied, 'Why be a second-rate Ravel when you are a first-rate Gershwin?'

"The writer Herman Melville once said that it's better to fail at originality than to succeed in imitation. From which I think it's clear to infer that he agreed with Ravel: There's no point trying to be something or someone other than what you are. True art lies in the cultivation of that which is unique unto you."

Jon looks confused. "You just contradicted yourself. If true art lies in the cultivation of what's unique to us, why are we doing these Imitation exercises?"

Bill gives a little shrug, but his eyes are shining. "I don't know," he says. "What do you think?"

Joyce says, "I think I know."

Bill waves an invitation for her to explain.

"When you told us what the assignment was, I went to a coffee shop near Penn Station," Joyce says. "Everyone wanted their cup of coffee, but the line was long and people were getting exasperated. I sat down at a table and I noticed how everyone dealt with their frustration differently. Some people acted loose and cool. Some folks shook their heads and commiserated with the person standing next to them. But this one woman really caught my eye. She was doing this thing with her hips."

Joyce demonstrates the bull-getting-ready-to-charge posture she'd adopted for her exercise with Dom.

"Why do you think that woman did that?" Bill asks.

"I didn't know and I started to get curious." Joyce blushes. "I followed her after she got a latte. She left the store and walked down Thirty-Fourth Street, heading for Eighth Avenue. I watched her meet some people on Eighth and all of a sudden she did it again. The hip cocking. It struck me that maybe she could only deal with people once she'd taken an aggressive stance. I'm no expert on psychology, but that's what I took away from her."

"And what happened then?" Bill says.

"I left her and started home. Along the way, I tried to walk the way Coffee Shop Woman did. It was awkward at first. I felt odd and uncomfortable. Then I realized I was starting to get really agitated. It was like that woman's posture, her way of walking . . . It began to create a sense of power in me. A kind of tough . . . like I was looking for trouble. A pugnacity. I'm sorry if I'm not describing this well."

"Actually, I think you are," Bill says. He turns to the class. "We do Imitation exercises to realize another way of working. Most people think of American acting styles as working always from the inside out, meaning that you cultivate your inner life through imagination and experience, then allow that inner life to grow until it fills you and becomes your performance. But there's another way of working which can also be very effective: *working from the outside in.* Stanislavsky spoke of this. He compared it to building a barrel and filling it."

"Is that what British actors do?" says Mimi.

"I think it's probably safer to say 'Like most British actors do.' Even today, the majority of British actors work exclusively from the outside in, though, in recent years, there's been a lot of cross-pollinating of acting styles across the Atlantic. Peronally, I love to watch actors like Maggie Smith and Judi Dench. Ralph Richardson was wonderful; I saw him in Pinter's *No Man's Land,* as well as in several films. But take your classic British stage actors— John Gielgud, Laurence Olivier, and so on. They always worked from the outside in. Olivier used to say that he always began work on a part in the same way: by finding the proper prosthetic nose. He used those noses for most of his career."

Quid snickers. "He put on a false nose every time he acted?"

Bill looks at him. "It may seem strange to us, but it's a valid way to work. And many American actors do it. I once heard that Nick Nolte starts every character he's working on by asking himself, What kind of bar does this fellow drink at?"

The class laughs.

"There's a story about Stanislavsky," Bill says. "He was in a play that was about to open but he felt that he hadn't found the character yet. So one afternoon, he went to his dressing room and started playing with his makeup, hoping to get some ideas. He made himself up and checked his look in the mirror, but it still felt wrong, so he impatiently picked up a handful of cold cream and wiped it over the makeup to remove it. But after smearing the makeup, he caught sight of himself in the mirror again and realized: That was the character. That blurred face was what he'd been looking for.

"When I was a student at the Neighborhood Playhouse, John Gielgud came to do a Q and A with our class. He was starring on Broadway in *No Man's Land,* which had just come over from London. He told us how he prepared for that role. First, he said, he read the script to become acquainted with his character, this impecunious poet befriended by Ralph Richardson. Then he took a walk around London. He saw a suit hanging in a thrift store window. The suit was old and worn and definitely out of style, and Gielgud said, 'Yes. That's it. That's the suit I shall wear.' So he went inside and bought it.

"He put the suit on and showed it to the play's director. 'What about this?' he said. And the director said, 'It's perfect. Absolutely perfect. And what do you think about sandals?' Gielgud loved this idea. 'Sandals!' he said. 'Of course. With socks!' They agreed that this was the way to go. So Gielgud put on the suit, the sandals, the socks, and he stood in front of the mirror to see the full effect. 'Aha!' he said. 'Now all I have to do is to find a character who can wear this!'"

The class laughs again.

"So you see?" Bill says. "There's many different ways we can work. Up until now, we've focused on bringing your inner life to the surface. But now that we're tackling character acting, we can expand our parameters. Imitations help us access hidden parts of ourselves that fit the characters we play. They help us to turn up the volume on different aspects of our personality. By presenting these different aspects to an audience, we have, in essence, created a character. What I want you to avoid, however, is creating effect for the sake of effect. Take Olivier and Gielgud again. These men were big international stars. Audiences loved their performances. To me, however, they could often feel shallow and empty. These days, when I watch most British actors, I feel like I'm looking at a lot of empty barrels. Interesting? Yes. But empty."

He turns back to Joyce. "You imitated the physicality of this woman you saw at the coffee shop. And you say that something happened to you internally?"

Joyce nods. "I don't want to give you the wrong impression. I wasn't trying to *be* her or anything like that. But just by doing that walk, that thing she did with her hips . . . Each time I did it, it triggered feelings, which I sort of let knock around inside me. And that's what inspired the rest of the posture. The way I walked with my torso tilted forward. The snarling. The tendency to go off half-cocked. I never saw Coffee Shop Woman do anything like that, but I guess you could say that her walk gave me permission to find all those things within myself. And of course they all came out in my interaction with Dom."

"Boy, did they ever," Dom groans.

The class laughs, and Bill smiles.

"I think you just answered the question," Bill says. "Why do we bother with these Imitation exercises? And what's the proper place for imitation in art? To be clear, we don't set out to repeat the accomplishments of other artists. *We use Imitations as a springboard to inspire our individual responses, and to expand our range as actors.* In terms of character acting, any idea is a good idea if it changes your straight behavior.

"By the way, take any really good character actor and chances are she's a wickedly talented mimic. Put her in a room with someone, she'll have that person down in five minutes flat. Paul Sorvino is like that. I've seen him do it time and again. In five minutes, he'll have your walk down, your voice, your posture. Everything. Like that." Bill snaps his fingers.

Vanessa says, "I heard a story about Robin Williams. Did you see the movie *Awakenings*? Williams plays Dr. Oliver Sacks, a real-life neurologist who helped revive patients who'd spent their whole lives in catatonic states. Well, Robin Williams is a gifted mimic. According to the story, he got Dr. Sacks down so well that when Sacks came to visit the set one day he got very uncomfortable. He found it so strange to see Williams walking around as his doppelgänger that he had to leave."

"Bill?" Melissa has raised her hand. "Do you think it can be taught?"

"What's that?" Bill asks.

"The ability to mimic someone."

"No," Bill says. "I don't. Mimicry is one of those things you're either born with or you're not." He turns to Dom. "I like what you did in this exercise. Today, we saw a milquetoast version of Dom. Your high-strung, nebbish alter ego. Where did that come from?"

"I worked with a gesture I saw a man make last week." Dom demonstrates by holding his hands up in front of his chest and rubbing his palms together, the way he did in the exercise. "I was so intrigued by this gesture that I started doing it all the time. Grocery shopping. Standing in line at the post office. Dealing with the cable guy who came over to fix my TV reception. It's funny. The more I did it, the more I got really anxious for no good reason at all. I felt like I had this whole other person living inside me, someone who hated confrontations but carried a lot of angst around and didn't know how to let it out."

Bill nods. "That's the outside working in." He turns back to Joyce. "I meant to ask you, what was your activity?"

"I was inspired by a fantasy I had when walking like Coffee Shop Woman," Joyce says. "She was so belligerent, I wondered what she would do if she found out her boyfriend was cheating on her."

The class laughs. Bill smiles. "What would she do that involves a computer?"

Joyce grins wickedly. "The way I imagined it, she would post an ad on certain dating websites. The ad would have her boyfriend's picture, address, and phone number, and . . . Let's just say the part where the person describes himself would be very creatively done. And colorful."

Trevor winces. "Oh, that's ugly."

Vanessa shrugs. "I did that once. The bastard deserved it."

No one elects to comment on that.

"It was a very good activity," Bill says. "It really activated you. I also noticed you gave yourself an expectation. Something about that white envelope you brought to the door. It looked as though you wanted to give it to someone."

Joyce nods. "That also came from my Imitation work. While I was walking like Coffee Shop Woman, I got this flash of insight. She's so aggressive with human beings, but I bet she'd get all mushy and sweet with dogs and cats. Especially abandoned dogs and cats. I had this fantasy where she loves to give away checks to animal shelters throughout the city. For her, that's the most pleasurable thing she does."

Bill narrows his eyes and smiles. "I wonder, Joyce. How do you feel about animals?"

Joyce blinks. "Me? Kind of the same way I feel about kids. They're nice to play with so long as they're someone else's. I'd never own a pet myself."

"Would you ever give money to an animal shelter?"

Joyce makes a bitter face. "No way."

"Why not?"

Joyce shrugs. "I don't see how people can give money to help animals when there's plenty of people who need help, too."

Bill nods. "Thank you."

Joyce looks perplexed. "Did I say something wrong?"

"No," Bill says. "On the contrary. You just introduced a topic that's very important to character work. We call it Point of View."

■ ■ ■ ■

Bill turns to Quid. "Do you remember what you and I talked about earlier this year? I asked what you would do if someone slapped you in the face."

"Right," says Quid. "I said I'd slap him back. Still would, if you want to know the truth."

"Good," says Bill. "So again, I pose this challenge to you: Suppose you were playing the part of a Christian in some period play. Your character believes with all his heart in turning the other cheek. That's his Point of View. But how could you play that part in an honest, authentic way if turning your cheek runs contrary to your true nature?"

Quid chews his lower lip for a moment. "When you asked that before, I said I didn't know. I'm sorry, I guess I still don't."

Bill nods. "Fair enough. But Joyce just gave us a very big hint. In her exercise with Dom, she incorporated a Point of View that's very different from her own."

"I get it," Quid says. "The thing about the animals. But how did she *do* that?"

Bill looks at Joyce, inviting her to explain.

Joyce shrugs. "Like I said, personally I would never give money to an animal shelter. But I *would* give money to my sister if she was sick. So for me, the check I made out to the shelter was as if

I was writing a check that would save my sister's life, and that's what got me so excited."

Bill nods. "This is practically a prerequisite for actors: the ability to empathize with different perspectives. What is the definition of 'empathy'? It's the ability to so identify with what another person is experiencing that you literally feel what the other person feels. Most human beings have the ability to empathize. The ones who do not are very dangerous indeed. But all good actors *must* have empathy. It's that thing that allows them to argue passionately for the right-to-life movement, then turn right around and argue just as passionately for pro-choice. It's the thing that allows them to say, 'This president is the worst thing that ever happened to our country. Ever! He's a thief and a charlatan, a socialist who'll steal your money and give it to all the lazy bastards who should get off their asses and find a good job!' Then to turn around and say, 'This president is what we've been waiting for. He understands the state of our country like nobody else in four generations. He's got this economy back on its feet and he's fixing social problems that have existed since the eighteenth century. I'd vote for him again in a heartbeat!'

"The truth is," Bill says, "any good actor should be able to take a subject like pets and find ten good reasons why he loves them and ten why he detests them. This issue comes up all the time when you have to play that you love or you hate somebody. In the end, of course, you only need one good reason to fulfill the needs of your role, but you may have to wade through the other nine or more until you find the one that activates you."

Bill turns to the class. "Some schools of acting insist that character work begins and ends with Point of View. I disagree. It's true that you can create a character just by taking on a Point of View that's not your own in life. But Point of View is only one tool when it comes to creating a character. It shouldn't be overemphasized."

▌▌▌▌

A few classes later, Bill tents his fingers and nods, satisfied. Each student in the class has done the Imitation exercise twice. Some have done it three times. In each exercise, they used Imitations to alter their normal behavior. Occasionally, Bill would offer suggestions. Most of them urged the actor to relax more into the behavior being imitated.

"How subtle can you make it?" Bill asks, which is usually all the actor needs. Hearing that question, he or she will pull back and explore more nuanced ways of expressing their imitated behaviors.

It doesn't surprise me that Bill directs actors by constantly asking them questions. Actors are very creative people. Ask them a question, they'll come up with answers. And better than that: The answers they offer are unique unto them. Organic, inimitable performances.

Many directors do not ask questions. Instead they command their actors. They tell them, "Do it like this" or "Cross here now" or "Cry here." What these directors gain by having their instructions followed, they often lose in the failure to collaborate. Actors are not puppets. They are artists willing to lend their gifts in exchange for the director's guidance. By dictating what an actor should do, a director places a lid on the actor's imagination. By asking questions about what might be, a director activates the actor's imagination, empowering them to create performances that are uniquely their own, and sourced from their inimitable creativity.

"This work with Imitations has certainly been worthwhile," Bill says, "and I hope you'll draw on these skills as we move deeper into character work. For now, however, it's time we move on. We're ready for our first round of second-year scenes."

Bill goes through his roll book and groups new sets of partners. He then assigns scenes from plays such as *Diff'rent,* by Eugene O'Neill; *Speed-the-Plow,* by David Mamet; *The Boys Next Door,* by Tom Griffin; *Lou Gherig Did Not Die of Cancer,* by Jason Miller; and *The Rainmaker,* by N. Richard Nash.

"I selected these scenes because each offers a clear character challenge for the actor," Bill says. "You should get a copy of your script and read it all the way through."

"The whole script?" says Donna. "Last year, you only wanted us to read the scenes we were acting in."

Bill smiles. "That was a first-year device to keep you out of your heads. I didn't want you hatching a lot of ideas about relationships, plot, and character. I wanted you to focus on contact with your partner, on listening and responding from your unvarnished Point of View while using the writer's text as a tool for your improvisation. We've moved beyond that now. We're tiptoeing into the waters of interpretation, so it's essential that you read the whole script. Read it twice, as a matter of fact: the first time to acquaint yourself with the story, the second time to acquaint yourself with your character."

Quid raises a hand. "Should we rehearse with our partners before we meet for the next class?"

"No," Bill says. "Because the process of working on your scripts is about to change, too."

Dom perks up. "How so?"

"I'll describe that next time," Bill says. "For now, just read your scripts and be prepared to work on them with your partner in front of everyone next class."

SIX

COME, SIT AT THE TABLE!:
THE ESSENCE OF THE CHARACTER

"The very essence of the creative is its novelty, and hence we have no standard by which to judge it."

—CARL ROGERS

"The oldest form of theater is the dinner table. It's got five or six people, new show every night, same players. Good ensemble; the people have worked together a lot."

—MICHAEL J. FOX

When class meets next, a table and two chairs have been set up in the playing space.

"Do you all have copies of your scenes?" Bill asks. When everyone nods, he says, "Good. Let's have Tyrone and Amber come up first. What play do you have?"

"*The Rainmaker*, by N. Richard Nash," Amber says.

"And you've each read the whole script? Read it twice?"

"We have."

"All right, let's hear it," says Bill.

Amber and Tyrone enter the playing space and take seats across from each other at the table. They open their scripts and begin to read in flat monotones. The effect is a bit like waiting for a train in one of New York City's many subway stations and hearing some disembodied voice crackle over the loudspeaker.

The mumble-talking about blah-blah-blah service interruptions and blah-blah-blah keep an eye on your personal belongings and blah-blah-blah thank you for riding the MTA. A tone so lulling, your eyelids droop.

I look over at Bill and he's cringing. He endures the read for a few more moments before cutting off the actors midsentence.

"Enough," he says. "You must really hate us. You're killing us with boredom."

Chastened, Tyrone frowns. "You said read our scripts, so that's what we did."

"Listen to me. When they call you in for an audition, they assume you can read. The burning question is: Can you act? It's interesting. During their first table read, most actors read vigorously *at* one another. Yours was the opposite: it was deadpan, no interaction, no life. I was hoping to see two people really listening and really responding to each other. But alas, my hopes were dashed."

Amber grumbles. "That's not fair. It's hard to really listen and respond when you have to hold a script in your hands."

"Is it?" Bill says. "I'm not so sure. I'm going to tell you about two towering American actors. The first is Laurette Taylor. How many of you have heard of her?" A few hands go up around the room. "Laurette Taylor was widely considered one of the greatest actors of the early twentieth century," Bill says. "Sandy thought she was brilliant. Uta Hagen said she was her idol. Even Stanislavsky agreed; Laurette Taylor was so talented, she was the only American actor he ever invited to perform at the Moscow Art Theatre. If you've never done so, I recommend that you read her essay 'The Quality Most Needed.' She writes about how important imagination is to an actor, about the importance of staying true to your instincts. Taylor affirms everything you're learning to do here at the Studio. That essay is something every actor should read."

Bill pauses and thinks for a moment. "Why was she considered so talented? I never saw her act myself, she was a bit before my time, but I recall something Martin Landau once said about her. He said that watching her act was 'almost like this woman had found her way into the theater through the stage door and was sort of wandering around in the kitchen.' Another fine actor, Charles Durning, agreed. He saw Taylor perform once and said he thought someone had pulled her in off the street, she was that natural. But how did she do it?

"Maybe this is a clue: People say that Laurette Taylor never learned her lines until just before the show opened. During rehearsals, she carried a script and put her entire attention on the other actors. She would get so fascinated by what they were doing that whenever somebody tossed her a cue, it seemed to startle her. She went to her script like she'd forgotten it was there. For all we know, she probably had. She would take a moment to find her line, deliver it, then go back to being fascinated by what everyone else was doing. Odd, right?

"Now let's talk about another great American actor, Paul Muni. He operated a bit differently than Laurette Taylor did. Whenever Muni did a play, he came to the first rehearsal with his lines all memorized."

"The way we learned last year," says Adam.

Bill nods. "I once read an interview where Muni was asked how he prepared for a role. Was it true that he learned his lines by rote before rehearsals started? Yes, Muni said. I do, that's true. This way, when rehearsal begins, I can look at the other actor and let myself get interested in something about them, their sweater or maybe the brooch they're wearing, or the highlights in their hair from the glow of the stage lights. And that's where the work begins, he said. Right there, in that connection."

Bill leans back in his chair. "So here we have two great American actors who approached their work from opposite ends of the spectrum. Or did they? That's my question to you."

"They sure did," Ray says. "One actor memorized all his lines while the other flew by the seat of her pants."

"I disagree," says Vanessa. "Their approaches look different at first blush, but I think they're the same."

"Tell me why," Bill says.

"Their means might have been different, but the end was the same. Both actors were trying to get the text out of the way so they could listen to and work off the other actor."

Bill grins. "Exactly." He turns to the class. "Remember what we learned last year? Acting comes alive only when you invest in the contact between you and your partner, then work from unanticipated moment to unanticipated moment. You play a game of ping-pong with your impulses while the words of the script just ride on top like a boat traveling down a river. The boat's not in charge, the river is. Your job is to jump on the river and get carried along by the flow."

Bill spreads his hands. "Working this way, from unanticipated moment to unanticipated moment, means that every line you speak is the last line before the curtain comes down, before the fade to black. But then something *else* happens and *that* becomes the last line. But something *else* happens, so *that* becomes the last line. And on and on like that. Do you see?"

Melissa nods. "It's not about actors reciting text, it's about how the text bubbles to the surface out of their connection to each other in the improvisation."

"Exactly," Bill says. "I once heard a story about actors reading for Edward Albee. When they finished the scene, Albee said, 'I congratulate you. You spoke every word and you spoke it perfectly. But I already know what the words are, I wrote them.' What does this mean? *The actor's job is not to speak the lines, it's to find the reason why those lines need to be spoken.* Or, to quote Stella Adler: 'The play is not in the words, it's in you!'

"Actors supply what writers cannot: the moments, the life, the human connection. And to do that, you have to work off your partner the same way we did last year. Let your partner affect you. Let him create an impulse which you express using the text as a guide to fulfilling the writer's vision."

"But how do we connect with someone while we're sitting at a table with scripts in our hands?" Tyrone asks. "I just don't think that's possible."

"Of course it is," Bill says. "A few years back, my wife, Suzanne, and I were invited to work with New River Dramatists. They're a nonprofit that pairs actors with playwrights to help the playwrights build and hone their stories. The writers would work all morning and arrive at the afternoon sessions with pages torn fresh from their typewriters. The actors would read the work sight unseen. Most of the time, they had no idea what role they would play or what their character wanted. They didn't know what the play was about. Didn't even know the title. And yet they created the most amazing performances."

"How?" asks Reg.

"I'll show you." Bill turns back to the partners onstage. "I want you to try this again, and this time I want you to do it like this: Sit up straight in your chairs. Relax. Open yourselves to each other physically." The actors do this. Bill smiles. "Good. Now I want you to allow the text to come to the surface. Who has the first line? Amber? Okay."

Amber starts to speak, but Bill cuts her off.

"Don't rush. I want you to take as long as you like. Work as Laurette Taylor or Paul Muni would. Forget about your script and concentrate on experiencing Tyrone. Really take him in. Find something about him that attracts your interest. It might be the smell of his cologne or maybe it's how his shirt looks so crisp, like he used enough starch it could stand up straight on its own. Whatever attracts your attention is fine. When you've got something, don't speak. Just nod and I'll know that you're there."

Amber focuses all of her attention on Tyrone. A few moments later, she nods.

"All right," Bill says. "Once you've made contact—and never before—I want you to glance down at your script. Pick up the first line, the first three or four words if that's all you can manage. Then lift your eyes off the page, put your attention back on Tyrone, and let your impulse move you to say the line."

Bill turns to Tyrone. "Same thing with you. Don't worry about your script. Just allow whatever she says to make an impact on you. No matter how small the impact is, it can still create a genuine moment. When it does, take your time. Pick up your first few words, put your attention back on Amber, and speak. If you work like this, from unanticipated moment to unanticipated moment, small things, real things, can start to happen between you. You'll experience a real conversation between two human beings who are really listening and really speaking to each other. Let's try it."

Amber and Tyrone start again. This time they really take each other in, and the change that comes over their work is amazing. The dismal flatness of their first attempt disappears and we follow their every word because we're interested in what's going on between them. A current charges the air around the table. The source of it? Their contact with each other.

When actors are really connected to each other, something spontaneous happens. Moments that are inimitable flicker into being and hover over the room. And who cares if the actors are using someone else's words? A passerby would never know. He would hear Tyrone and Amber talking and think he was eavesdropping on a private conversation.

From a technical standpoint, Amber and Tyrone maintain their contact even when they're out of words. Whenever they need a line to speak, they pause, check their scripts for the next set of words, return to the contact, and use them. It's interesting that, rather than halting the flow of their exchange, this method seems to connect them more.

When they finish, Bill nods. "That was very good. So tell me. What have you learned, Tyrone?"

The big man purses his lips. "In our first reading, nothing had any meaning for Amber and me. Because of that, it was completely dead. But you're telling us that the actor is there to seek meaning, not to deny it or block it or turn it into something that's mechanical or theatricalized. You're suggesting that, even though we're sitting at the table with scripts, we can still work the same way we did in our first-year exercises."

Bill jumps out of his seat, makes a megaphone of his hands, and shouts: *"Yes! Yes! Just! Like! In! The! Exercise!"* The class cracks up, and he sits back down. "So you're saying it's possible to improvise from unanticipated moment to unanticipated moment even while working with script in hand?"

"It's clear to me now," Tyrone says. "Yes."

"And further: You're saying that working this way allows you to achieve all the goals we set for last year's work. Like conversational reality. Working off the other person. Slowly allowing your responses to each other to bring you to an authentic life."

Amber smiles. "Yes."

"Think of it this way: The life of the scene is a beautiful plant which begins as a tiny seedling. The attention the partners pay to each other serves as the water and the light that seedling needs to grow. Without attention, the scene will never open. It will remain shrunk inside itself, lifeless and cold. Now, who here would want to do that to a helpless plant?" The class laughs, and Bill nods. "I think we're ready to move forward. Let's dig deeper into the material and figure out what's going on in this scene."

The Rainmaker takes place in the American West during the Great Depression. Lizzie Curry (played by Amber) is a plain-looking spinster whose father has tried to marry her off, but no prospective groom will have her. To make matters worse, the county has been stricken by drought and all the cattle are dying. So, too, it seems, are the Curry family's prospects.

Enter Starbuck, played by Tyrone. Starbuck is a charming drifter who promises he can call down rain but charges a fee to do it—one hundred dollars, cash money. Lizzie sees Starbuck for what he is: a confidence man who makes his living bilking people out of their funds. The Great Depression was full of them. Still, she can't help falling for him. Starbuck makes romantic overtures and Lizzie begins to succumb to his spell. But can she trust a man like this? Can anyone really trust him?

The scene begins with Lizzie bringing a blanket out to the stable. Her father has allowed Starbuck to sleep there while the Curry family considers his offer to call down the rain. When Starbuck has Lizzie alone, he argues that she should view herself in a different light. She isn't plain, Tyrone insists—that's just what everyone else thinks, but why should that matter? All that's important is how Lizzie sees herself. What matters is who she wants to be.

Starbuck wonders aloud: What would happen if Lizzie thought of herself as beautiful, charming, and attractive to men? He points out that even her name is dull and urges her to invent something new. What about Leonora? he asks. Desdemona? Mélisande?

Lizzie tells Starbuck to cut it out. She harbors simpler dreams, she says. She wants a husband. Children. A family. She doesn't want to be Helen of Troy. She wants an average, everyday life. She just wants to love and be loved.

Bill leans back in his chair and thinks. "Starbuck is quite a specimen," he says. "You know who would probably understand him? Norman Vincent Peale. Of course, these days, most people don't know who that is."

"I do," says Melissa. "He was a minister at Marble Collegiate Church. During the early 1950s, he wrote a very influential book called *The Power of Positive Thinking*."

Bill looks at her; he's impressed. "That's right," he says. "That book is based on the premise that you can make anything happen in life—anything at all—so long as you *believe* in it strongly enough." He turns to the class. "Can you see how that Point of View might appeal to someone like Starbuck? This is a man who lives for dreams, who longs to inspire them in others because they're essential to his own survival. If he can't get other people to believe their dreams, then maybe his own are worthless as well, and if that's true his whole universe will collapse. He'd have to face the fact that he's nothing but a small-time crook running from town to town, always one step ahead of the sheriff. How would that feel?"

Tyrone pouts. "That would be awful."

"So now you see why he does it. And now I feel we've come to the point where I can ask you a very important question. What's the Essence of your Character?"

Tyrone frowns. "I don't understand."

"The 'essence' of something is defined as its intrinsic nature or indispensable quality. In Latin, you might call it the sine qua non: a condition, bereft of which, a thing would simply not be. Let me ask you this: Can you summarize who your character is in a simple word or phrase?"

Tyrone's frown deepens. "Well," he begins. "I'm a con man, right? But also, you see, I'm charming. I mean, I really like Lizzie and I want her to grow. But then there's this thing about making the rain—I haven't decided whether Starbuck can really do that or not, you know? I mean, clearly he can't, that would be impossible. But the play has a certain magic to it and . . ."

He trails off, frustrated.

Bill nods, sympathizing. "Now you see what a morass character work can be. Diving into a character can be like diving into the ocean. The deeper you go, the more constricted you feel, the less air there is to breathe. You look around for help, but all you see is more water pressing down on you. So you start to panic. You flail toward the surface. But now you don't know up from down. You start to give up. You're drowning in too many concepts, too many ideas, too many tidbits to keep in mind. It can be awesomely discouraging. The actor who has too much on his mind can become paralyzed. I learned that the hard way years ago when I taught with Sandy."

Bill sits back in his chair. "One time, Sandy had a second-year class that didn't excite him, so he called me into his office and gave me a play to direct them in. Basically, he pawned them off on me so he wouldn't have to deal with them anymore."

The class laughs, and Bill shrugs as if to say, What can you do?

"The play was *Assembly Line,* by Marian Winters," Bill says. "It was a forty-five-minute one-act about a small business that assembled manicure kits. All the usual characters in a factory were there: the office boy, the bookkeeper, the owner, the women who worked the assembly line.

"Keep in mind, I'd never directed before. I was sort of flying blind. But I'd read somewhere that Elia Kazan, a director I admired, would get a notebook before each project he worked on. He'd read the play again and again and jot down all sorts of thoughts and impressions. So what do you think I did? The moment I left Sandy, I ran to the corner and bought a notebook. I read the play again and again, making notes on every character.

I imagined who their parents were, where they grew up, where they went to school, why they left school, what they wanted out of life, what scared them the most, and I wrote it all down. Pages and pages and pages of notes.

"Well. Every day I'd go to rehearsal and share what I'd written in this notebook with the cast. I hoped that my observations would help them deepen their understanding of their characters and come to life in their parts. But to my horror, their behavior grew deader each day. I fought back by giving them more and more information, which only made matters worse. Finally it was like watching a bunch of zombies up on the stage. No life. No spark. No nothing.

"One terrible day, Sandy and I passed each other in the hall. 'So, Bill,' he said. 'How's that play coming along?' I confessed that it wasn't going so well. 'It seems like every day the actors just get deader and deader.' Sandy shook his head and said, 'I'd better come take a look.'

"The next day, he came to rehearsal. After watching the play for about ten minutes, he said, 'You're right, this is really awful. The actors look like they're ready to be embalmed. Stop the play and call everyone out, I want to talk to them.'

"The cast assembled at the foot of the stage. Sandy looked at one of the actors and said, 'You. Tell me, what is your character?' The actor said, 'Well, Mr. Meisner, I grew up in Lithuania. My father worked as a glover. We fled the Soviet occupation just before the Nazis attacked. The Soviets put him in jail for a year because someone overheard him voicing sympathy for the independence movement—'

"Sandy cut her off. 'Good God, no! Forget all that! You know what you are? You're a Good Time Charley. You'll do anything for a laugh, get it? You want everyone to be happy. You think life should be a party. A Good Time Charley. Okay? That's your character.'

"He turned to the next actor and said, 'Tell me about your character.'

"The next actor said, 'Well, I was thrown out of grade school once for doodling in a textbook. In fact, I've always been very attracted to drawing and the visual arts. My mother was raised Greek Orthodox and my father was Russian Orthodox. They met and had a stormy relationship, which neither of their families approved of—'

"'Stop!' said Sandy. 'No, no, no! You know who you are? You're a Brownnoser. Everything that comes out of your mouth is, Yes, Boss! Sorry, Boss! Right away, Boss! A Brownnoser, see? Do that. That's your character.'

"Then Sandy addressed the actor who played the owner of the business. 'What about you? What's your character?' he said. The actor responded, 'All my life, I've wanted to own this business—' Sandy cut him off immediately. 'No, no, that doesn't help you. Your character is, you're a Nice Guy. You want everyone to like you. Okay? Do that.'"

Bill raises his eyebrows and sighs. "Sandy did that with every actor in my cast and we ran the play again. Can you guess what happened? The most amazing thing. Suddenly there was life onstage! My cast, which had died, was back to life!"

The class laughs. Bill grins and turns to Tyrone.

"You see why I told you that story just now? Back then, I made a big mistake by filling the actors' heads with useless information. It was like I'd injected their brains with glue. All that information paralyzed them. They couldn't act from anything I'd told them. In trying to work like Elia Kazan I'd failed to heed one of the most valuable pieces of advice he ever gave. He said, 'Acting is the ability to turn psychology into behavior.'

"Sandy knew what that meant, of course. *A character is not a complicated series of circumstances and life history and so on, it's one thing. One concrete idea. That's how the character lives in the writer's mind.* From what I can see, this marks a big difference between how artists like Lee Strasberg and Sandy approached the craft of acting. It's my impression that Strasberg thought that, in order for something to be profound, it had to be complicated. Sandy disagreed with that. Eventually, so did I. I believe that in order for something to be truly profound, it has to be truly simple."

Bill thinks for a moment and smiles. "You know what happened? Later on, I told Sandy about my magic notebook and he laughed. 'How many times have I told you?' he said. 'You cannot act complicated things. This notebook you have. Go home immediately and burn it.'"

Dom raises a hand. "Bill, I'm not sure I understand that last part about a character being an idea."

"It doesn't matter whether you're reading a play, a screenplay, or a novel," Bill says. "Regardless of what form it takes, good writing is really a statement the author's trying to make or an idea he's trying to express in dramatic terms. And all the characters in the piece are there because they contribute different aspects to the argument. You could say that each character is a lamp that shines light on an issue from a different direction, exposing different facets.

"Take *Death of a Salesman*. Arthur Miller used that play to force us to look at how corrosive the American dream could be to our humanity. Every member of the Loman family attempts to achieve the American dream in his or her own way, and it destroys them. Or take Ibsen's *A Doll's House*. That play is all about the search for self-worth. The characters undertake this central mission from drastically different Points of View."

Bill thinks for a moment. "I find it interesting that Freud built his whole system of psychoanalysis around a similar position. Psychoanalysts believe that an individual's whole personality generates out of a single predominant issue. How that issue plays itself out and influences every part of your life is the skein you try to untangle when you start to work with a therapist. For instance, you might discover that you had very critical parents, and that's the reason you've spent your whole life trying to excel to a point beyond criticism. Which reveals the Essence of your Character: you are a perfectionist."

Bill looks at the class. "Do you see where I'm going with this? In terms of our work, it couldn't be clearer. In the end, *you must distill everything you know about your character into a single word or short phrase which is the defining trait of the person you are playing. It's what I call the Essence of the Character.* All the rest is gobbledygook. If it takes you more than one sentence to explain your character, it's too complicated. Go back and try again, but remember: Do not overthink or overelaborate. It's easy to get in your head and to start intellectualizing. Be aware of something Michael Chekhov once said: 'An actor's intelligence sits in his head like a murderer, ready to kill any sign of life.'"

Bill turns to Tyrone. "So tell me. Knowing what you know about Starbuck, what would you say is the Essence of his Character?"

Tyrone thinks it over. "Well," he says, "he's an optimist."

"Excellent. And not just any old optimist, right?"

"No, this guy's *insanely* optimistic, almost like he's on another planet or spiritual plane. A visionary."

"I like that better," Bill says. "Can you work from that?"

"I know I can."

Bill turns to Amber. "What is Lizzie's Essence?"

"A pessimist," she says. "It couldn't be clearer. Lizzie refuses to let herself imagine that anything good could ever happen to her."

"Right," says Bill. "But let's try to be more specific. In fact, let me ask you this: Is there a part of yourself that you consider unattractive?" Amber looks uncomfortable and Bill holds up his hands. "A rhetorical question. You don't have to share that information with us. But I think it's something you need to ask yourself to understand a woman who feels that she's unattractive. Everyone has traits they consider unattractive. It could be your nose or your voice. It could be that you think you're too heavy or too thin. Maybe you don't like your smile. Whatever it is doesn't matter. As you work on this part, you must allow yourself to dwell on that thing or things. To magnify them. Let them become the lens through which you see the world, and interact with it."

Bill smiles. "Do you see what a good writer we had in N. Richard Nash? I once read an interview where he talked about *The Rainmaker*. He said, 'I tried to tell a simple story about droughts that happen to people, and about faith.' Well, that's just it, you see? Spiritual droughts are caused when our inner wells of faith run dry, and that's what Lizzie's going through. Her inner circumstances mimic those of the outside world. It wasn't whimsy that led Nash to introduce a cockeyed optimist like Starbuck into a situation like this. He was following every good writer's instinct to set up a conflict, raise the stakes high, and let the characters fight for themselves until they achieve resolution.

"A question I'm frequently asked is, How do you marry the Essence of the Character to your own experience? The answer, again, is that empathy is a key factor in an actor's talent. Empathy is your ability to identify with another human being, with what's going on inside the person. Without this quality, you cannot have a really good actor. It won't work to understand the Essence of the Character mentally, it has to resonate with you in some way." Bill turns to Tyrone. "I wonder: Is there anything in your life that allows you to empathize with Starbuck's irrational hopefulness?"

"To me it's like being an actor," Tyrone says. "I can draw from my own experience of waking up every day to a constant struggle, convincing myself that I'm talented enough to keep going, that one day my big break will surely come. It could be today. It could be tomorrow. I just have to keep at it."

Bill smiles. "I think that will do very nicely. Allow yourself to live in that place. Both in and outside of rehearsals, I want you to actively look for things to be optimistic about. Give yourself permission to be optimistic all the time for no good reason at all. In this way, you will bring yourself to the demands Starbuck makes of you." He turns to Amber. "What about you? Can you relate to a pessimist's Point of View?"

"I'm thinking of a friend of mine," Amber says. "Years ago, she suffered an accident that paralyzed her from the waist down, and she's been in a wheelchair ever since. I had a tough time coping with seeing this happen to her. I used to give her these crazy pep talks. But one day she told me, 'Amber, stop it. Dreaming that I'll be able to get up and walk someday won't help me get on with my life. I've got to be practical and focus on what I can do from this chair.' That was a big awakening for me. I realized then that all those pep talks were really more for my sake than for hers. She was much more realistic about her situation, and that's something I think I can use to play Lizzie. It sort of matches her perspective."

"Good," says Bill. "But don't work too hard at it. Sometimes finding a Point of View is really just a matter of allowing your actor's faith to accept it. You might take on a Point of View the same way you slide into a hot bath: gently, easing into it. Then, once you get there, allowing yourself to soak in it until the water doesn't scald, but feels natural. Don't leap into it, immerse yourself gradually. Throughout the course of a day, allow yourself to connect with the Point of View again and again until it becomes almost second nature."

The class, I notice, is taking notes.

Bill goes on. "Well. It's clear to me that you both have very good instincts about the Essences of your Characters. At this point, you should go away from each other and marinate in your own time. Allow yourself to experience the central issue of your character in daydreams. You must make the character's major issue your major issue. The more time you spend doing that, the more you'll find that your character begins to inhabit you. Meantime, let's return to some technical considerations. The next time you bring this scene in, you should have answered all the questions we asked ourselves last year. For instance: What happened just before this scene took place?"

Tyrone says, "Starbuck argued with Lizzie's brother Noah."

Bill nods. "Noah thinks Lizzie is so unattractive that no one will ever want to marry her and he thinks she's got to accept that. But what do *you* think?"

"I reject that notion," Tyrone says. "I think Noah's destroying her confidence out of spite, so I act as Lizzie's champion. Then I go out to the barn so I can turn in for the night."

"You've got it," says Bill. He turns to Amber. "Why do *you* go to the barn?"

"I'm conflicted," Amber says. "All my life, I've believed what people like Noah have told me. I should give up my dreams, be practical, face the facts: I'm an unattractive girl and I'll spend my life as a lonely old maid. But here's Starbuck, this good-looking, sexual man who says I can have so much more out of life. He says that he finds me attractive, and I can't help it, I want to believe him."

"But that creates another obstacle, right? Which is what?"

"He's a liar. A con man who makes money off people by saying he can make it rain whenever he wants."

"So why do you bring him a blanket?"

"That's just an excuse for me to go to him. What I really want is to find out if he's telling the truth. Whether or not he really believes what he said to my brother."

"Great," says Bill. "Now that you know what your characters were doing just before this scene begins, you can add an Emotional Preparation, the same way we did last year. What do you think you'll prepare for, Tyrone?"

"Like I said, I was just talking to Noah. From my Point of View, he's a pessimistic man who's destroying Lizzie's life with his negative attitude. But I just stood up to him! I told him off! I confronted my archenemy and won, which makes me feel vindicated. Glorified! So that's what I'll prepare!"

Bill smiles. "Very nice. If it helps, you can always go back and reread the chapter on Emotional Preparation in *The Actor's Art and Craft*. In case anyone's forgotten, does it matter where you go within yourself to conjure up the emotion you'll bring to the start of the scene?"

Tyrone shakes his head. "For all you guys know, I might be fantasizing about torturing defenseless chipmunks. In the end, you'll never know what daydreams I use to prepare and I'll never tell. It's deeply personal and, if it activates me, that's all that's important."

"Correct," Bill says. "But remind me: How long will your preparation persist once the scene begins?"

"Only for the first moment," Tyrone says. "At which point, the improvisation takes over. If my contact with Amber perpetuates the emotion I've prepared, so be it. But I have to work moment to moment and let the emotions change as they will."

Bill nods and turns to Amber. "What do you think you should prepare for?"

Amber frowns. "I'm not sure," she says. "I see two possible preparations. On one hand, I have this virile, sexual man who finds me attractive. He's telling me all these wonderful things, which is thrilling, but I'm also afraid of him because I know he's a con man. How do I know that he really means what he says?" She looks at Bill. "So which should I prepare for? The thrill or the fear? I remember last year you said that it's only possible to prepare for one thing."

"It is," Bill says. "But if you recall, last year we also talked about using the magic of *because* to boil down your circumstances to one preparation. In this case, that might go something like this: *Because* you feel so attracted to this man and *because* he's offering you attention that you've only ever dreamed about . . . and *because* you can't tell if he's lying through his teeth or not . . . and *because* you so desperately want to believe what he's saying . . . *because* of all that . . . *how would you feel?*"

Amber thinks about it. "Scared," she says. "Scared would encompass all of those things. I'm scared of him but nonetheless compelled to enter the barn and get some answers. I mean, what if he isn't lying this time? That's a really tough place to be."

"Correct," says Bill. "So that's what you will prepare for this scene. You're scared as hell, then you walk in, the contact begins, and who knows where it will lead you?"

Bill nods, satisfied. "We're off to a pretty good start with this, so there's two more elements I want you to add for next time. The first is heat. The script says you're caught in the middle of a drought. It's 110 in the shade—which, by the way, is the name of the musical they made based on *The Rainmaker.* So you both need to start working with heat. How do you think you'll do that?"

"I'd treat it like any other Physical Impediment," Amber says. "Practice until it becomes second nature."

"But how can you create the illusion of heat?"

"When it's really hot, people move around ponderously, as if the heat leaches all strength from their bodies. They're always dabbing at sweat on their face and they get cranky because the heat is so much to put up with."

"I like this," Bill says. "Here's a piece of advice for playing heat.

Always begin by isolating some part of your body that's warmer than the rest of you. Close your eyes and place your full concentration on that area and imagine it spreading throughout your entire body. If you really concentrate on that, the heat will become very real for you. Then you can add the external touches—tugging at sticky clothing, mopping your face. And so on."

"But this way we'll be anchored to something real," Amber says.

"That's right. Try building that in for next time. The second thing you should start working with is the accent. *The Rainmaker* takes place out west, during the Great Depression. Think Kansas or Missouri. Both those states will work fine for this play and both have very particular accents. You two should agree on a place, get hold of some recordings of people who hail from there, and practice until you've got that dialect down pat. And yes, *just as with a Physical Impediment, you have to have mastered a dialect to the point where it's second nature.* You should become so deft at speaking in that dialect, you could speak to a native and he wouldn't know you weren't from that region. Who has questions?"

Jon raises his hand. "Bill, I'm concerned. This business of picking the lines up off the page." He hesitates.

"Yes?"

"I'm just not very good at it," Jon admits. "I read kind of slowly."

"You have to practice it, just as with anything else," Bill says. "There's a knack to it, the same way there's a knack to crafting activities or responding to a knock when your partner comes to the door. Here's a suggestion: Go home and pick up a book. Open it to a random page. Start at the top, pick up the first two or three lines, and deliver them to your dog or your cat. Eventually, you'll get the hang of it."

Adam raises a hand. "Going back to the difference between Laurette Taylor and Paul Muni. Should we memorize these scenes by rote before we bring them in?"

"No," Bill says. "I had you do that in the first year to keep you away from line readings. It was a tool that helped you focus on your instincts and what they were telling you. That way, you would learn to trust them and recognize how much your instincts will do for you if you only get out of their way. You've surpassed that now. Focus on creating the acting. Memorize the acting instead of the lines. The words will come to you easily once, as Edward Albee said, the acting you've created demands that they be said."

■■■■

Later, back in his office, Bill sits down in his chair and sighs. "I'm throwing a lot of concepts at them, and fast."

I nod. "They can handle it. They're a good group."

Bill agrees. "They *are* a good group, and there's really no way to avoid this learning curve. Advanced character work demands a lot from actors. They have to have certain tools at their disposal, the tools I'm giving them now. It'll take them years to figure out how to use them properly, but at least they can begin to experiment. When an actor understands who his character is, when he understands what's really going on in the scene, *then and only then can a scene begin to come to life.*"

I finish jotting a note in my book. "I love that story from *Assembly Line.*"

Bill nods. "The ability to understand the character's Essence provides a solid foundation for all the advanced work in character and interpretation. It clears the decks of all nonessential information, freeing the actor to pursue one clear, concrete concept. Unless that element is discovered, the actor may find himself falling off a cliff and landing in a whirlpool of meaningless detail. Did I ever tell you about that movie Sandy shot back in the 1950s?"

I shake my head.

"At one point, Sandy left the Neighborhood Playhouse and went to Los Angeles," Bill says. "This was during the days of the old studio system. Twentieth Century–Fox hired him to start an acting school for contract players. Fox brought Sandy beautiful people whom he tried to teach how to act, though many of them could not.

"While he was in Los Angeles, Sandy did a movie called *The Story on Page One,* written and directed by his old friend Clifford Odets. In the film, Rita Hayworth and Gig Young were having an adulterous affair, but Young accidentally killed Hayworth's husband while wrestling over a gun.

"Sandy played the role of Phil Stanley, a driven prosecutor who was certain the couple had plotted the murder so they could be together. Sandy was wonderful in that film. Such a zealot! An uncompromising, snarling megalomaniac.

"One time, I asked him about how he prepared for that role. He told me he'd based his entire performance on Savonarola, the fanatical fifteenth-century monk who took control of Florence and nearly destroyed the Renaissance. Savonarola despised art. He had his acolytes gather books, statues, mirrors, cosmetics—anything he thought signified beauty—and burn them all in the Piazza della Signoria."

"The Bonfire of the Vanities," I say.

Bill nods. "Savonarola was a fanatic, convinced beyond all reason that his Point of View was correct. Sandy commandeered his essence to craft a militant prosecutor and turned in a brilliant performance."

"Working with the character's Essence seems to fit perfectly into Sandy's creed."

Bill grins. "Simplify, simplify, simplify!"

SEVEN

STILL AT THE TABLE:
ACTIONS AND SUPER OBJECTIVES

"We become just by performing just actions, temperate by performing temperate actions, brave by performing brave actions."

—ARISTOTLE, *NICOMACHEAN ETHICS*

"Action is the real measure of intelligence."

—NAPOLEON HILL

The actors spend their next few classes exploring their scenes at the table. They quickly catch the trick of lifting words off their scripts and using them to improvise. Even Jon gets the hang of it—Jon, who once claimed to have trouble reading. I stop him after class one day and ask what method he used to improve.

He smiles. "I took Bill's advice and started practicing at home. Every night, I pick a book off my shelf, open it to a random page, and deliver lines to my bird."

"You have a bird?"

Jon nods. "Hippolyta, my African gray parrot. She's very smart, but now there's a problem."

"What's that?"

"I've been giving her lines for over two weeks and she's started to give them back!"

The work in Bill's studio continues apace. Each time a scene returns to the table, we start to identify less with the actors, more with the characters they're playing. For instance, I no longer recognize Reg and Vanessa; instead I see Val and Alea Johnson from Dennis McIntyre's play *Split Second*. Trevor and Cheryl have morphed into Captain Caleb Williams and his fianceé, Emma Crosby, from Eugene O'Neill's *Diff'rent*. Melissa and Donna have transmogrified into Georgie and Lydia from Theresa Rebeck's *Spike Heels*.

Adam and Uma have just finished improvising their way through a scene from William Gibson's *Two for the Seesaw*. Adam plays Jerry Ryan, a lawyer from Nebraska who discovers his wife is cheating on him and moves to New York City while his divorce is being finalized. He meets a struggling dancer named Gittel Mosca (played by Uma). Jerry and Gittel fall in love, but their relationship is hampered by obstacles. Gittel finds it hard to abandon her gypsy ways and move past her insecurities to embrace the man of her dreams. Jerry spends hours on the phone with his soon-to-be ex-wife. Both characters are encumbered by the past. The question is, Are they so encumbered they won't be able to move forward and start a new life together?

Their relationship reaches a crisis point when Jerry invites Gittel to a party thrown by Frank Taubman, the boss of his law firm. Gittel declines, so they agree that Jerry will go to Taubman's alone, but as soon as he's finished he'll pick Gittel up at her friend Sophie's party.

Jerry turns onto Sophie's block and sees Gittel leaving the party with another man, a down-and-out painter named Jake. Mortified, Jerry tracks Gittel to Jake's apartment building on Bleecker Street and waits outside. An hour later, Gittel and Jake reemerge. Jerry trails them as Jake walks Gittel home and kisses her good night. Gittel goes into her building and Jerry follows, intent on confronting her.

Uma and Adam finish their table read and Bill smiles. "This was good. You took your time and worked off each other moment to moment. I'm pleased. This scene from *Two for the Seesaw* is perfect for second-year work. It offers roles with very rich emotional lives and it's replete with character issues. Let's make sure you can integrate some of the concepts we already know. Uma, what happened just before the scene began?"

"I stood Jerry up, and instead of waiting for him at Sophie's party, I went home with an old boyfriend, Jake the painter. I just got home and now I don't feel so hot."

"What's wrong?"

"I've had this ulcer for a while and it started bleeding again."

"What do you know about bleeding ulcers?"

"Not much. I had to look it up. A bleeding ulcer is tremendously dangerous. Sometimes you can die from it."

"Are there any symptoms?"

Uma nods. "Nausea and intense abdominal pain, especially when I eat or drink, and most especially when I drink anything with alcohol. Sometimes you vomit blood."

"So how do you think you'll play that?"

"It's a pain exercise, like we did at the beginning of this year. I started working on it at home. Should have it ready for next time."

"This pain that you're in. Does it hint at a possible Emotional Preparation?"

"It sure does—I'm frightened! I come home thinking I'm in mortal danger, so that's what I'll prepare for."

"Ah, ah, ah." Bill wags a finger. "Not so fast. You didn't mention a pivotal circumstance that precipitates this scene. It's written right there in the script."

"Do you mean the phone bills?" Uma asks.

Bill's eyes go wide. "You mean you found some phone bills?!?" The class laughs. "Of course I mean the phone bills. What information did those bills convey to you?"

"They told me that Jerry's been calling his ex-wife in Omaha, Nebraska, almost every day."

"And what does that mean?" When Uma frowns, Bill says, "It means that he's still very connected to her. In light of that, what do you feel your chances are with Jerry?"

Uma considers this. "I don't know."

"Then let me ask you this: What do you think Jerry's wife looks like?"

"She's beautiful, I guess."

Bill nods. "Is she educated?"

"Sure."

"Is she rich? And are you any of those things?"

Uma looks at her shoes. "No."

"So what's the handwriting on the wall say?"

"Oh God . . . I don't stand a chance."

"You're about to lose the most precious thing in the world to you because you're not good enough. Meanwhile your ulcer is bleeding and you think you're going to die. So preparing that you're frightened is a bit too shallow for Gittel Mosca. You should prepare that you're a fucking emotional basket case—do you see the difference?" Uma nods and Bill nods back. "Now there are other technical considerations for building this character. For instance, where is Gittel from?"

"The Bronx," Uma says.

"Correct. And people from the Bronx speak in a very specific way. You'll have to study that accent and master it, just as you would a Physical Impediment. In other words, you should be able to speak like Gittel and forget that you're doing it." Bill thinks. "To a certain degree, being from the Bronx also informs how you deal with your emotions. How do you think a lifelong dancing gypsy from the Bronx deals with feelings of inadequacy and vulnerability?"

Uma laughs. "I live in the Bronx right now and I love it there, the people are great. But it's true. They have a certain edge to them."

"Does the script make use of this?"

"It sure does. Gittel uses sarcasm a lot to mask her true feelings. That's something I'd like to key into some more. Whenever something strikes close to my heart, I throw up a wall and blow a Bronx cheer." She does this, blowing a raspberry that makes the class erupt.

Bill grins. "That's good. Start working with that." He turns to the class. "Have you noticed how I'm working with Uma? By asking her questions. Someone wise once said that correctly identifying a problem is ninety percent of the solution, and that's very true of creative work. A lot of great art comes about when the artist sets up a problem, then works to conquer it.

"Years ago, they hired Sally Jacobs to head the set design department at Rutgers' Mason Gross School of the Arts. Sally designed a number of Peter Brook's productions, including the famous circus production of *A Midsummer Night's Dream*. I asked her once how Brook and his team came up with such a fantastic concept. Sally said the concept evolved from a single problem that Brook posed to his production staff: How do you go about creating magic on the stage? Eventually, the designers figured that a circus is one of the last true instances of magic on earth. So they set about imagining every aspect of *A Midsummer Night's Dream* as it would appear under the Big Top."

Bill shoots the class a pointed look. "You should approach every character you play like a detective approaching a crime scene. Meaning that you must look for every clue you can find embedded in the text. Focus on taking in everything. Nothing can fall beneath your scrutiny. The clues you discover will fill you with many questions, which, one by one, you will set about answering.

In doing so, you create your performance." Bill turns to Adam. "What technical challenges will you face in creating Jerry?"

"His accent, for one thing."

"That's right. Where is Jerry from?"

"The Midwest."

Bill darkens. "No, not the Midwest, that's too general. Don't you remember our discussion last year about general choices versus specific choices?"

Adam nods. "Specific choices breed art, whereas general choices breed mishmash."

"Well put. *The Midwest* tells you nothing, whereas specific information like *Omaha, Nebraska,* tells you how to craft your accent, and possibly even your temperament. Omaha, Nebraska, is very different from Chicago, Indianapolis, Cleveland, or St. Paul. Do you see what I'm getting at?"

"I do," Adam says.

"Then work on that for next time. Just as I mentioned with Uma, rehearse your accent and Omaha behavior until they become second nature. Go to the dry cleaners or the drugstore in character."

"I will," Adam says.

"You should be able to walk down Main Street, Omaha, and chat up the natives without them ever suspecting you're from big bad New York City." The class laughs, and Bill grows suddenly serious. "Okay. Now listen very carefully. Today is a very special day. Because today is the day when I reveal to you the whole secret of being a great actor."

The class looks shocked. They lean in and listen.

"Just kidding," Bill says. "But it really is important, what I'm about to say. So pay attention. I'm going to introduce an important tool that will help your acting a lot. Think back to last year. What did we say was the actor's job?"

Cheryl jumps in. "To create behavior."

"Correct," Bill says. "But if that's true, tell me this: What is it *exactly* that creates human behavior?"

The class falls silent, thinking it over. Bill turns abruptly to Dom. "What are you doing?"

Dom is startled. "I— What do you mean?"

"Just now. What were you doing when I interrupted you?"

"I was thinking of an answer to your question."

"Good," says Bill. "Would you do that again?"

"Would I think of an answer? Sure."

Dom's expression grows vague. His eyes drift off while he ponders.

Bill smiles and turns to the class. "Do you see how clear that behavior is? What do you see?"

Reg nods. "I see a man deep in thought."

"Right. And what's causing this behavior? Dom is really doing an Action. You see him Trying to Think of an Answer because he really is trying to think of an answer."

Joyce nods and jots something down in her notes.

"In his *Poetics,* Aristotle proposed that plays are imitations of Action. Tragedies imitate serious Actions, he said, while comedies imitate Actions that tend to create carefree, lighthearted behavior. With all due respect to that ancient Greek, I'd like to propose something different. To my way of thinking, plays aren't imitations of anything. Rather, *a play is a series of Actions that are truly and authentically performed.*

"Actions have two aspects that are very helpful to actors. First, the number of Actions is not infinite. I don't know that anyone's counted the Actions it's possible for human beings to perform, but there is a limit. Which means that, when you sit down to apply Actions to your script, you're not inundated with choices. Second, Actions are universal. They are the shared vocabulary of our species, a lexicon human beings have been developing since the dawn of time. For example, every woman who's ever lived has known how to sing a lullaby to put a child to sleep. It doesn't matter what country she's from. Chinese women do it, Spanish women do it, Eskimo women do it, African women do it. The song may change, the melody may alter, and the words will be sung in different languages, but the Action is always the same.

"By the same token, since people lived in caves, men have been interrogating their wives. How do I know? Because it's written in the ancient Greek and Roman plays, as well as in the work of Shakespeare, the Jacobeans, Molière, the Victorians, the Edwardians, and playwrights up to modern times. For thousands of years, whenever a man enters his home and spots something expensive that wasn't there yesterday—a vase, some drapes, a new pair of shoes—you can bet he'll corner his wife and Interrogate Her."

The class laughs, and Bill grins. "Whether they know it consciously or not, audiences understand Actions because they've all spent their lives doing them. From the moment we're born to the moment we die, human beings are constantly in Action. In fact, one could argue that life is a series of Actions strung together, moment to moment, from cradle to grave.

"Remember the discussion we had on our very first day of class last year? We realized that even before you started your training here, in a very real sense, you'd been performing specific, concrete Actions throughout the course of your lives. Did you tie your shoes in the morning? Congratulations, that's an Action. Did you make a pot of coffee? Write checks to pay bills? Make love? Watch a movie? Wonder where your life is going? Make the bed? Do the laundry? Walk the dog? Greet your doorman? Look for your keys? Try to remember a dream you had? All of these are Actions, but of course you performed them in real life. If you performed them under imaginary circumstances, you would enter the world of acting. And if you *really* performed these Actions—not pretended or indicated that you were doing them, but really did them without the slightest tinge of pretense—you would enter the world of *good* acting."

Amber frowns. "Bill, is it me or have we come full circle? On our first day of class last year, you talked about what it takes to play Hamlet. You asked us, what does Hamlet *do* throughout the course of the play?" She ticks off Actions on her fingers. "First he confronts his father's ghost and listens to its secrets. Then he pretends to be insane. He breaks up with Ophelia. Hires the players and writes a special script for them and trains them to perform it precisely the way he wants them to."

Adam jumps in. "He contemplates suicide. 'To be or not to be!' He kills Polonius."

Reg nods. "He tricks Rosencrantz and Guildenstern. And he fights Laertes."

Bill offers a sly smile. "You know, I *do* remember all that. That was the day we came up with a definition for acting. What was it again?"

Cheryl smiles. "Doing truthfully under imaginary circumstances."

"'Doing.'" Bill nods. "Which means: identifying and executing Actions. Amber's right. It's taken us over a year to travel full circle. I hope it was worth the trip."

The actors nod, though some of them seem a bit stunned to find themselves back where this journey began. I wish they could see what I see. Having been with this class from the start, I have marked firsthand each student's growth, and in every case, the student's work has deepened. Their art has gained tremendous strength as well as the particular accent lent by each actor's unique personality.

Bill leans forward. "It might surprise you to know that you

began using Actions last year. Remember how you trained yourselves to do only what your partner made you do?" The class nods.
"And because you only did what your partner made you do, everything you did, you *really* did. Now you've reached a point in your
training where your awareness of Actions must deepen to a more
sophisticated level. *Now you, as the actor, must know what you
are doing at every single moment in your script. And whatever that
Action is, you must execute it accurately, and never merely pretend
to do it.*"

Bill turns to Adam and Uma. "Now, in light of all this, let us
examine your scene from *Two for the Seesaw*. We'll start with Gittel, since she appears first onstage. You come in the door and
what do you do?"

Uma thinks. "I go to the phone and call my physician, Dr.
Segen. But all I get is his answering service."

"So what's your Action?"

"To Call My Doctor?"

"That's certainly true, if a bit general," Bill says. "Once again,
I'll point out that general choices create general performances.
You want to be much more specific. I'll give you an example. Suppose you're working on your script and you select an Action for
a moment, or more probably a series of moments: To Share. You
might pull that off in the acting, but it won't produce behavior
that's as clearly recognizable and interesting as you'd get from a
more specific choice. For instance, what would it be like if you
tried To Share the Innermost Secret of Your Heart? Would that
be more evocative?"

Uma nods. "It certainly would."

"Take note here," Bill says to the class. "A lot of college and
university theater departments insist that Actions must be boiled
down to simple infinitive verbs. To share. To flirt. To argue. That's
what they did in the college I went to. If you went to a college like
this, you should try to get your money back."

The class laughs.

"If it takes three or four or five words to phrase your Action evocatively, that's what you do." Bill winces. "Sandy hated colleges and universities. When I first went to Rutgers, graduating MFA actors were required to perform an important role and accompany that with a written document that analyzed their work in the part. Upon hearing this, I recovered myself with great difficulty and started pounding the table. Actors do not write essays, I said. Dancers dance. Sculptors sculpt. Painters paint. And actors act. They do not write theses. If you want to judge their acting, you must go and see their performance. What academics don't understand is that art is not created in someone's brain. You should beware of pedagogical takes on acting. When it comes to art, all rules should really be rules of thumb." Bill turns back to Uma. "That being said, why are you calling your doctor?"

"To Plead for Help."

"Much better. So what happens next?"

"I leave a message with my doctor's answering service. So I guess that's my Action: To Leave a Message." Uma frowns. "Actually, here again I can be much more specific."

"How so?"

"Well, the text says the woman who answers the phone sounds like a robot. I can't tell if she's really there or if it's an answering machine, but I have to make her understand that this is a life-or-death situation. A more specific Action would do that. If she's mechanical in her response to my message, maybe I really have To Spell Everything Out for Her and hope to God she passes on my message."

Bill nods. "I like that better. So you hang up the phone and Jerry enters. You say something like, 'Hey, Jerry. Where'd you blow in from?' What do you think you're doing with that line?"

"It goes back to me being a sarcastic girl from the Bronx. I've just been with another man and I feel guilty about it. I'm really upset. So I guess I'm just being defensive."

"Fine," Bill says. "But what will you *specifically do* to defend yourself?"

Uma thinks. "I could Mock Him."

Bill grins. "Now you're getting it." He turns to Adam. "So you, Adam/Jerry, enter. Why are you here?"

Adam smiles. "Well, Jerry wants answers—"

"Wait a minute. Who?"

"Jerry."

Bill scowls. "Who's playing this part?"

"I am."

"So what are you talking about 'him' for? Don't externalize your character—it sounds like you're going to job someone else in to do the work. The Brits talk like that all the time. 'I think my character would speak this way' or 'Certainly, he would smoke a pipe.'"

Adam chews his lip. "I just thought—"

"Don't do that. Stop thinking. You went to college, didn't you?" The class laughs.

"A college taught you to think too much. We're here in America, do you understand? We've been deeply affected by Stanislavsky, the Moscow Art Theatre, and the Group Theatre. We therefore believe that the actor's approach starts from somewhere inside him. Talk about the character from your own Point of View. Talk from 'me' or 'I.' When you refer to 'he' or 'him,' you're distancing yourself from your character."

"Got it," says Adam. "Then I don't know why Gittel stood me up. I thought we had something great together. But now I've got hard evidence that she cheated on me, and I want to know why."

"So what do you do? What's your first Action?"

"I start To Cross-examine Her."

"Spoken like a true lawyer, which of course Jerry is," Bill says. "Why are you frowning?"

"It's just . . ." Adam flips through his script. "I've never been good with memorization and this is a complicated scene. I've tried to get off book, but I keep getting the words all wrong."

"So what's your goal in life?" Bill says. "To play small parts?"

The class laughs, and after a moment, Adam does, too.

"Actually, I'm glad you brought this up," Bill says. "You're reminding me of an interview I once read with Mark Rylance, who I believe is one of the finest stage actors in the world. He played Valere in *La Bête*, by David Hirson. The play opens with Valere's first speech, which runs about forty minutes. The interviewer asked Rylance how he was able to memorize all those lines. To paraphrase, Rylance said that he doesn't memorize lines. He's more concerned with figuring out what his character's doing in every moment. Once he has that figured out, the lines just sort of fall into place, hopefully by opening night."

Bill turns to the class. "Sandy used to compare a script to an opera's libretto. Have you ever read one? The words make for pretty dismal reading. They might go something like this: 'The sun! The sun! Our love is like the sun! It rises! We're in love! In love, just like the sun!' Simple. Even silly, right? Thankfully, there's a lot more to opera than that. That art form isn't about the words so much as it is about everything underneath: the emotions, the behavior, the conflict. Sound familiar?

"Frankly, I think musicians and actors share a core skill. Music is written in code, is it not? A trained musician can study sheet music and hear what the composer intended by looking at all those dots. Well, actors do that, too, in a way. An actor's script is a coded message for what the playwright intended. When composing a script, the playwright imagines what each of his characters is *doing* in the most minute detail. But, apart from a stage direction here and there, he only writes down what the characters say. It therefore falls to the actor to pick up the script, examine the playwright's words, and figure out why his or her character utters that dialogue. In other words, work backward from the script and try to understand what the character is doing and why the character is doing it.

"As the actor begins to understand his character more deeply, he becomes empathetic to the character's situation. He begins to sense what the character is feeling and begins to see why the character does what he does, why the playwright chose the words that he or she did to express the character's needs. When you feel this connection beginning to happen, congratulations. It means that you and the character are becoming one. The character's Actions become yours, and vice versa."

Vanessa seems perplexed. "Aren't we sort of reversing the way we've worked all along up to now?"

"No," says Bill. "Think of it this way: We're expanding what you've learned before, not changing it. There are really two possible bridges to building your character. The first bridge is built by identifying with the character's emotional life. You discover what everything means to the character, then find those meanings within yourself. The second bridge is built by first identifying your character's Actions, then really performing those Actions yourself. To quote Epictetus, another famous Greek: 'First say to yourself what you would be, and then do what you have to do.' Or, as Stella Adler once purportedly said, acting is easy. Just live under the imaginary circumstances and do what you would do, and don't do what you wouldn't do."

Vanessa nods and jots something down in her notebook as Dom raises his hand.

"Bill, are all verbs actable?"

"No," Bill says. "Recently I saw a so-called dictionary of actor's Actions being sold in a bookstore. I flipped through it and found that most of the verbs were too general to act. General verbs make good objectives, not Actions. Suppose I want To Persuade

You to Give Up Acting. I know that's an objective because the only way to do that would be to ask myself: *How* will I achieve that? One thing I might do is Laugh at Your Aspirations. Or I might Lecture You on the Economic Realities of Being an Actor in Our Capitalist Society. Remember: The only way to find out if a verb is actable is to try doing it. Can you Introduce Yourself to Another Person? You can? Good. That's an actable Action. Can you Try to Recall an Important Phone Number? You can? Good. That's actable. Can you Share a Piece of Scintillating Gossip? Yes, so that's an Action.

"Now, this is also important: Once you've determined what your Action is at any given point in the scene, isolate that Action and practice doing it away from the script, using your own words or perhaps no words at all, depending on the Action. Do that until the doing of the Action becomes a comfortable habit. Gertrude Stein wrote that a 'Rose is a rose is a rose.' I'm saying that flirting is flirting is flirting. It doesn't matter what words you use, the Action is the same. Once you feel secure that you have an almost kinesthetic understanding of the performance of that Action, bring it back to the work at hand and integrate it with your text. You should use the words of the script to help you execute the Action. In other words, if you're going To Let Someone In On a Secret, you need a secret to let them in on. That's one very important role the text fulfills."

Quid raises his hand. "Bill, if we're thinking about Actions all the time, won't that interfere with our moment-to-moment work? What should we concentrate on—our Actions, or working off the other person?"

"Both," Bill says. "I'll clarify. You won't be thinking about your Actions, you'll have worked those out ahead of time as part of your homework. That way you can come to rehearsal, put your attention on your partner, and let your partner's behavior take you for a ride, the same way you've done all along. You'll still work unanticipated moment to unanticipated moment. Only this time the Actions you've chosen and practiced will guide your responses to what your fellow actor brings you. In other words, do your homework, then improvise, the same as you've done all along."

"Now, forgive me," Bill says, "I don't mean to wax academic." He shoots a look at Adam, who holds up his palms. The class laughs. "But Actions fall into three basic categories, and it will be important for you to know them. First you have Physical Actions. We incorporated a lot of these in your activities first year: Sweeping the Floor, Closing the Door, Mending a Broken Plate, Learning to Juggle, and so on. Physical Actions are simple. You do them with your body and no dialogue is required.

"Next we have Interpersonal Actions. These are Actions we do to another person. For instance, we might Share a Dark Secret with someone. Or Make a Joke. Or Toot Our Own Horn. Or Cut Someone Down to Size. Or Gently Break a Piece of Bad News. Interpersonal Actions are, by far, the broadest category of Actions. You'll find that you use them a lot.

"Finally we have Inner Actions. These are Actions we do internally, and again, we started to do them last year. For instance, To Take Someone In is a really important Inner Action that comes into play very often—the whole first year's work is based on it. Another Inner Action could be To Figure Something Out, like you saw Dom doing earlier."

Trevor says, "Bill, I tried doing an Inner Action in a play one time. The director didn't like it. He said, 'Whatever you're doing, it isn't translating.' Isn't it true that Inner Actions aren't legible to an audience?"

"Nonsense," Bill says. "Projection—that is, getting the performance across to an audience—always depends on the clarity of the doing. In this case, it sounds like whatever you were doing wasn't clear. But the fact is, people are continually in Action throughout their lives, so they will always recognize the same Actions when they see them in performance.

"Consider this: Whenever you read about some great piece of acting, something legendary, it's always about something the actor did, not said. I once saw Eva Le Gallienne play Queen Elizabeth I in Friedrich von Schiller's *Maria Stuart*. There's a scene in which Elizabeth makes a suggestion to one of her courtiers in a very subtle way. She needs a man to kill Mary, Queen of Scots. So a man is brought in and he kneels before Elizabeth. I still remember how Le Gallienne played that moment. She leaned forward on her throne and stared at the man for what seemed like a half hour. She never uttered a word, but her Action could not have been clearer. She was Looking into His Soul and Deciding if She Could Trust This Man.

"Remember, too, the words of Tommaso Salvini. In the early 1900s, he was considered the greatest actor ever to play Othello. Stanislavsky loved his work. Early in his career, Salvini said that acting is voice, voice, and more voice. But toward the end of his career, he said that he never really started to act until, one time, he lost his voice.

"If you'd like a more modern example, you could just watch the movie *GoodFellas*. Has everyone seen that film?"

The class nods.

"There's a classic example of an Inner Action in that movie. Robert De Niro is a gangster having a drink at a bar. He's just pulled off the heist of a lifetime and he's hidden a fortune in loot. He lights a cigarette and the jukebox clicks over to an Eric Clapton song just as his partner in crime walks in. De Niro doesn't like this guy. The camera zooms in for a close-up and we see what he's thinking: What if I killed my partner and took his share? Keep in mind: De Niro doesn't have a single line to express what he's thinking, but that's okay; he doesn't need lines. His behavior is clear as geometry. Up close, we can see his mental wheels turning. *Should I? Shouldn't I? Should I? Shouldn't I?* His process is written all over his face and it's riveting to watch."

Adam laughs. He remembers that moment, as do I. Once you've seen it, you'll never listen to Eric Clapton the same way.

"Working in film allows the actor to concentrate less on being heard, and a close-up can certainly capture a great deal of subtlety in the face," Bill says. "But make no mistake: Inner Actions should be as legible as any other type of Action so long as they're performed clearly.

"Here's another example of an Inner Action. Have you ever needed To Buck Yourself Up?" Bill takes a deep breath. Slowly, his spine straightens and a look of resolve comes over his face. What he's doing is clear as day. "You see? Just as with Physical Actions, Inner Actions require no words. You do them within yourself."

Growing serious, he turns to the class. "I predict that things will get rough in here for a few weeks. It always feels like you're hitting a speed bump the first time you work with Actions. From now on, I'll frequently stop your scenes and ask, 'What are you doing right there?' or 'I don't understand that, what are you doing?' You'll find yourself obsessing over that question both in and out of class, on the street or at home, while walking the dog or washing dishes. Unfortunately, the only way to really master the use of Actions is to drive yourself out-of-your-mind crazy. 'What am I doing? What am I doing?' Every single second. This is the only way to know that you're learning how to utilize Actions in your work. One day you will feel yourself instinctively translating any text that you look at into Actions, and then you will know that the work was worthwhile."

Bill checks the clock on his desk. "I have just enough time to give you one more skill that will help your acting. It's called the Super Objective. Let's suppose you meet a young man and you notice certain things about him. One: He carries a toothbrush wherever he goes and brushes his teeth five times a day. Two: He lives in a cheap basement apartment in a very bad neighborhood in Brooklyn. Three: He spends most of his money on a membership to a health club. Four: When his girlfriend presses him to get married, he dumps her even though he cares deeply for her. Five: He works as a waiter, but when his restaurant asks him to become a manager, he refuses the promotion."

Bill spreads his hands. "What are all five things I just mentioned?"

Melissa answers, "Actions."

"Correct. But now I ask you: How are they connected? What does brushing your teeth five times a day have to do with breaking up with your girlfriend? Why does the young man spend all his money on a gym instead of a nice apartment? And who would refuse a promotion? What do these Actions have to do with one another?"

Donna blinks. "As far as I can see, they don't share any connection at all."

Bill frowns. "The Actions will look unrelated until you understand the young man's Super Objective. Think of a Super Objective as the trunk of a banana tree, the spine that leads to bunches of fruit, which are the character's Actions. The Super Objective organizes these Actions into a logical pattern or structure. Once you understand what your role's Super Objective is, you can confidently select Actions that best illuminate your character.

"For instance, what if I told you that the thing this young man wants more than anything else in the world is to become a great actor?"

Mimi fairly jumps out of her seat. "I get it! He wants his teeth to look perfect for head shots, auditions, and close-ups. The gym keeps his body in shape so he can get hired for pilots and soaps. Like lots of young actors, he's probably living hand to mouth, so that explains his cheap apartment."

Jon nods. "I bet he can't commit to his girlfriend because he's already committed to his career. Same reason he can't take the job as a restaurant manager: he needs a flexible schedule."

"You've got it," Bill says. "All characters are ships out on the ocean at night, tossed about by the storms of circumstance. It's easy for them to get blown off course, but their Super Objective acts like a distant lighthouse, the beacon that's trying to guide them home. It's that thing they will follow with all their might, hoping that, one day, they'll make it to shore. Your character's Super Objective is his life's ambition, the thing he wants more than anything else in the world, the goal he will fight to obtain with all his heart and his will. Therefore, *every Action a character commits should fall under the umbrella of his or her Super Objective.*"

"I'm thinking of *Hamlet* again," says Quid. "Look at everything Hamlet does in that play. He visits the castle's ramparts and confronts his father's ghost. He swears everyone to secrecy. Pretends to be insane. Hires the players and writes a scene for them to play in front of the king. None of these Actions makes a discernible pattern until you find out he's trying to avenge his father's death."

"Right," Bill says. "Now remember: *You cannot act a Super Objective.* Super Objectives are big, general statements, and therefore impossible to act. To Gain Financial Freedom. To Live a Happy Life. To Marry the Girl of My Dreams. You can't get up and act I'm Avenging My Father's Death. But you can Instruct the Players in How You Want Your Script Played Before the King. You can Observe Your Uncle to See if He Reveals His Guilt. The Super Objective helps you understand the logic behind Hamlet's behavior. Let's see how we can apply this to scene work." He turns to Uma. "What do you think Gittel's Super Objective is?"

"More than anything else in the world, I want to marry Jerry. I see him as the key to living a happy life."

"Exactly." Bill turns to Adam. "And what do you think your Super Objective is?"

"I want a stable, loving relationship with a woman I can trust. That's why I'm thrown for such a loop when the second woman I thought I was in love with betrays me."

"Correct." Bill turns back to the class. "Isn't it interesting? These characters have similar Super Objectives. This happens a lot in well-made plays. Both characters search for commitment from a romantic partner. But they go about achieving their Super Objective in very different ways, which of course breeds conflict, the playwright's friend. If a protagonist obtains his or her Super Objective by the end of the play or script, you get a happy ending. If he or she does not, you have a tragedy. *Whether or not you obtain your Super Objective at the end of a scene dictates what the next scene will be about.*" Bill turns to Uma. "For instance, if you can't convince Jerry to marry you, what will you do the next time you see him?"

Uma laughs. "Try harder!"

"That's right," Bill says. "Or try something different: Change tactics to find another way around the mountain." He turns to Adam. "Suppose you don't get the answer you came looking for. What do you think *must* happen in the next scene?"

"I'll have to look even harder, since it means the stakes have risen."

Bill nods. "So now you know about Actions and Super Objectives. Incorporate this knowledge into your work, and good luck. We'll see you next time."

EIGHT

BEATS, HOMEWORK, INNER EMOTIONAL LINES, AND PARTICULARIZATIONS

"Some actors prefer to start with [external details]. It is more difficult . . . and the result is not so subtle, the choice of elements not so wise as it might be if you followed the inward thread of the part first. It is like buying a dress without being measured."

—Richard Boleslavsky

"The basic components of the characters we play are somewhere within ourselves."

—Uta Hagen

By the next class, Bill has permitted the partners in about half the scenes to start working away from the table. The actors use the studio's furniture and props to appoint themselves a set. Some of them work with costumes. The scenes are now being played as they might be in front of an audience, but they're still a bit shaky.

Bill stops Dom and Jon halfway through a scene from David Mamet's *Speed-the-Plow.*

"Something's wrong here. Tell me about your rehearsal process."

"We do everything we learned last year," Dom says. "We emotionally prepare, come to the door with our objective, and try to work off the other person. Only this time, we've each identified our Actions at home, really pinned them down. That way, when we come together, we can focus on living out the scene."

"Your process sounds right, but the scene hasn't grown much since you started bringing it to class," Bill says. "Tell me something. Do you ever stop in the middle of a scene to examine or rework what you're doing?"

"No," says Dom. "We just run it."

"That's your mistake," Bill says. "In your rehearsals, you should break the scene down into sections. Start working the first section. Work it several times, until you feel like you've gotten it down. Then and only then should you go on to the next section. In acting, we call these sections Beats. They're important tools for crafting performances. Think of Beats as the building blocks for scenes. A play is composed of acts, the acts break down into scenes, and the scenes break down into units called Beats. *Each Beat is a series of moments that have to do with the same subject.* I'll give you an example.

"Suppose we have a scene involving two brothers: Jim and Tom. Jim comes to the door and knocks. Tom lets him in and welcomes him effusively. He takes Jim's coat and seats him in the most comfortable chair. He asks Jim if he wants something to drink or something to eat. All these moments are basically about the same thing, aren't they? So let's call this Beat: Welcoming the Brother to His Home. Then suddenly Jim says, 'Tom, we've got to decide what to do with Mom.'" Bill looks at the class. "Right away, what do you know?"

"The subject has shifted," says Trevor. "So has the Beat, I guess."

Bill nods. "And what might this new Beat be called?"

"What to Do about Momma?"

"Sounds good. And the What to Do about Momma Beat will continue until the subject matter shifts again. Like whenever someone enters or exits the stage, the Beat automatically changes."

Bill spreads his hands. "Can you see how Beats are a useful tool for rehearsing a script? They help us chart the progress of a scene and clarify the chain of cause and effect that every good script has. The concept of Beats came from Stanislavsky himself. He once compared performing a role to the act of eating a turkey. You can't eat a turkey all at once, he said. You have to eat it bit by bit, piece by piece, one piece at a time. Actors move through scenes in a similar fashion. You can't do a whole scene at once. You have to break it down into manageable sections with clear goals. Complete each task in order, do it well, and move on to the next. Before you know it, the curtain comes down and it's time to take your bow."

Donna raises her hand. "Bit by bit—I get that part. But why call them Beats? Why not *bits*?"

Bill grins. "That's a funny piece of theater history. During the 1920s, a director named Richard Boleslavsky emigrated to the United States. Boleslavsky had worked with Stanislavsky at the Moscow Art Theatre. When he got to New York, he opened a school called the American Laboratory Theatre. His students included Harold Clurman, Stella Adler, and Lee Strasberg, all of whom went on to become founding members of the Group Theatre, as did Sandy Meisner."

Bill raises his eyebrows. "Can you imagine how excited the Americans must have been? For years, they'd been reading about Stanislavsky and his revolutionary acting techniques. Now they had a teacher who'd studied with the master himself! Boleslavsky repeated Stanislavsky's turkey metaphor, but his accent was so heavy that when he said 'Eat a turkey bit by bit,' his students heard it as '*beat* by *beat*.' So that's what they wrote in their notebooks. Not bits, but *beats*. And from that moment forward, it's always been Beats." Bill spreads his hands and chants aloud: *"Beats, beats, beats!"*

The class laughs. Jon shakes his head. "I don't believe it."

Bill shoots him a look. "It's true nonetheless. Take your scripts home and break your scenes into Beats. It shouldn't be hard. In any well-written script, the Beats are clear and well defined. Establishing where the Beats are and what happens to change them will make your scripts more manageable to work on. Rehearse your scenes one Beat at a time. Stop and rework the Beat, if you have to, before moving on to the next."

Dom frowns. "Finding the Beats almost sounds like drawing up a blueprint for how the scene fits together."

Bill looks at him. "Blueprints are helpful things. Can you imagine trying to build a house without one?"

Dom shudders.

Joyce and Mimi are up next with the final scene from Lillian Hellman's *The Children's Hour*. First produced in 1934, this classic play tells the story of two women, Martha and Karen, who run an all-girls boarding school. To further her own ends, one of their students accuses them of having a lesbian affair. The ensuing scandal ruins the women's reputation, and that of their school. They sue their accusers and lose.

Throughout their entire ordeal, Karen's fiancé, Joe, defends the two women. Joe is a local doctor and a good man. He gives up his practice and arranges a research job in the Midwest. He tries to persuade Karen that both she and Martha must come with him. But in the course of this discussion, a slip of the tongue reveals that he has repressed a doubt about the two women's innocence. Karen feels that this doubt will never be erased, and so she sends him away. Reluctantly, Joe leaves.

A moment later, Martha enters expecting the three of them to sit down to dinner; she suddenly realizes that Joe has gone. In the course of the following conversation, Martha blurts out that she has always been in love with Karen. Karen dismisses this and says that, in the morning, they should talk about relocating. Martha says she doesn't feel well and goes to her room. A few moments later, Karen hears the shot. Martha has killed herself.

It's the fourth time these actors have worked during class. They're still at the table, and Joyce has clearly grown frustrated. In the middle of working, she slaps her script down on the table and fumes. "It feels all wrong! I hate working at the table. I want to get up on my feet."

"And do what?" Bill says. "Continue indicating?"

Joyce throws her hands in the air. "I know, I know! I can feel it's all out of whack, but—Bill, I swear. I'm trying so hard to work out these fucking moments!"

"That's part of the problem," Bill says. "You're playing each line as though it were its own reality, separate from all other moments. It's as if you've created a fistful of beads. Each one is interesting, but you have nothing connecting them, no string that runs through them. That string is the Inner Emotional Line."

Joyce shakes her head. "Have we talked about that? The Inner Emotional Line?"

"No," Bill says. "But now's as good a time as any." He turns to Mimi. "Would you sit for a moment? I want to demonstrate something."

Mimi takes her seat in the bleachers. Bill gets up from his desk, walks into the playing space, and sits at the table, across from Joyce.

"Want to do a scene?" Bill says.

Joyce grins. "I'm game."

"This is my Famous War Play. In this play, I'm an army major. Every officer above me in rank has been killed, leaving me in command of the regiment. For six months we've been fighting to take a pivotal hill, and the effort has cost us a lot of men. Too many men. Well, today is our last chance. I've committed all our forces to the final push. If we take the hill, we'll win the war and I'll be a hero. If we don't take the hill, we'll lose the war and I'll be court-martialed for incompetence. That would end my career, I'd be ruined. Got it?"

Joyce nods.

Bill gestures toward the studio. "This is army headquarters. It's six a.m. and the battle's just begun. Everyone's waiting to see how it goes. You're a sergeant, my adjutant. Go outside, wait a minute, then come in and take my breakfast order. Ask me what I want to eat. Some cereal? Eggs? Some toast? Like that."

Joyce goes out the door and closes it behind her.

Bill sits at the table, alone, and a darkness falls over his face, the shadow of consternation. Seething, impatient, he taps the tabletop with his fingernails—a rapid tattoo. *Tap-a-tap-tap! Tap-a-tap-tap!* He is the picture of a man caught in a vise of anxiety.

There's a knock at the door. Joyce enters and Bill looks up at her, glaring. "What is it?"

Joyce stiffens as though she's been slapped, and she bows her head, obsequious. "Take your breakfast order, sir?"

Bill mutters. "Right, right. What do we have?"

"Cereal?"

Bill winces like he's been stabbed. "No. What else?"

"We have eggs."

Bill shakes his head, enraged. "No, no, no! What else?"

"Toast?"

Bill slams his palm on the table. "No!" he says. "Coffee! Just bring me some coffee!"

Joyce has already beaten a quick retreat. She calls back over her shoulder. "Want milk or sugar with that?"

"Black!" Bill snarls like he's speaking to an utter incompetent. "Just! Black! Coffee! Please!"

"Okay," Joyce whines. "Yes, sir." And bolts out.

Bill returns to his brooding. The studio crackles with tension until he looks up and grins, and just like that the volatile major is gone.

"So," he asks. "How would you describe my character?"

"Worried," says Mimi.

"Frazzled," says Cheryl.

Quid snorts. "You kidding? That guy's headed for a nervous breakdown."

"Good," says Bill. "That's what I was going for."

Joyce slips back into the room and Bill turns to her. "Let's try it again. See if you can use the same words we did last time."

Joyce nods and exits, closing the door. The moment she's gone, Bill's face lights up. Elated, smiling, he hums a little ditty to himself and puts both feet on the table, making himself at home. He crosses his arms across his chest and heaves a contented sigh like a man taking sun at a beach resort.

There's a knock at the door. Joyce enters.

Bill looks up. "What is it?" He practically sings the words. Bill doesn't just smile at Joyce, he beams like someone welcoming a long-lost friend. Joyce blinks, surprised, and she can't help herself. She smiles back.

"Take your breakfast order, sir?"

"Right, right!" Excited, Bill swings his feet to the floor and rubs his palms in anticipation. He's got all the pep of a man who just won the Mega Millions jackpot. "What do we have?"

"Cereal?" Joyce offers.

Bill makes a show of thinking it over. Hmm, hmm, cereal might be nice, who doesn't like cereal? Ultimately he shakes his head. "No." His tone is that of a precocious child selecting desserts from a silver tray. "What else?"

"We have eggs."

Bill chuckles. "No, no, no." The wave of his hand says eggs are cute but a silly, ridiculous choice. The gesture is so whimsical, so affectionate, the class bursts out laughing. "What else?"

Joyce is clearly enjoying herself. Bill's happiness is infectious. "Toast?"

Bill clutches his temples and moans in mock agony. "Nooooooooooo." He grins. "Coffee. Just bring me some coffee."

Joyce nods, smiling. "Want milk or sugar with that?"

"Black." Bill sighs as though, in heaven, all coffee is free from sugar and milk. "Just black coffee, please."

Joyce looks only too happy to serve. "Okay! Yes, sir!" She skips out, closing the door behind him.

Bill smiles after her a moment, then looks to the class and waggles his eyebrows. The class cracks up.

"How would you describe my character now?"

"Relieved!" says Donna.

"Exalted!" says Uma.

"The attack on the hill must have been a big success," Trevor says. "You were a totally different person!"

"Good," Bill says. "Let's review what happened from a technical perspective. If I'm not mistaken, the lines of dialogue were the same in both scenes, correct? But the men I played were, as you say, totally different. How can this be? The first time, I played the major as a Man on the Brink of Disaster. The second time, I played him as a Triumphant Man. And perhaps you noticed something else, something very important: Each Emotional Line set the tone for the overall scene. The individual moments in each scene molded themselves to fit my character's Inner Emotional Line."

"The same way Joyce adjusted herself to fit your reactions," says Cheryl.

"Exactly. Sometimes you can create a character just by identifying that person's Emotional Line. A Depressed Man is a character. A Happy Girl Who's Deliriously in Love is a character. Or a Frightened Person. Or Mr. Happy-Go-Lucky. *Once an Emotional Line is created, it persists unless or until something happens to change it.* For instance, remember the second scene? I played the major as a Triumphant Man; life was a grand parade when Joyce came to take my order. But suppose Dom walked in right after Joyce left. Imagine Dom, pale as a ghost, standing in the door, bereft. 'I—I'm sorry,' he stammers. 'There's been a tragic mistake. Intelligence got fouled up and we lost the hill after all, along with the entire regiment.'" Bill raises his eyebrows. "What do you think will happen once I've processed that news?"

"If you're really leaving yourself alone and working improvisationally, you'll be swept down a different Inner Emotional Line," Dom says. "Perhaps this line will be the major as The Man Condemned to Die."

"Perhaps." Bill grins. "But regardless of which direction it goes, this new Emotional Line will continue until something else happens to change it." He turns to Joyce. "Remember that handful of disconnected beads I was talking about? In order to string them together, you must emotionalize yourself from the very beginning of your homework. Are you doing that?"

Joyce shakes her head. "No."

"No wonder the scene isn't working. Your homework starts and ends in your head. But we know that acting is emotional. So you must begin your homework emotionalized and let that emotion carry you through the scene moment by moment. Think of it this way: Doing your homework is sort of like building a raft and putting it on a river. When you're on that raft, the river's swift current picks you up and bears you along. You respond to the direction you're going in, but then you find yourself stalled in a whirlpool, paddling like crazy to stay out of the vortex you know will destroy you. Suddenly—*shoosh!* The current shoots you down a tributary, and you have to fight like mad again to stay afloat as you bounce along. But if you work each moment and ride that current, you'll come to the end of the rapids, and you'll have had one hell of a ride.

"Let's take this back to your scene," Bill says. "You're setting the table for dinner and, because of what happened in the prior scene, you feel there's a possibility that you and Karen can finally live a normal, happy life. So that's your first Beat: Joe's commitment to Karen has edified you. But then comes this terrible moment where Karen tells you she's sent Joe away and he's never coming back. At that moment, your Action must be *To Take in This Terrible Piece of News.* You've ruined the life of the person you love more than anything else in the world. Whenever you're confronted with moments like this—your whole family just died in a plane crash, for instance—of course your Emotional Line will shift, and you must go wherever it takes you. Does that help you?"

Joyce looks at Mimi, who nods. "Can we work on this and give it a try next class?"

"Of course."

"And you still want us to work at the table?" Joyce says, frustrated. "I've done a lot of plays with a lot of directors and I have to say, most of them never worked this way."

"That's a shame," Bill says. "But we don't have to repeat their mistakes. I once had a student who was cast in *The Glass Menagerie* at one of the country's most prestigious regional theaters. The production was allotted a nine-week rehearsal period, unheard of in this country. The first day the cast met, the director said, 'Okay, everyone, up on your feet! Today we're blocking the show!'"

Bill shakes his head. "Can you imagine? The actors had barely shaken hands, let alone read through the play as an ensemble,

and here they were being pushed to decide where their characters would move and why. You might as well ask someone who's
never played the piano to sit at the keyboard and render a Mozart
sonata. The actors had no idea what they were doing onstage
because they hadn't had time to explore their roles. To work off
one another. To *play*. They began to get confused. The more disoriented they became, the more irate the director got. 'No, no!'
he shouted. 'Don't go over there! Come over here! That's it. Now
raise your arm when you say that line, it makes a prettier picture.'
Care to guess how this production turned out?"

"Five bucks says it bombed," says Trevor.

Bill shrugs. "Of course it did. Do you know the actor Lee J.
Cobb? He played Willy Loman in the first Broadway production
of *Death of a Salesman,* directed by Elia Kazan. Kazan always
started rehearsing a play by seating his cast around a table and
letting them take their time, making contact, reading the script
aloud. For days on end, Cobb just sat there, mumbling his lines.
He looked vague and distracted. The show's producers got nervous. They didn't believe Cobb had what it took to do the part,
so they went to Kazan and urged him to find another actor. But
Kazan refused. 'Just wait,' he said. 'I know this man. You'll see.' A
few days later, in the middle of rehearsal, Lee J. Cobb stopped
mumbling, pushed his chair back, and stood up from the table.
And there was Willy Loman."

"I get it," says Mimi. "Cobb wasn't slacking off, he was getting
a feel for the role, letting it work on his subconscious."

"He was doing what actors do," Bill says. "Feeding on the
material, letting it digest, not judging it, trusting his process. You
discover the character's inner emotional journey and begin to par-
ticipate in it, lending yourself to the character's needs and giving
what is required of yourself to fulfill them. Stanislavsky said that
unless the actor connects to the character from inside himself,

there's nothing there to nurture, and the character becomes an empty shell bereft of humanity. Sandy shared a similar view. He believed that if you don't work from inside yourself to create your character, in the end you will give a performance which is louder and faster, but never deeper."

He looks at Joyce. "This is difficult work. It takes a supreme amount of patience. You can't think your way through the challenge of creating a character and you certainly can't rush it. The work may feel like it's taking forever or it may feel like it's never going to happen, and that can be daunting. It rattles the nerves. But then, all of a sudden, it's like somebody snuck up behind you and gave you a push. And just like that, the character takes over."

■■■■

Toward the end of class, Bill says, "I have another very useful tool I want to introduce today. It's called Particularizations. With any role you play, you will be confronted with the same problems and issues. Here am I, the actor"—Bill gestures toward himself— "and somewhere out here"—he extends his arm and wiggles his fingers—"is the character I want to marry myself to. How do I connect them? By using associations to fuse the meanings in the text to meanings I already understand. I'll give you an example.

"I once worked with an actress who was in a play about a troubled woman in love with a handsome RAF pilot, who leaves her. The actress was having a very difficult time in the scene where the pilot packs his clothes and walks out the door. She dreaded having to rehearse this scene; it felt so empty and mechanical to her. One day, however, a memory drifted into her consciousness. She remembered an incident when she was eleven years old and her father left the family. As a girl, she had stood in the vestibule and watched him carry his suitcases down the front walk to his car; he put them in and he drove away. Once she saw the parallel between the real event and the fictitious one, she realized that her character was an abandoned child, just as she was, and she immediately understood every moment of her scene."

Bill spreads his hands. "Human beings make associations all the time in life—they're a naturally occurring phenomenon. That's good news for actors. Let's say you go to a party where you meet a woman, a perfect stranger. You exchange a few pleasantries, some banter. Then, for no good reason at all, you find yourself getting upset. 'Hmm,' you think. 'Now, isn't that odd?' You excuse yourself and leave. A little while later, you're riding home on the crosstown bus when it suddenly occurs to you: That woman at the party had the same high-pitched, nasal voice as your older sister, The Family Critic. Your older sister's the one who's always on your case, saying, 'Why do you want to be an actor? You'll never make it. Don't waste your life chasing pipe dreams. Get a real job!' Well, no wonder you didn't like the woman at the party! Her voice was so close to your older sister's that you *associated* the two. And because of this, the dislike you have for your older sister attached itself to a complete stranger."

"You know the experiment 'Pavlov's dog'? It's one of the earliest exercises in classic conditioning. Ivan Pavlov would ring a bell, then feed a dog. Consistently. Over and over again. Eventually, Pavlov rang the bell and the sound alone was enough to make the dog salivate because the dog had associated the ringing of the bell with being fed.

"But whereas most people experience associations unconsciously, actors put them to conscious use. In the metaphor of Pavlov's dog, the ringing bell is the actor's cue and the food is the homework he does to develop a given meaning: a Particularization. Once the actor has stimulated himself repeatedly, he becomes sensitized to the cue. It's as if your Particularization is the shell of a walnut. When you crack it open and extract the meat, you don't need the shell anymore, you can cast that aside. The meat is what's important.

"Suppose I'm acting in a play and there's another character who reminds me of my six-year-old nephew. Well, I know how I feel about my nephew; I know how I talk to him and how I respond to him. So now I know how to work with this other character. Therefore, I don't need my nephew anymore. I can throw him under the bus." The class laughs, and Bill grins. "Particularizations supply the meat your performance needs, which is behavior."

Bill turns to Joyce. "You know that moment when Karen says that Joe's not coming back? The wise actor playing Martha will have explored that moment over and over again in her homework. After rehearsals have ended, she will sit with her script, she will daydream through the scene from start to finish, taking as much time as she wants. The trancelike state of a daydream is very important because it's only when you're in that condition that lost personal associations rise from the unconscious. As personal associations come up, the actor will incorporate them to clarify and connect herself to the meanings of the text. At the next rehearsal, she'll be in a different place with the part. At that point, she'll leave herself alone and see how much of her homework has carried over."

"So how will we know when our homework is working?" Joyce asks.

"Simple," Bill says. "You'll be emotionalized."

Joyce nods, and Cheryl raises her hand. "Bill, should we find Particularizations for every moment?"

"Oh God, no," Bill says. "Remember, Particularizations serve one purpose: to clarify anything in the script that's opaque— those things which you feel you do not completely understand. If you already understand something, leave it alone. Particularization can be for a moment, a scene, your relationship with another character, or—sometimes—your entire part. I'll show you what I mean.

"You could Particularize a moment by leveraging the power of 'as ifs.' For example, when your partner says a certain line, it's *as if* she's slapped you in the face. Or when you hear him say a certain word, it's *as if* your heart is melting. Particularizing individual moments can lead to ingenious performances. I still remember a performance I saw more than fifty years ago: Maureen Stapleton in Tennessee Williams's *The Rose Tattoo*. Stapleton played Serafina, an Italian-American woman who's crazy in love with her truck driver husband. One day, he dies, and she's devastated. Then she gets a phone call. The person on the other end of the line says that Serafina's husband died in the arms of another woman. I still remember how Stapleton played that moment."

Bill mimes holding a phone to his ear. He listens intently, then his body snaps forward as though he's been punched in the stomach. He stays bent over, clearly in agony, then straightens back up and looks at the class.

"Stapleton Particularized that moment *as if* the news hit her like a kick in the gut. Of course, it helped that she had an emotional life powerful enough to back up the choice. Was it good acting? It made such an impact on me that I'm still talking about it more than fifty years later."

Bill scratches his chin. "I mentioned that a good Particularization can provide the key to your whole performance in a role. For instance, what if you played your character *as if* she had a chip on her shoulder? Or *as if* he had a hole in his heart? Or *as if* today was the day you won the Lotto jackpot?

"I once directed an actor in a scene from Clifford Odets's *The Big Knife*. The actor was playing a movie star whose girlfriend will be murdered to save his career. In one scene, she comes in to see him—smiling, bubbly, and infatuated. He knows what's going to happen to her, but he can't say anything about it, of course. It's quite a predicament. The actor playing the movie star had a hard time finding that relationship. As a result, the scene was dead in the water. I thought about it and finally suggested, 'Try it like this. Every time you look at her, you see a bullet hole right in the middle of her forehead.' That did the trick. When the actor adopted that Particularization, the scene became much more compelling."

Bill thinks. "You know, literature is full of Particularizations. Any simile or metaphor is, essentially, a Particularization, and can be useful to actors. 'She walks in beauty, like the night. . . .' You hear that line, you have a way of walking."

Bill turns to Uma. "Let's see if we can add Particularizations to your scene from *Two for the Seesaw*. What's all this business about a party you didn't go to?"

"Jerry invited me to a party at Frank Taubman's place," Uma says. "But I didn't go."

"Why not?"

"Because if it involved Jerry's boss, and it was on Park Avenue, it had to be too ritzy for me."

"Right. It's like you got invited to the White House."

"I wouldn't fit in."

Bill nods. "So you skipped Taubman's party to pass the night carousing with your going-nowhere bohemian friends. And that's where you ran into Jake, the guy you ended up going home with. Why do you think you did that?"

"I've been having trouble with this. I don't know."

"In the text, Jerry refers to Jake as 'the wrestler,' 'the fat-necked one' who brought you home. What's that mean?"

"Well," says Uma. "He's big and fat and not real attractive."

"I was once in summer stock," Bill says. "An attractive young lady who worked in the costume shop fell head over heels in love with a very handsome, wealthy young actor in the company. The way these things go, at the end of the season, when we all returned to New York, he dumped her. She was devastated. Over the next couple of years, I would run into her at parties. And you know what? You could always predict which guy she would go home with. All you had to do was look around the room and find the biggest dirtball: that would be the guy. Now, tell me why that was."

Uma frowns. "I guess because she didn't believe that she was good enough or smart enough or pretty enough to deserve better."

"And who else do we know who fits that profile?"

Reluctantly, Uma nods.

"Have you ever done something like that, Uma? Something so nakedly and brutally self-destructive? Have you ever taken a willful misstep that was predicated utterly on your lack of personal faith?"

The look on Uma's face is all the answer anyone needs.

"Good," says Bill. "So work with that for next time. Now, before I forget, let's check the rest of your work. What's the Essence of your Character?"

"I'm Just Not Good Enough," Uma says. "To me, Jerry's the catch of a lifetime, but I don't believe I'll ever measure up to him, his money, or his glamorous wife. There's a line in the text where I say, 'Spend a penny, get a piece of penny candy.' I get it now. When I say that, I'm talking about Jake. Jake is cheap, which is just my style. Not like Jerry, who's this big box of chocolates, totally out of my reach."

"Sounds like you're on your way," Bill says. He turns to Adam. "Your turn. Where were you before this scene began?"

"I was at Taubman's party," Adam says. "But I didn't stay long. I wanted to be with Gittel. So as soon as I could, I rushed down to the Village to pick her up at Sophie's place. And that's when I spotted her leaving with Jake. I was mortified; I followed them to Jake's apartment building and waited outside for an hour."

Bill gives him a pointed look. "What do you think they were doing in there? Knitting doilies? Can you Particularize how being cheated on makes you feel?"

Color rises to Adam's cheeks. His jaw clamps tight.

"Right," Bill says. "So what happened next?"

"They came out. Jake walked Gittel home and I followed them. I saw Jake kiss her good night at her door, then I went to confront her and that's how the scene begins."

"Why do you confront her?"

"It's like I told you before: I thought we had something, but she just cheated on me and—" Adam stops. "You know what? It's more than that. My wife cheated on me, too, back in Omaha. So it's like I'm having this awful case of déjà vu."

Bill nods. "Now you're getting it. Your wife was having an affair, which is why you left Nebraska and came all the way out to Manhattan. You were hoping to start over."

"That's right. I even thought about taking the New York State Bar Exam to cut my last ties with Omaha. But then I met Gittel and fell for her and that was confusing enough. But now my wife is calling, saying she wants to make amends."

"So what's the Essence of your Character?"

"I guess I'm confused."

Bill shakes his head. "It's stronger than that. This isn't simple everyday confusion, it's a massive life conundrum. Go back to the text. Jerry says, 'When lightning strikes twice, I have to know why.' And that's why you confront Gittel. You need to know why *both* these women you love so dearly have betrayed you. What is it about you that keeps inviting this kind of tragedy? Jerry also says, 'I'm at a crossroads here.' Don't let this line slip away, it's pivotal to the character. When you say that you mean: Should I go back to Nebraska or stay in New York? Should I reconcile with my wife? Or stay with Gittel? Or ditch them both? Should I give up my practice, my license, my friends, my money? All to start over with this crazy gypsy invalid dancer with her thick skin and her crass Bronx accent but something better, more soft underneath?

"Think of how high the stakes are, Adam. You haven't a clue which way you should turn, but, worse, you know you'll be ruined if you march down the wrong path. So no, you're not confused; instead you're a Man on the Horns of Dilemma. Do you see the difference? One wrong move and your world will explode. Can you find a Particularization that will help you understand Jerry's desperate need for an answer? Something within yourself that identifies with not knowing up from down, left from right, and right from wrong?"

Adam pales, then nods.

"Then that's where your homework should start," Bill says. "And again: I don't care where you go inside yourself to make that become a reality. But you must bring a full, specific, and clear emotional understanding to the stage in order to activate this role. The more you invest in your Particularization, the better your performance will be."

Bill turns to the class. "From now on, you must train yourselves to think in terms of Particularizations. You must constantly ask yourself: 'What does this part of the scene mean to me? What emotional chord does it strike in me? How do I understand it in terms of my own experience?' *Your art will take on clarity only when you take ownership of yourself and all that you have experienced. At that moment and never before, you will gain the ability to reach out, take hold of a character's hand, and marry the character to yourself.*"

Reg has been scribbling furiously in his notebook. "You've used that phrase before and I like it: 'marry the character to yourself.'" He looks up. "For me, that dispels a lot of illusions about character work."

"It's never about creating something from nothing," Bill says. "It's about revealing the character within yourself. In this regard, I often think of Michelangelo."

Reg turns a page and keeps writing. "How so?"

"Have you ever seen his statue of David?"

"I have," Reg says. "In Florence."

"Then you know that Michelangelo was an artist beyond compare. His attention to detail, his love and understanding of the human form, his skill with his tools—all flawless. Michelangelo would look at a block of marble and see the statue within. He claimed he could visualize the finished piece in every detail—every line and every curve. Therefore, when he set to work, he wasn't really sculpting so much as he was freeing the statue from the block that held it prisoner.

"This, to me, is how the actor should work on a character part. *You're not creating something new, you're finding the parts of the character that are already present within yourself.* Once you identify those, you just get rid of everything else."

Mimi nods. "You make it sound easy."

"Easy?" Bill shrugs. "Sure it is. It's so easy it only takes twenty years to understand."

■ ■ ■ ■

Eventually, all the students get their scenes up on their feet. Some scenes develop in fits and starts, but most succeed by a wide margin. Often, I find myself overwhelmed by the awesome (and sometimes subtle) transformations each actor undergoes.

Take Uma, for instance. To me, Uma has *become* Gittel Mosca: crass and snide on the outside, wide open and unprotected on the inside. Her accent twangs away, reveling in Bronx borough glory even as her thick walls crack and tumble as she argues with Jerry.

Adam matches her moment for moment. Despite the roughness of earlier rehearsals, his Jerry is superb—a Man on the Horns of Dilemma, indeed. It takes a very brave and talented actor to leave himself completely open as life administers blow after blow and there seems to be no way out. Adam plays Jerry as stoic and still. Bill remarks on the strength of this choice and wonders how Adam selected it, since it's very un-Adam-like behavior.

Adam shrugs. "I have a really good friend from Nebraska and he's solid as a rock, this guy. You know that expression 'salt of the earth'? I bet whoever coined that phrase was trying to describe my friend. He comes from a long line of farmers, simple folks who listen a lot and choose their words very carefully. I thought it would be interesting to play Jerry like that because of the contradictions. How compelling is it to watch someone with bedrock principles and a simple, abiding truth have his world turned upside down?"

And yes, he nailed the Omaha accent, exactly as Bill asked him to do.

"Good," Bill says. He smiles at Adam and Uma, who have taken seats in the playing space. "I'm very pleased. A lot of nice things are happening—"

Uma bursts into tears and begins to sob. The class falls deathly quiet.

"Uma?" Bill says.

She turns her face away and, shaking her head, she bawls. Bill waits until the worst of the spell has passed. Then, once Uma's breathing evens out, he prods her very gently.

"Talk to me," he says.

"I'm not good enough," she says. "Not smart enough. Not beautiful enough—oh God!"

Again she sobs, heart-wrenching, inconsolable, and again Bill waits for her to recover herself. It takes a little while.

"Bill," she finally says. "I'm scared."

"Of what?"

"I feel so . . . I just . . ." She makes a gesture with one hand that conveys everything: she is helpless. Cast adrift.

"Listen to me," Bill says. "Few actors can do what you've done. You played Gittel Mosca completely and her world disintegrates in this scene. It's just as you said: she realizes she'll never be good enough to have someone like Jerry. A kind man, an educated man who's caring and well-to-do. He's the man of her dreams, the key to the life she's always wanted, but she learns that she can never have him and it crushes her. She's a lamb being led to slaughter, but one that knows all the while what's happening to her and knows, too, how unfair life is. But you did it, Uma. You did it."

Uma nods vaguely and keeps her eyes trained on the floor. "I don't know if I can do this," she says. "Suppose I was cast in this part and had to play it night after night over a long run." She sniffs and wipes her nose with the back of her hand. "I don't know if I'm strong enough for that. I'm exhausted just doing one scene in class. How can anyone be that strong?"

"You need to have a philosophy," Bill says. "You need to believe in the importance of art and you need to believe that, in the best of hands, the actor's work is one of the most powerful forces on the planet. That will make it worthwhile for you."

He turns to the class. "Recently, Suzanne and I were invited to teach a seminar in Sarajevo. It's a small city, about a half million people, in a valley surrounded by mountains. We learned that during the civil war the Serbs positioned their artillery on the ridges and rained fire on everyone below, a constant bombardment. They cut off the water and food supply. They cut off the fuel in the middle of winter. Blockades kept the citizens from escaping, while snipers shot them dead in the streets. But every night, the national theater remained open. The actors performed and an audience came.

"Imagine," Bill says. "The people of Sarajevo knew they could be killed at any moment, but they still came together. They acted. They watched. I was very moved when I heard that. To me, it affirmed what I've always believed: that a theater is our temple to humanity, and art the force that binds us irrevocably, regardless of race, color, or creed. That the boundary lines of nations cannot divide us, nor can the ravages of time, war, or simple neglect tear us down. By going to the theater night after night, those people upheld an eternal truth: Without our humanity, both life and death become meaningless."

Bill turns back to Uma. "Why do it?" he says. "Why trouble ourselves to create a living, breathing part for the stage, a character who is vivid, real, and alive in every way? I can't speak for each of you, but I bet the answer goes back to why you want to act in the first place. There's something within you you want to share, something you know will make a difference in this world if only you find a way to release it, polish it, show it to others. We are connected to one another in ways we cannot possibly comprehend, but it's easy to forget this. Life seems hell-bent on breaking the few timorous connections we maintain with one another. But the child in each of us never dies and the signals we want to emit over this massive web were not meant to be kept to ourselves. The hard work is hard for a reason: in the end, it's the work worth doing."

Bill looks around at this class and nods.

"I'm satisfied. You're ready for the next exercise I want to give you. For this, you'll need a book of nursery rhymes."

Mimi was taking notes, but stops. She looks up. "What on earth are we going to do with a book of nursery rhymes?"

Bill grins at her. "You'll see."

NINE

NURSERY RHYMES

"Simple Simon went a-fishing
For to catch a whale,
But all the water he had got
Was in his mother's pail."

—ANONYMOUS

Bill begins the next class by saying, "I need someone to help me. Amber, would you mind?"

"Not at all," she says.

"You have your book of nursery rhymes? Does your book have 'Jack and Jill' in it?"

Amber checks. She nods.

"Would you read it out loud for us?"

Amber reads:

"Jack and Jill went up the hill
To fetch a pail of water.
Jack fell down and broke his crown
And Jill came tumbling after."

Bill thinks for a moment and nods. "All right. It's not exactly the Saint Crispin's Day speech, but it'll do. Can you remember the text, Amber? If you need to take a moment and look it over . . ."

Amber says, "I think I can manage."

"Good. Now, suppose I asked you to turn that text into acting. What would you have to figure out first?"

Amber thinks about it. "I guess I'd have to decide who Jack and Jill were, specifically."

"That's right." Bill's tone becomes grave. "Let's suppose they're your little niece and your nephew. Jack is four, Jill is two, and they're adorable. The lights of your life. But a few minutes ago, they wandered up the hill in the backyard to get some water from that old well that's up there. Jack fell down and broke his crown, meaning that he had fractured his skull and he's in the hospital. And little Jill fell down right after him—"

"Stop!" Amber stares at Bill, horrified by where this is going.

"Tell me," Bill says. "If this really happened, do you know how you'd feel?"

Amber nods.

"Can you go outside and prepare emotionally for that, and when you're ready, come in and break the awful news to me using the text from the rhyme?"

Amber gets up and goes to the door. She's already starting to tremble as she slips from the room. After a few minutes, the door opens and Amber is there. She looks a fright. Her body has stiffened with grief and shock. She's the picture of a woman who just saw a tragedy happen and couldn't do anything to prevent it.

"My God!" Bill says. "What happened?"

Amber tries to speak but can't. Her voice has caught in her throat. She blubbers, sobs, and tries again.

"Jack." She starts to breaks down but gets hold of herself and tries again. "Jack and Jill . . . went up . . . the hill?" She points backward, out the door. "To fetch a pail of water. Jack . . ." Amber can barely breathe. ". . . fell down . . ." She starts to moan. ". . . and broke his crown . . . and . . . Jill . . . came . . . tumbling *after*!"

Her agony swells, too much to contain. Collapsing against the doorjamb, she bawls, inconsolable. Bill gives her a moment to gather herself.

"That was pretty good," he says. "Now I want you to do it again using the same nursery rhyme, but this time let's say that Jack and Jill are those two little pains in the ass who live next door to you. You know, those two spoiled brats? They run around doing whatever the hell they want. Yesterday they broke one of your windows playing ball too close to the house. You understand what I'm saying? How many times have you told them to stay away from that well?"

The change that comes over Amber's manner is instant. She wipes her nose and narrows her eyes. "A hundred, at least."

"You've told those little bastards time and time again: Stay away from that damn old well! But do they ever listen?"

Amber snorts. "Not hardly."

"Well, they took some fall and it serves them right. Am I right or wrong?"

"You're right."

"Okay. Then go outside and do it again, but this time from a completely different Point of View."

Amber departs. This time, she's only gone a few moments before she storms back in, flushed with absolute pleasure. I once saw the same euphoria consume a long-suffering employee who got a new job and told her lousy old boss to go screw a barnyard animal.

Infected by her mood, Bill grins at Amber. "What's up?"

Amber throws up her arms in triumph. "Jack and Jill went up the hill to fetch a pail of water? Jack! Fell! Down!" Her subtext: *Thank God! My prayers have been answered!* "And broke his *crown*!!!" Amber laughs so hard, she's nearly in tears. The last bit hits like a punch line. "And Jill! Came tumbling after!!!"

Amber claps her hands and actually hops up and down. She

and Bill have a good laugh. It's such an absurd, vindictive, spot-on performance, the whole class starts laughing with them.

"Can we do it one more time?" Bill says. "This time, Jack and Jill are the two most adorable kids you've ever seen in your life. They're both really young, maybe two years old. We're at a playground and they crawled up this little hill in the sandbox to get a plastic pail of water. And Jack was wearing one of those little crowns they give to tots at Burger King. You know the kind I'm talking about?"

Amber presses her hands to her heart and gushes. "Oh!"

Bill smiles. "Well, it was so cute! He rolled down the hill and the crown came off." Bill pouts to show how Jack reacted. "A second later, Jill rolled off, too. It was the most adorable thing you ever saw. Right? Go outside and get as fully connected as possible to that. Then come back in and use the text to tell me what happened."

Amber does. This time she uses the lines like a proud parent describing her child's first game of peekaboo. Enraptured, she pouts and rocks back and forth. Half her lines are delivered in baby talk. Again the actors erupt with laughter.

Bill turns to the class. "I think you get the idea. As an exercise, nursery rhymes train you to take any piece of text and make it mean what you want it to mean. The theory being that if you can act a text which is completely without any dramatic intention or content, then you can act anything. In addition, as with any good acting exercise, nursery rhymes force us to focus on behavior. Again and again, they confront us with the actor's great dilemma: *I see what I'm supposed to say, but what do I mean?*

"In the nursery rhyme Amber just did, the text came to the surface and explained the emotional preparation that was alive inside the actor. Now I'd like to show you another kind of nursery rhyme exercise."

Bill gets up from his desk and walks into the playing space. "Let's suppose I'm the boss of a factory. I have three employees. Dom, you play a guy named Hickory. Jon, your name is Dickory. Reg, your name is Doc. Okay?"

The actors nod, and Bill leaves the room but bursts through the door a moment later. His cheeks are flushed. His manner is that of Lieutenant Commander Queeg from *The Caine Mutiny Court-Martial*: tyrannical and unhinged. Storming straight to the front of the seats, he jabs a finger at Dom.

"Hickory!"

Stunned, Dom places a hand on his chest. *Me?* Bill nods and jerks his thumb toward the playing space. *Get over here now!* Dom leaps to his feet and does as he's told, and Bill repeats the process, pointing to Jon and Reg.

"Dickory! Doc!"

Jon and Reg jump down from the bleachers and join Dom in the playing space. The three actors stand in a straight line facing the audience. They look honestly apprehensive.

Squaring his shoulders, Bill marches up and down before them like a drill sergeant reviewing his troops.

"The mouse!" he explodes, glaring at each of his workers in turn. Clearly, this is somehow their fault. Dom, Jon, and Reg respond with hangdog faces.

Bill sighs and throws up his hands, exasperated. "Ran up the clock."

Aha. Now it's clear. The factory has fallen prey to an infestation and these guys are to blame.

"The clock struck one, the mouse ran down . . ."

Bill paces before them, wringing his hands, bemoaning what he saw. Amazingly, Dom, Jon, and Reg shake their heads, empathizing with a situation that's not only fictitious, but one for which they were given no preparation whatsoever.

Bill stops pacing. His face darkens and he turns on his men, having reached a decision.

"Hickory." His eyes ablaze, he points to Dom, then points to the door. Dom gets the hint and hastens to leave, presumably to bait traps.

"Dickory." Bill points to Jon and then to the door. The look on Jon's face is comically sincere: *Please Let Me Keep My Job!* Someone in the audience titters, but Jon doesn't hear it. He follows Dom out the door.

"Doc!" Bill turns to Reg, but the big man is already hustling his portly frame toward the studio door. At the last possible moment, Bill whirls and delivers a kick to Reg's ample ass. Reg lets out a little squeal and grabs the seat of his pants as he leaves the room. The class breaks into laughter and applause as Bill stalks after his vanished crew. He is clearly determined to kill every mouse he can find.

A moment later, everyone's back in the studio.

"Do you see what I was going for here?" Bill says. "Nursery rhymes can also be used as exercises to justify even the most nonsensical pieces of text. In other words, to do a good nursery rhyme exercise, you have to invent a plausible reason to speak each word. That reason must be imaginative, since we're essentially forcing each rhyme to tell a story against its will. And I hope it goes without saying that your reasons must also be grounded in truth."

Cheryl laughs. "It's like you just gave us a two-minute play," she says. "It had a beginning, a middle, and an end."

"The characters were all very specific," Ray notes.

"And the situation was clear," says Joyce.

"The moments," says Melissa. "That's what I liked the best. Each moment was carved in specific detail."

Trevor grins. "Mother Goose is turning over in her grave. I never would have looked at 'Hickory Dickory Dock' like that."

"And that's the point," Bill says. "Part of your job as an actor is to bring your unique take to every piece of material you're given. Nursery rhymes demand that you come up with concrete and imaginative answers to the problem of ambiguous or misleading text. So give it a try. Take your books home, select a rhyme, and come up with at least two interpretations that satisfy all the requirements we just talked about. Three interpretations would be even better. Just so you know: I once had a student who brought in eight separate viable pieces crafted from the same verse."

Vanessa looks shocked. "Eight interpretations of the same nursery rhyme?"

"No," Bill says. "Eight *completely different* interpretations of the same nursery rhyme. But this was an exceptionally gifted student, and I can't expect you all to be like him. I'll settle for three.

"You'll continue to work with the partners I assigned you, but please understand: Your partner is really only there as a resource to help you flesh out a situation, the way I just used Dom, Jon, and Reg. If your partner isn't enough, you can pull in anyone else from the class to help you. Naturally, you'll have to give them a bit of direction to make your scenario work. But that shouldn't be very difficult if you've justified everything well. Any questions?"

No one seems to have any.

"Good," Bill says. "Let's see how you take to these."

▊ ▊ ▊ ▊

"Which rhyme are you doing?" Bill asks.

Jon holds up a piece of paper. "This one is simple. It's called 'Go to Bed, Tom.'" And he reads:

"Go to bed, Tom.
Go to bed, Tom!

Tired or not, Tom.
Go to bed, Tom."

Bill grins. "Simple is right. In fact, that might be the simplest one of the lot. Let's see what you do with it."

Jon flicks off the lights and the studio goes black. We wait in darkness for several minutes, during which we hear furniture being shuffled around and the scurry of footsteps. What is going on?

When the lights come back up, the space has been transformed. We're in a studio apartment. Quid sits on the sofa clawing tortilla chips from a plastic bag and stuffing them into his face. He crunches, crunches while staring at a football game playing on a TV set.

Jon reclines on the bed nearby. He's reading from a book, or trying to—it's impossible. The TV distracts him again and again. He flips a page and squints and frowns and glares at Quid, who, oblivious, stuffs more chips in his mouth and keeps his eyes focused on the screen.

Finally Jon slams his book shut. "Go to bed, Tom."

Quid/Tom acts as though he didn't hear. He loads his mouth full of chips. *Crunch, crunch.* A moment later he mutters, "Go to bed?"

Jon sits up, annoyed. "Tom! Tired?"

The way he says 'tired,' he might as well be saying, 'Hey, doofus, what am I, chopped liver, here?' He's demanding that Quid pay attention to his needs.

Unfortunately, Quid does not. He acts as though he couldn't care less. Snickering, he says, "Or not." And shoves a handful of chips in his mouth.

"Tom!" says Jon. To remonstrate with him. Grabbing a pillow, he hurls it at Quid's head. *Smack!* The bag of chips jerks out of

Quid's hands. He turns, a look of surprise on his face as another pillow hits him. *Smack!*

Jon laughs. "Go to bed, Tom!"

Grinning, Quid grabs a cushion off the sofa and leaps toward the bed. A pillow fight ensues with both men laughing, enjoying themselves. They tackle each other and roll around like kids in a playpen. Their affection for each other is so contagious, the class roars with laughter.

The lights come up, and Bill nods, smiling.

"That's exactly what I wanted. You worked out every detail and imbued the scene with life so the story came across perfectly, as did your characters. Do you have a second interpretation?"

Jon grins. "Give us a minute to set up."

The studio goes dark again. When the lights rise, we're in the same tiny apartment, only this time Jon is alone and standing in front of the dresser, whose top drawer is open, with shirts lolling out.

Something is wrong. We know from the look on Jon's face. His eyes have gone wide, features slack with disbelief. He holds a stack of letters and he reads the top one, his pupils darting over the words. Dropping the top letter, he reads the second while starting to pace. He drops the second one. Reads the third. Drops it. Reads the fourth. The fifth. The letters now cover the floor like so many autumn leaves, and still he paces. Reading. Reading.

The door opens. Quid enters. Jon turns and freezes.

Quid has a cell phone cranked to his ear and he's laughing with whoever's on the other end of the line. Until, that is, he sees Jon, the apartment, the letters scattered across the floor. His eyes dart at once to the dresser drawer, which has obviously been rifled. In shock, Quid lowers his phone and thumbs it off. Then he squares his shoulders and his features compose themselves in a look of intense resolve.

The two men stand there, staring at each other. The studio has gone utterly quiet. The tension in the room is immense. You can practically feel the bonds of this relationship that held us so charmed dissolving into thin air.

Quid breaks the stalemate. Setting his jaw, he closes the door and puts his bag down, taking his time. Aloof, he takes off his jacket and hangs it deliberately on a hook. Kicking his shoes off, he moves to the dresser while Jon stays rooted, frozen in shock, his expression morphing like quicksilver through sadness, hurt, confusion, and rage.

Quid picks up the shirts that have spilled from the dresser, folds them, replaces them, shuts the drawer, then moves past Jon as if he isn't there and starts to get undressed.

"Go to bed," he says. Though it's a simple statement of intention, under the circumstances, it lands as a devastating blow. Jon rocks backward, as if struck.

"Tom!" he says. His voice is a ruin.

Quid turns and regards him, but the look on Quid's face holds nothing—no guilt, no remorse, just a steely-eyed *Well, What Did You Expect?* It's a powerful moment, the kind that, in just a few seconds, tells you all the backstory anyone needs to know about these two characters. And yet not a word was spoken.

Jon notes that look and opens his mouth to say something, but stops himself. He drops his eyes. Softly, almost inaudibly, he says, "Go to bed, Tom." Dismissing him.

And just like that, the tables have turned. Miraculously, we watch Quid shrink, losing height and weight to become less substantial, insignificant in his guilt. Agony creeps across his face. He watches Jon move to the couch and sit and stare straight down at the tips of his shoes.

"Tired," Quid offers. The meaning is clear. He's explaining his position. *This relationship. The two of us. It's not working anymore.*

You knew it and I knew it, he's saying. *The only difference is that I went out and did something about it. How can you blame me for that?*

Jon pays him no attention at all. He's become captivated by his shoelaces. Reaching down, he toys with one, remarkably calm. So calm, in fact, that Quid takes a step toward him, crumbling.

"Or," Quid says. His Action couldn't be clearer. He's Offering an Olive Branch. But Jon has made his decision. He doesn't react when Quid walks over to the couch and slowly sits beside him. Or when Quid reaches across and begins to knead Jon's shoulder, looking intently into his face as if saying, *Can we? Maybe? Try again?*

Quid's cell phone rings. He freezes.

Jon turns his head very slowly, his face a burning torch of resentment, his expression an indictment. *That's him, isn't it?*

The phone rings twice. Jon drops his head. It's over. So clear. It's over.

Three times the phone rings. Four. It stops. The silence that opens between the boyfriends, or former boyfriends, is deafening.

"Knot," Jon says. He picks at a snarl in his shoelace.

Quid decides to try again. He reaches for Jon's shoulders but—

"Tom."

Quid stops. Jon has not lifted his eyes. He speaks in a pleasant, grounded voice, as if speaking to a child.

"Go to bed, Tom."

Quid looks stricken. He knows he screwed up, but what can he do? The damage is done. Rising slowly, he moves to the bed and starts to remove his clothes.

Left alone, Jon picks up the remote and thumbs the TV to life. A football game. We hear the announcer, the roar of the crowd. Lights from the screen flicker across Jon's face, but he isn't really watching; his eyes are a million miles away.

The two men sit mere feet from each other, but they're already living in two different worlds as the lights fade slowly to black and the class breaks into applause.

"Another good exercise," Bill says. "Plus you have a real epic unfolding. Is there a third variation?"

"Yes."

The set remains the same, only this time the apartment is empty and dark. It stays that way until the door opens and a knife blade of light cuts into the space. Jon's silhouette fills the threshold.

He flicks on the light. He wears a light jacket and his face is drawn. He turns and goes back out in the hall and reappears moments later, pushing Quid in a wheelchair.

Donna is sitting beside me. She gasps.

Quid has become a shell of himself. He's bundled into heavy clothes with a blanket wrapping his torso and legs. He wears a heavy wool cap that, like the rest of his outfit, looks markedly out of place beside Jon's light jacket. Quid is sick, that much is clear. When he coughs, his whole body wracks as with spasm. His head falls forward—he's fighting to raise it. When he moves, he does so with the eerie economy of someone rationing vigor, whose energy has been leached from his body. Someone who's probably dying.

We can see only small patches of Quid's skin—his face, the backs of his hands. They are spotted with purple-black lesions.

Jon rolls Quid to the side of the bed and starts fussing with his blanket, making sure he's bundled tight against a nonexistent chill. It's like watching a mother tend to her helpless infant. Sour and feeble, Quid waves him away.

"Go," Quid says.

Jon shakes his head. "To bed."

He continues to fuss. Quid fights him at first, but gives up. He can't win. He lets Jon pull his hat lower over his ears and adjust the winding of his thick wool scarf. Satisfied, Jon kisses Quid's cheek. Quid offers no reaction at all. Smiling, Jon holds up a *One moment* finger, turns, and exits the apartment, leaving the front door open.

Quid waits until he's gone and seizes the opportunity. Gripping the wheels of his chair, he spins it around and rolls toward the couch. The remote control rests on the armrest. Quid reaches out slowly, a shaking hand. He grabs the remote and points it at the TV, thumbing it on.

Football blinks into life on the screen. Quid heaves a heavy sigh.

A few moments later, Tom reenters the apartment, hauling what can only be Quid's luggage. He stops in the threshold and stares.

"Tom!"

Quid shoots him a look that's somehow innocent and wily all at once.

Dropping the bags, Jon stalks forward, grabs the remote from Quid's weak grip, and thumbs the TV off.

"Go to bed, Tom," he orders.

Quid shivers and yawns.

Jon looks triumphant. "Tired?" He sets the remote on top of the TV, just out of Quid's reach, and leaves him alone while he goes to collect the bags.

"Or not," Quid mutters.

Jon hauls the luggage over to the dresser, opens the suitcases, and starts to unpack. He turns his back to Quid, who—checking to make sure the coast is clear—wheels himself slowly, softly toward the TV and tries to find an on button. He can't. The remote is the only way to activate the set, but the remote is on top, and well out of his reach. Unless . . .

Wincing, Quid struggles to rise. Tough work on legs now stripped of their strength, but he does it. Halfway. He stretches

one hand out, steadies himself on the arm of the wheelchair, straining, straining toward the remote. His fingertips brush the plastic
case. They struggle to close. He is almost there, but the wand
slips back off the top of the set and hits the floor with a crash.

Caught off balance, Quid falls as well, his brittle bones slam-
ming the hardwood.

"Tom!"

Jon rushes toward him and kneels and the two men start to
grapple. Jon tries to help Quid rise but Quid bats his hands away
and, desperate, claws across the floor. Given his superior strength,
Jon should win this struggle easily, but Quid is obsessed. He
wants the remote, must have the remote, but he never gets it. All
at once, his energy deserts him and he collapses, weeping.

Jon starts crying, too. He gathers Quid up like a bundle of
sticks and rocks him, crushing him tight to his chest.

"Go to bed, Tom!" he sobs.

The lights fade on a picture of two people, down on the floor
and wrapped up in each other. Their limbs have so intertwined
that, as shadows lengthen, we cannot tell where one man ends
and the other begins. Then darkness falls.

Applause, applause. When the lights return to full, Bill looks
pleased.

"Three scenes," he says. "Each one carved exquisitely, like a
jewel. But dare I ask? Can you give us a fourth?"

Jon nods and gestures to Dom, who's been working the wall
switch. Once again, we are plunged into darkness.

Two minutes later, the lights rise again. The same apartment,
but this time Quid lies in bed, his mouth an open and senseless
O, his head hung back and his body utterly still. Tom stands over
him, looking down, his face a mask, unreadable.

"Go to bed, Tom," Jon says.

Nothing. Long moments pass. Again, the disembodied tone.

"Go to bed, Tom."

Quid's chest rises. Holds for an agonized moment. Then falls. A rattle rolls around in his chest. His lips work, straining to structure a word.

"Tired," he gasps.

Jon waits.

More labored breaths, each a battle hard won. Then, slowly, tenuous as spider's silk, Quid's hand lifts an inch off the sheet. It reaches toward Jon.

"Or . . ."

Was that a word or a cough? If a word, was it the whole word or simply the start of one? What is he trying to say? *Organize? Order? Ornament?*

Beside me, Donna strains forward in her seat.

"Not . . . ," Quint gasps. Barely audible now, and perhaps this is just another fragment of a word. We'll never know.

His hand drops onto the sheet and lies still.

For a long moment, Jon regards him. Then he picks up a pillow, his face still blank. It remains that way as he presses the pillow over Quid's face and leans in, using his weight.

Beside me, Donna has started to sob. Her release hits the studio like a bursting dam. Sniffles and chokes spill out from the bleachers, but the scene isn't over. Not yet.

After a while, Jon pulls the pillow away and examines what he has done. His expression is half fright, half childlike wonder.

Fluffing the pillow, he sets it beside Quid's head and arranges it just so. Then he sits on the edge of the bed and takes one of Quid's hands in his own.

"Tom," he says, and stays that way for a long, long time, which doesn't feel long in the least. It's like Bill said: When actors work from moment to moment, it's as if every split second earns the right to be the one where the curtain falls and the lights return.

Except that another moment passes. Then another. And another. As audience members, we await each one eagerly, not knowing where they lead because, like all things truly alive, each one contains possibility.

Jon lifts Quid's hand to his lips and kisses it before placing it gently on Quid's chest.

"Go to bed, Tom."

He pulls a pistol from his pants and looks at the thing, which is ugly and black. He smiles at it. Cocks the hammer with a shaking hand. Puts the barrel in his mouth and closes his eyes.

A strange sound like a *clickety-clack* fills the studio. It takes me a moment to figure out what it is: gunmetal rattling against Jon's teeth.

Blackout.

■ ■ ■ ■

A moment later, everyone's back in the room.

"That was very, very good," Bill says.

Jon blushes. "Thank you. There's one thing I've begun to discover."

"Yes?"

"Well, it seems to me that, if you craft a performance just so, a good actor can say a whole lot without speaking a single word."

"Very true," Bill says. "Dialogue isn't necessary to create human behavior. If it were, silent movies would never have become popular and Charlie Chaplin would never have had such a stunning career. Mimes and dancers would go out of business. Life would lose all the subtlety and grace of lovers batting their eyes at each other, or the beautiful poetry of all that goes unspoken between human beings as we navigate through our lives. They say that the best things in life are free. Likewise the most powerful moments an actor will ever supply come frequently without words, since words would only mar them, take what is priceless and render it cheap."

Bill thinks for a moment. "Good," he says. "So let's summarize. What are nursery rhymes teaching you?"

"How to take even the most unlikely text and turn it into acting," says Jon.

"How to carve out moments in a script," says Quid.

"How to justify absolutely anything," says Vanessa.

"All very true," Bill says. "Nursery rhymes provide a simple way for you to practice the skills you've learned so far. We'll do a few more of these over the next couple days. I want you all to succeed in a nursery rhyme before we move to the next exercise."

Uma looks up from her notebook. "Which is what, Bill?"

"The next step is to apply your skills to more challenging text. For that, I need you to get a copy of Edgar Lee Masters's *Spoon River Anthology.*

"*Spoon River* is a collection of short free-form poems. Read the whole book. When you hear a piece that you empathize with, mark it. I'd like you have four to six pieces picked out. We'll avoid overlap this way; if someone does a piece you wanted to do, there's flexibility. Also, I might tell you that a piece you want to do so desperately isn't right for you, either because you don't really understand what it's about or because you want to do it so desperately."

Bill thinks for a moment, then nods.

"Who's up next?"

"I'll go," says Joyce. "I'm doing 'Three Blind Mice.'"

"All right. Let's see how they run."

TEN

SPOON RIVERS

"A poet's work is to name the unnameable, to point at frauds, to take sides, start arguments, shape the world, and stop it going to sleep."

—SALMAN RUSHDIE

"An artist must understand the reality he depicts in its most minute detail."

—FYODOR DOSTOEVSKY

"Are there any questions before we begin?"

Mimi raises her hand. She looks perplexed. "You didn't tell us the poems in *Spoon River* are about dead people."

"Don't get hung up on that," Bill says. "Spoon River is a fictional small town in southern Illinois right after the Civil War. It's true that everyone in the book is deceased, but a livelier bunch you'll probably never meet. These people want to talk about their lives. They have lessons they want to share and secrets to divulge. Today I'll show you how we use these speeches to help us integrate everything we've learned so far about character work, but with one important addition: the use of heightened language. Who would like to go first?"

"I will." Cheryl walks into the playing space and sits at the table. "I considered five poems, but I'd like to start with Pauline Barrett."

Bill waves for her to begin and Cheryl reads:

"Almost the shell of a woman after the surgeon's knife!
And almost a year to creep back into strength,
Till the dawn of our wedding decennial
Found me my seeming self again.
We walked the forest together,
By a path of soundless moss and turf.
But I could not look in your eyes,
And you could not look in my eyes,
For such sorrow was ours—the beginning of gray in your hair,
And I but a shell of myself.
And what did we talk of?—sky and water,
Anything, 'most, to hide our thoughts.
And then your gift of wild roses,
Set on the table to grace our dinner.
Poor heart, how bravely you struggled
To imagine and live a remembered rapture!
Then my spirit drooped as the night came on,
And you left me alone in my room for a while,
As you did when I was a bride, poor heart.
And I looked in the mirror and something said:
'One should be all dead when one is half-dead—
Nor ever mock life, nor ever cheat love.'
And I did it looking there in the mirror—
Dear, have you ever understood?"

Bill nods to Cheryl and turns to the class. "Edgar Lee Masters possessed a genius that was almost Shakespearean. Consider his accomplishment. He created an entire town, and he peopled it with scores of characters who are distinct but nonetheless universal. And while each of these pieces is short, do not be fooled by their brevity. Masters wrote each epitaph as poetry, which is language at its most condensed. That's why a whole human life can take shape from a few lines of text. Masters was a man of great sensitivity and insight into the human condition. To realize his work, the actor must bring his or her whole self, as well as all his or her knowledge of what it means to be human.

"From a technical point of view, these poems are like puzzles. Each piece challenges us to analyze it, figure out what the character's really saying, and find a way to translate that into acting. I want you to start by going through your speech line by line. Examine it thought by thought in order to understand what you're saying in plain English." Bill turns back to Cheryl. "You start by saying, 'Almost the shell of a woman after the surgeon's knife.' What do you think you are talking about?"

"Did I have a hysterectomy?"

"No, but I'm actually glad you said that. Very often, these pieces deceive the actor. You believe they're about one thing when they're really about something else. I think that might be the case with you. Let's look at the second line. It took you 'a year to creep back into strength.' Even then, you were only your 'seeming self.' I don't think a hysterectomy would put you in the hospital for an entire year. What else could devastate your health in such a fashion?"

Cheryl blanches. "Cancer?"

Bill nods. "Sometimes, just before a patient dies, their cancer seems to go into complete remission. Sometimes it lets you get well enough to take a trip home from the hospital, but you're not really cured. In this case, why did the doctors let you go home?"

". . . I'm not really sure. . . ."

"What does the text say?"

"It's my tenth wedding anniversary." Cheryl frowns. "Bill, are you certain it's cancer? I honestly didn't read it that way."

"Did you ever see Penn and Teller perform?"

Cheryl shakes her head.

"They're terribly funny comic magicians, and they do a skit featuring Mofo the Psychic Gorilla. Mofo is a fake gorilla head whose eyes light up. He has a voice like the wizard in *The Wizard of Oz*. In the skit, Mofo knows all, tells all! Well, a script is like Mofo. It knows all, tells all! Everything you need know about your part can be found in the text. So let's put that thought to the test. Do you really have cancer? Well, we know that you and your husband take a walk in the woods. 'But I could not look in your eyes,' you say. 'And you could not look in my eyes, / For such sorrow was ours.' What do you think you were sad about, Cheryl? Why couldn't you look into each other's eyes?"

Cheryl chews her lower lip. ". . . I thought it was because we couldn't have a baby."

"It's bigger than that," Bill says. "This speech says that you had a very large elephant in the room, and neither you nor your husband could acknowledge its presence. That elephant was the fact that you were going to die in the very near future. The biggest taboo in our society is not sex, it's death. That's the one subject almost no one is able to confront head-on. Watch how people behave when someone they know starts to fail. So many empty platitudes get spouted. 'Chin up. You'll be out of here in no time. You can beat this thing. You're going to be okay.' We go on and on like that without any real grounds to justify what we're saying. And why do we spout this bunkum? To avoid the topic, and thereby our own mortality."

Cheryl thinks it over and nods. "My next line is, 'The beginning of gray in your hair, / And I but a shell of myself.' I guess this goes with what you're saying. Time is passing for both of us. We probably had all these dreams about what we wanted our life to be like, but now . . ."

Bill nods. "Those dreams are gone. And what's left? What could you and your husband possibly talk about?"

"'Sky and water, / Anything, 'most, to hide our thoughts.'"

Bill gives her a very direct look. "What thoughts do you think you're hiding from, Cheryl?"

She starts to answer, but tears well up in her eyes and she bites them back before reading on.

"And then your gift of wild roses,
Set on the table to grace our dinner.
Poor heart, how bravely you struggled
To imagine and live a remembered rapture."

Cheryl looks up. "He must have loved me so much."

"He did, and you loved him. More than anything. More than life itself. Keep reading."

"'Then my spirit drooped as the night came on.'"

"You got exhausted," Bill notes. "That happens to sick people. What happened next?"

"'And you left me alone in my room for a while, / As you did when I was a bride, poor heart.'"

"Why did he leave you alone on your wedding night, Cheryl?"

". . . So I could change clothes?"

Bill shakes his head. "Remember, this was a much different era. Near the turn of the century, most people didn't sleep with each other before they got married. Most times, they barely knew each other before they consummated their marriage. The night you got married, your husband respected your modesty, your youth and inexperience. He didn't want to frighten you, so he gave you time to be by yourself. To change clothes, yes, so you wouldn't have to undress and put your nightgown on in front of him."

"Oh!" says Cheryl. Clearly this gesture has touched her.

"So why does he do it now, ten years later?"

". . . I'm not sure."

"Because he still adores you, even though you look like a concentration camp survivor. You're emaciated, with scars all over your body. There's practically nothing left of you, you're the walking dead. But he adores you and he wants you to be able to retain some dignity, do you understand?"

Cheryl has to choke out the next words. "'And I looked in the mirror and something said: "One should be all dead when one is half-dead— / Nor ever mock life, nor ever cheat love."'"

"That 'something' you speak of. That was an impulse. It took you by surprise. And what did that impulse goad you to do?"

"'. . . I did it looking there in the mirror— / Dear, have you ever understood?'" Cheryl looks up, in agony. "I took my own life."

Bill nods. "And you didn't leave a note. That's very important."

". . . But why . . . ?"

"Because your sadness was unimaginable. It consumed you to the point where you saw yourself as a mockery to the dreams the two of you once nurtured. So this impulse struck and you acted and—"

"How?"

"A gun, I imagine," Bill says. "Anything else would have been too slow. You'd have had time to pause and reconsider. So you shot yourself, but you forgot one thing."

"My husband." Cheryl looks deeply moved. "I had no idea this speech was about all those things."

"Now you understand the last line," Bill says. "'Dear, have you ever understood?' Remember before? We talked about actors being like detectives examining the scene of a crime. That's never more true than when you're dealing with elevated text. No detail can fall outside your scrutiny." Bill turns to the class. "Once you've figured out what you're saying, it's time to move on to the next stage, which is pinning down technical points. The first of these technical points is, What person or thing are you speaking to? In other words, what is your Acting Object?

"You cannot create acting unless you're connected to an Acting Object. Most often, your Acting Object will be another character in the script or a group of people. But people in life, and therefore people in a script, also connect to inanimate objects. We talk to plants or to pets, for example. We talk to stuffed toy animals, ghosts, mementos. In Eugene O'Neill's *Mourning Becomes Electra,* the character Orin speaks both to his father's corpse and, at another point in the play, to his father's portrait on the wall. The possibilities are endless.

"In cases where the Acting Object isn't specified, selecting one becomes a vital decision on the part of the actor. Trying to communicate with any of these Objects will create its own particular challenges. In all cases, the actor must capture the reality of trying to communicate with his specific Object. If he doesn't, he won't create acting—he'll be stuck with a mere recitation of text."

Melissa raises her hand. "Bill, what's the technique for acting with something that isn't there?"

"Good question," Bill says. "That situation happens a lot. Actors doing monologues must imagine they're speaking to another person. If you're shooting a film, you may find yourself delivering lines to a stand-in, a production assistant, or even someone's hand. You may find yourself acting with a green screen where they fill in the character you're talking to in postproduction. In all cases, the challenge is the same.

"Take the case of acting with a corpse. You have to believe that even though this person's been in the grave thirty years, even though he or she can't respond, some essential part of the person still exists and can hear what you're saying. The same goes for acting with a picture in a locket. You have to believe that the picture can hear you as keenly as the person it depicts."

Melissa nods and jots in her notebook.

Bill turns back to Cheryl. "So who are you speaking to as Pauline Barrett? Who or what is your Acting Object?"

"That's pretty clear. My husband."

"'Husband' is a legal term, it won't help your acting. What if you were talking to your best friend, or to the love of your life? Would that activate you more?"

Cheryl nods.

"Again," Bill says, "*until you've pinned down an Acting Object that has real and deep meaning for you, your speech won't produce any acting. Instead you'll just be reciting the lines.*

"So now that we know who you're talking to, let's figure out what you're doing. In other words, what's the Action of this piece? Here again, we have a helpful tool. In all of these Spoon Rivers, the key to the character's emotional Point of View lies in the last lines. Knowing your character's Point of View will often help you discover the character's Action. What's your last line, Cheryl?

"I say, 'Dear, have you ever understood?'"

"Why do you think you say that?"

"Because I'm dead and my husband is still alive and he misses me terribly. But mostly he's suffering because he's never been able to figure out why I did what I did."

"That's right. So what are you trying to do? What's the Action of your piece?"

"I'm trying to make him understand why, after this beautiful day we had, I killed myself and didn't leave a note."

"Trying to make him understand is an objective," Bill says. "What Action do you do to make him understand?"

"I'm Leading the Man I Adore Through a List of the Events That Happened the Day I Killed Myself. That way he'll understand that it wasn't his fault."

Bill nods. "So let's review. You've gone through the speech line by line and you understand what it's about. You've pinned down the Acting Object and now you've found your Action. This next step is very important. I want you to do an actor's paraphrase of the speech. Do you understand what I mean by that?"

Cheryl thinks. "You want me to speak the text in my own words."

"Yes and no," Bill says. "I want you to perform the Action of your piece in a way that connects you to the material's *essential meaning*. You don't have to dwell on the details of Pauline Barrett's speech. You don't have to try to use her words. Just do what Pauline Barrett does in a way that you understand. In other words, go through a list of everything that happened to you leading up to your big decision."

Cheryl frowns. "I'm not sure I follow you."

Bill shrugs. "Here's an example of What Not to Do. Suppose you're doing Hamlet's speech 'O, what a rogue and peasant slave am I!' A bad actor would paraphrase it like this." Bill hunches forward and furrows his brow. "Hmmm. Okay. I say I'm a rogue, but what's a 'rogue'? Well, a rogue is sort of a scamp, a scalawag, a ne'er-do-well. Possibly wearing a doublet and hose. Okay. I know what a rogue is now, but what about 'peasant'? Well, a peasant is a poor farmer in medieval Europe. So! I'm a scamp wearing a doublet and hose who moonlights as a poor medieval European peasant!"

Bill's muttering is so odd, so disembodied and emotionally shut down, the class erupts with laughter. He looks up.

"Can anyone act that? Did I just hear a resounding no? I hope so. Say it again, please."

"No!" the class says.

"This kind of paraphrasing is just a literary exercise in substituting the words of the text for words that are just as meaningless to the actor. Working like that won't help your acting at all because the associations are intellectual. Whereas I want your paraphrase to come from here." He taps his gut. "From someplace deeply personal. So forget about Pauline Barrett's lines. Forget about Pauline Barrett, if you must. How would you, Cheryl, list all the things that happened to you so that someone very dear to you could understand why you did something?"

"I'm not sure where to begin the process."

"Do you ever daydream?"

"All the time."

"Good," Bill says. "Every actor should say that without hesitation. Let me ask you: Have you ever found yourself walking down the street having that same argument with your father, your mother, your sister, or your brother you've been having for the past twenty years?"

Cheryl laughs. "Are you kidding? I did that this morning!"

"Then you know how to live out a scene with someone in your imagination. So let's try something. I want you to sit in your chair. Lean back and close your eyes."

Cheryl does.

"Choose some person who has real meaning for you," Bill says gently. "Someone to whom you once did a grave disservice, something you've regretted ever since. When you've found that person, just wiggle a finger."

A few minutes later, Cheryl signals she's ready, but it's a redundant gesture. We know she's found the right person when, even with eyes closed, the look on her face undergoes a dramatic change. Her breathing quickens. Her face flushes.

"Good," Bill says. "Now forget that we're here. Forget about your text and forget about Pauline Barrett. Just make your loved one understand why you did what you did. And speak out loud whenever you're ready."

Cheryl's voice has gone dreamy and soft. "Oh, darling," she says. "I'm so sorry. I know I must have hurt you so badly and I never meant to do that. It was me. You see that, don't you? I was broken and tired and you were so kind. You took me outside and we walked down our favorite path and I saw the little brook that we used to sit by and the alder tree with the old gnarled roots. And we didn't know what to say. Neither of us could find the words and we couldn't look in each other's eyes because I was dying and we both knew it. Then you took me home and made me such a lovely dinner. You put my favorite flowers on the table and I loved you so much right then. I thought, He's the best man I've ever known. He's always so sensitive, so nice to me. I was lucky we'd found each other. And later that night. You were always so decent. You told me to take my time getting ready, so I went in the bedroom and took off my clothes and I looked in the mirror and saw what they'd done to me. My ribs. My bones. The scars. So many scars." Cheryl pauses. Her eyes roam under her eyelids. "I was already dead, don't you see? You had so much to live for, but my time was done and I knew it. I knew we would never go walking again and I wanted that day to last forever, so I picked up the gun that you kept in the drawer and I shot myself. Do you know why, my love? Do you understand now? You gave me the best gift of all. Our life. And that wonderful, wonderful day."

Bill turns to the class. "There it is. That's the performance. Cheryl chose to stick to the details of Pauline Barrett's speech, but she could just as easily have been telling her loved one why she had an affair or threw out his favorite bowling shirt. Again, the details don't matter so long as you work from the essential meaning of the piece. So long as you create the performance out of your deepest empathetic response to the person you're portraying.

"And do you see how the performance springs from the reality of doing? Cheryl is really trying to make her loved one understand, and that creates behavior, which is much more important than the lines and, ultimately, has very little to do with them.

"I want you to consider something," Bill says. "There are only two reasons why text is ever important. The first is to create context. For instance, without text, we might never know that Pauline Barrett was talking to her husband. The second reason we need text is to supply building material for our Actions. Suppose you're apologizing to someone for some grievous thing you did. Well, you'll need words to make that apology, right? Just as, if you're telling a joke, you need a joke to tell."

Melissa raises her hand. "Bill, I understand how the paraphrase taps the part's essential meaning. But we still have to speak the writer's lines, don't we? How do we make the journey from our paraphrase back to the author's text?"

"Very carefully," Bill says. "And that's the next step. Once your paraphrase captures the heart of the character, drip the author's text back in a little bit at a time. It's delicate work and you must do it slowly, as though you're making mayonnaise. Has anyone here done that?"

Donna nods. "It's difficult. Mayonnaise is oil blended into egg yolks mixed with lemon juice. But you have to add the oil very slowly, very evenly. Add too much too soon and the mixture will curdle."

"Now tell me. What does mayonnaise, curdled or uncurdled, have to do with acting?" When the class doesn't answer, Bill says, "Aha! I see you stand mute. Here's the point: You should be just as careful when working with your poems. Once you've made your paraphrase, don't rush to return to the author's words. Reintroduce them slowly. Did you see how simple and genuine Cheryl's paraphrase was? She should drip the text for Pauline Barrett into her paraphrase gradually enough to maintain the authentic life she discovered. Working in this fashion might take a couple of hours or a couple of days. But if you keep it up—moving slowly and evenly, never pushing—sooner or later you'll arrive back at the author's text. And when you do, you'll have brought something unique with you, something that you alone can supply: the character's living soul. Do you understand?

"The final step is to add character elements to your performance. Remember that acting is doing truthfully under imaginary circumstances. But character work is an exploration of *how* you do things. So maybe you add an accent or throw in a Physical Impediment. Or work from an imitation of someone you saw walking down the street or waiting for a bus. And I hope it goes without saying that any character element you add must be rehearsed to the point where it's second nature. And however you choose to play your character, remember this: The reality of doing must always be your first and utmost concern. Are you clear on how to work on your piece?" When the class nods, Bill says, "Good. Then let's see who's next."

▌▌▌▌

Dom takes the stage and reads Walter Simmons:

"My parents thought that I would be
As great as Edison or greater:
For as a boy I made balloons
And wondrous kites and toys with clocks
And little engines with tracks to run on
And telephones of cans and thread.
I played the cornet and painted pictures,
Modeled in clay and took the part
Of the villain in the 'Octoroon.'
But then at twenty-one I married
And had to live, and so, to live
I learned the trade of making watches
And kept the jewelry store on the square,

Thinking, thinking, thinking, thinking,—
Not of business, but of the engine
I studied the calculus to build.
And all Spoon River watched and waited
To see it work, but it never worked.
And a few kind souls believed my genius
Was somehow hampered by the store.
It wasn't true.
The truth was this:
I did not have the brains."

"This is another good one," Bill says. "Where do we start?"

"With a line-by-line." Dom reads: "'My parents thought that I would be / As great as Edison or greater.'"

"What does that mean?"

"My parents had high expectations for me."

"How high?"

"They thought I'd be as great as Edison."

"I heard that, but what does it mean?"

Dom frowns. "Well, Edison was a great inventor."

"That's too general. It doesn't activate you when you say it. I want you to consider something. When you lived in Spoon River, the lightbulb hadn't been invented yet. Then Edison came along and suddenly people all over the world could flick a switch and *voilà!* Darkness had been banished. These days we take electric lights for granted. But can you imagine what a miracle it must have been for you back then?"

Dom thinks it over and nods. "It'd be like if I was a writer and my parents honestly thought I'd be as good as Shakespeare someday. That kind of limitless talent."

"You see the difference?"

"Yes."

"Keep going."

"For as a boy I made balloons
And wondrous kites and toys with clocks
And little engines with tracks to run on
And telephones of cans and thread."

"What does that mean?"

Dom shrugs. "A telephone of cans and thread? I made a bunch of cute toys. Lots of kids do that."

Bill throws up his hands. "Why do you make choices that devalue the character? Listen. Suppose you had a three-year-old son who created a tiny working hot air balloon that flew his pet mouse across the Hudson River to deliver telegrams in New Jersey. Would that be cute? Would that be kid stuff? Or would that be amazing? Miraculous?"

"Actually, that would be pretty miraculous."

"I agree. So here's our good friend Walter Simmons. Today we'd call him gifted. Precocious. As a kid he could do anything. He invented things, he played a musical instrument, painted pictures. He even played the villain in *The Octoroon.* Do you know what that is?"

"I had to look it up. It's a nineteenth-century play and the villain is Jacob McClosky."

"So what?"

"McClosky is not a nice man. He connives to steal a plantation, kills people, and tries to ruin the life of a slave who spurns his advances. Then he has this incredible death scene."

"High drama and an incredible death scene. Does that sound like kid stuff to you?"

Dom frowns. "When you put it that way, no. It's a pretty meaty part."

"And what if you nailed that meaty part when you were just fifteen years old? You were a phenomenon, do you understand?"

"I'm starting to."

"Keep going."

"The text says when I turned twenty-one I got married. I had to make a living somehow, so I kept the watch store on the town square. But I wasn't really focused on my business."

"How do you know?"

"The text says I was thinking all the time."

"No," Bill says. "The text says you were 'Thinking, thinking, thinking, thinking.' Why would the poet repeat that word four times?"

"Because I wasn't just thinking, I was obsessed."

"Correct. And what were you obsessed with?"

"An engine I was trying to build. The damn thing had me so mesmerized, I went back to school and learned calculus so I could perfect it."

"Right. But what happened?"

"The whole town was waiting for me to debut my invention."

"That's another clue to your character. How bright must you have been if the whole town was waiting to see what you produced?"

Dom nods. "I get it now. Pretty damn bright."

"So what happened?"

"I let everyone down because I never got my engine to work. But that wasn't the worst part."

"Oh really? What was the worst part?"

Dom reads from the text. "'. . . a few kind souls believed my genius / Was somehow hampered by the store.' But it wasn't true. I just wasn't smart enough."

Bill nods. "Remember when I said these poems are crafted like monologues or a good joke? Walter Simmons's punch line is 'I did not have the brains.' Dom, tell me. Why do you think Walter Simmons is telling us this story? What's his Action?"

"I'm confessing. That last line is like my ultimate sin, the dirty secret I've kept hidden all these years because it was too painful to admit."

Bill nods. "I like that. *To Confess*. So who are you confessing to?"

"I imagined I was speaking to the whole town. Is that okay?"

"Absolutely. So how could you paraphrase this speech?"

Dom frowns. "I had something in mind, but it's kind of fallen through now that I see I've devalued the character."

"It's probably simpler than you think," Bill says. "Every actor I know can relate to Walter Simmons. Suppose you paraphrased him like this: 'From the time I was in kindergarten, I got all the leads in all the school plays. I was the star of every spring musical and everyone said, "You're amazing! Someday you'll be the greatest actor who ever lived!" And I believed them. I went to college and played all the great parts—Richard III, Macbeth—and people kept telling me, "You're fantastic! Someday you'll be famous!" Well, of course I thought they were right. I was obsessed about being an actor! So I moved to New York and I was so excited! My dream was going to come true! But the rent was so high in the city that I had to get a job waiting tables. And every night I got home and worked and worked to prepare my auditions. Meanwhile, everyone back home kept waiting for me to be on TV. They'd call and they'd write, saying, "When will it be?" But I wasn't getting any work. Ten years went by, and I had nothing to show for it.'" Bill spreads his hands. "'Don't you see? I was a star in high school and college, but New York City is full of actors who were high school and college stars. Finally I had to admit the truth. I didn't have the talent necessary to succeed.'"

Dom shudders. "That's my worst nightmare."

"Then that's what you should work from," Bill says. "*Only work from a paraphrase that holds genuine meaning for you*. So now you can add in your character elements. If you worked from the

Emotional Line, you might play Walter Simmons as a Crybaby, moaning about what became of his dreams. Or maybe you play him as The Bewildered Man, astonished at how completely he's failed when, at one point, he held so much promise. Or maybe he's an alcoholic, drowning his sorrows and ruminating over his glory days."

Dom smiles and nods. "I've got an idea."

Trevor brings in Fiddler Jones.

"Good," Bill says. "A happy piece. Spoon Rivers aren't all doom and gloom, you know."

Trevor reads:

"The earth keeps some vibration going
There in your heart, and that is you.
And if the people find you can fiddle,
Why, fiddle you must, for all your life.
What do you see, a harvest of clover?
Or a meadow to walk through to the river?
The wind's in the corn; you rub your hands
For beeves hereafter ready for market;
Or else you hear the rustle of skirts
Like the girls when dancing at Little Grove.
To Cooney Potter a pillar of dust
Or whirling leaves meant ruinous drouth;
They looked to me like Red-Head Sammy
Stepping it off, to 'Toor-a-Loor.'
How could I till my forty acres
Not to speak of getting more,
With a medley of horns, bassoons and piccolos

Stirred in my brain by crows and robins
And the creak of a wind-mill—only these?
And I never started to plow in my life
That some one did not stop in the road
And take me away to a dance or picnic.
I ended up with forty acres;
I ended up with a broken fiddle—
And a broken laugh, and a thousand memories,
And not a single regret."

Bill grins. "This is one of my favorites. Tell me about Fiddler Jones."

"I'm a musician," Trevor says. "Playing my fiddle is like a love affair. Anytime there's a dance going on and someone hollers my name, I can't help myself. I drop whatever I'm doing to play. My neighbors spend all their time worrying over business decisions and I don't understand that. How can anyone be concerned about making money or having more stuff? All I ever wanted was my fiddle, so that's what I got in the end, and it made me the happiest man in Spoon River."

Bill nods. "Have you ever read Joseph Campbell's work? One of the principles he espoused was 'Follow your bliss.' By which he meant, Do what you love in life and, no matter what else, at least you'll be happy. Fiddler Jones understands why people say you never see hearses with luggage racks. So who are you talking to in this speech? And what are you doing? What's your Action?"

"I decided I'm talking to everyone in town—that's my Acting Object—and my Action is I'm Sharing the Secret of a Truly Happy Life."

"Right," Bill says. "It's as if Saint Peter gave you a special dispensation so you could come back down to earth for ten minutes and share the secret of true joy with everyone in Spoon River.

You're just tickled pink with the life you've led—tickled, too, with this opportunity to let everyone in on how you did it. What else? Fiddler Jones is pretty ancient, isn't he?"

Trevor nods. "Another poem in the book says I'm ninety years old and still a real hellion."

"This brings up an interesting point," Bill says. "A text can supply information about your character from three principal sources. Obviously the first source is *what your character says and does*. But the second source is *what other characters say and do about your character*. And the third source is *what the playwright says about your character in the form of stage directions*. When making acting choices, you should consider all three perspectives." He turns back to Trevor. "Are you clear on how you should work on this piece? You need to start with the bliss. Can you prepare for that?"

Trevor nods. "And once I have that, I share it with these poor dopey people who think that happiness can be achieved by hard work. My philosophy is, Forget hard work. If you really have a good time every day, you'll have a happy life."

Bill nods. "So go find your bliss, paraphrase the speech, and bring it back. Leave the details for last. Once you work out the broad strokes of a speech, a lot of the details will fall into place on their own. And where they don't, you'll work that out."

■■■■

Later, Bill tells me: "The paraphrasing might be the hardest part."

"I noticed," I say. "The actors seem to get hung up on the details of the text. It's like they want the contours of their paraphrase to match the contours of the *Spoon River* speech, when that isn't the point at all."

"Exactly. Most actors try sticking to the text like a swimmer afraid to kick off from the dock. But they have to be brave and head out into the deeper water that lies within themselves. They have to dive deep into their own understanding, grab the gold at the bottom of the pool, and bring it back up to the surface. No great art was ever made from being literal."

"The details of the paraphrase don't matter," I say. "They'll add those later using Particularizations if they need to."

"And sometimes they won't need to," Bill says. "Many years ago, I had an actress in class who got the part of Laura in *The Glass Menagerie* on Broadway. I went to see the production; afterwards I went back to congratulate her on what I thought was a truly wonderful performance. She said, 'This part is as clear to me as the palm of my hand.' Sometimes an actor will pick up a script and have an instant sense of recognition. I once spoke to Paul Sorvino about his part in the movie *Reds*. He said, Oh, that was easy. That character was my uncle Guido."

"You're saying that, sometimes, the actor won't have to work at all."

Bill nods. "When that happens, he should say thank you, and then have a good time. But when it doesn't happen, that's when you need craft. Getting back to the Spoon Rivers, what matters is that the actor express the speech's active meaning. If the actor truly understands his part, he'll paraphrase it easily. If he doesn't understand the part, he can only turn in a half-assed, intellectualized, surface-deep performance."

"Not good," I say.

"That's right. Not good."

▮▮▮▮

A few classes later, Cheryl brings Pauline Barrett back in, but she can't complete the exercise. Midway through her performance, she starts to weep. Her emotion grows until it keeps her from speaking and she can't recover herself. Bill asks her to stop.

"This speech presents a very special problem. This emotion you have. It's very deep and I think that it's pure. It could also be counterproductive."

Cheryl sniffs. "I'm not sure what you mean."

"I think I mentioned last year someting Bobby Lewis once said: If crying was all there was to acting, his aunt Tessie would be a great actor. On a film set, directors call 'Action,' they don't say 'Emote.' In other words, emotion can't be the only ingredient to good acting. If it rises to the surface at all, it must do so unlooked for and unmanipulated, and you can never hang on to it. That would rightfully alienate your audience. Think of it this way: Actions are the bricks with which you construct your performance. Emotion is the mortar that binds the bricks together. You can make a wall of bricks without mortar. It won't be strong, but it will be a wall. Not so the other way around. A wall made of mortar is no wall at all.

"I think the emotion you have, Cheryl, is very deep and very personal. But, at the moment, it's incapacitating you. And you can't really act if you're incapacitated. One thing you can do: When emotion rises up within you, when it's about to overwhelm you, do exactly what you'd do in life. Take a breath and let it out. Take a moment, get control of yourself. Then go on with what you've got to do. In this speech, that means you've really got to make your husband understand why you did what you did."

Bill turns to the class. "I mentioned the work would get difficult, didn't I? By which I meant it would start to change. The first year was all about emotional freedom. Very often, students come back from the summer break and I hear them say, 'My life is changed! My work is changed!' Then they hit the second-year exercises and I hear things like 'What? I have to Particularize something? I have to craft something? I hate this class!'"

The students laugh, and Bill shrugs.

"A lot of actors are afraid to let their process change. They don't understand that it *must* change if it is to evolve. When I visit Los Angeles, I often hear people say, 'Don't do so much work, it'll ruin your spontaneity!' I hate that. What a misguided thought. *Spontaneity doesn't arise from doing no work. It comes when you do all your work beforehand, carve everything out, then forget it.* The forgetting—that's the important part. You have to let go and receive."

Bill turns back to Cheryl. "I'm mentioning this now because you're a bit hung up on your emotional life and it's time you moved past it. Emotion is formless, like water. It must have a vessel to give it shape, and that vessel is your Action." Bill holds up the bottle of water on his desk. "You see what happens to water with no form to contain it?" He spills some water onto the floor. "What a mess. It's no good to anyone. Sandy used to say that emotion is like oil in a tank within the actor. The pipe reaching down into the tank represents your Actions, the reality of doing. If you're not doing something, or if you're not really doing what you say you're doing, the pipe won't make contact with the tank and therefore won't draw up any emotion."

Ray raises his hand. "Bill, I thought Cheryl's emotion was very genuine."

"It's not a question of whether it's genuine," Bill says. "It's a question of proportion. I once heard that Stella Adler could never play parts that dealt with unrequited love. The very notion of unrequited love affected her so deeply, she couldn't perform. Every actor has those places he or she can't go personally, and therefore professionally. When you're a very young actor, you can expect that time and life experience will gradually stretch your range. As you get older, you realize you can still stretch, but there's no point in trying to reinvent the wheel. Respect your limitations and move on to parts you're more suited to play."

When the various elements come together, the work produced is nothing short of astonishing.

A few days later, the lights in the studio dim and a small, hunched man shuffles into a solitary spotlight. The man wears a tweed coat, frayed at the elbows, and a cap pulled low above small round spectacles. Pausing, he checks right and left before deciding the coast is clear. With shaky fingers, he pulls a flask from his pocket, unscrews the cap, whips the flask back, and drinks. Wiping his lips with the back of his hand, he grunts, caps the flask, slips it back in his pocket. At which point, he looks up and starts. He didn't know we were watching him, but now he's seen us. He's caught. Recovering, he sways a bit, then waves a dismissive hand, and sneers.

"My parents thought dat I vould be as great as Edison. Or greater!" he says, his accent guttural German. "For as a boy I made der balloons! Und vondrous kites! Und toys mit clocks! Und little engines mit tracks to run on! Und telephones of cans und tread!"

The small man's hands dance gracefully, his fingers showing us how they worked. It hits me then like a kick in the skull. This hunched little man is Dom!

His transformation is as stunning as it is seamless. By hunching, Dom has erased his natural willowy height. This—plus his costume—conjures a man long used to leaning over worktables, squinting at tiny sprockets and gears. But his physical presence isn't the only thing that's changed. Dom's normally upbeat, laid-back manner has devolved into something much darker. Inflexible. Driven.

Reaching the end of the piece, he howls out the final line, in agony, demanding that we hear him.

"I did not haf der brains!"

A few moments later, the lights rise again.

Bill nods. "Where did the German accent come from?"

"There was something about this image of a watchmaker," Dom says, pulling off his cap. "I felt I was someone meticulous, obsessed with precision, so I started with that. Spoon River was supposed to be in southern Illinois, but the U.S. is a nation of immigrants. Lots of Germans settled in the Midwest through-out the nineteenth century. I figured my family was among them. Then I remembered this guy who comes into the bar next door to my apartment building. He's older and Swiss, and every time I see him, he's sitting on the same stool, alone. He drinks to excess and he talks to himself. He's there every time I go in.

"I talked to him once. It was clear right away he was very bright. I learned that he was an engineer, but we never got much beyond that. His accent was thick and I had trouble understanding him. I've always wondered what tragedy, mishap, or failure turned him into a drunk. But I never realized how useful he might be until I read Walter Simmons."

"We use what we have been given," Bill says. "I think that's the nature of art. When you capture what's real to you and marry it to the character—when you really do what the character's doing—it doesn't matter what period you're in, whether you're onstage or in front of a camera. It doesn't matter whether the character is like you or not. You use technique to demystify the process of playing another person, break down the steps so you can execute them, and build them back up.

"It's like walking past a skyscraper. We admire a building that's so tall and magnificent because we are the audience. The archi-tect is the artist. He or she knows that building quite differently, the location and purpose of every beam, of every bolt and screw."

Bill looks at the class. "I want each of you to complete at least one good Spoon River," he says. "Doing so will help you where we're headed next."

"Which is where?" says Adam.

"It's time we dive off the cliff and plunge headfirst into periods and styles."

ELEVEN

PERIODS AND STYLES

"A people without the knowledge of their past history, origin, and culture is like a tree without roots."

—MARCUS GARVEY

"Our own epoch is determining, day by day, its own style. Our eyes, unhappily, are unable yet to discern it."

—LE CORBUSIER

At the start of the next class, Bill says, "We're about to begin a journey into some of the most important work composed for the stage throughout human history. These plays are considered classics of the theater, and they're written by our greatest playwrights. Shakespeare. Ibsen. Chekhov. Shaw. Molière. O'Casey. Williams. O'Neill. Each piece will challenge the actor in many ways. By the same token, each will offer fantastic artistic rewards.

"Classic plays such as these involve two new elements—period and style—about which misconceptions abound. I want to discuss these notions at length before we turn to the scripts I'll assign."

The students, I notice, have all taken out their notebooks and started to jot things down.

"Let me start with a story," Bill says. "There's an actor I know who's based in Chicago, where she frequently works. A few years back, she was in New York, taking my summer intensive class. While she was here, she booked a part in an Off-Broadway run of *Mrs. Warren's Profession,* by George Bernard Shaw, at a very reputable theater. This should have been cause for celebration. Instead, this actor was worried.

"She told me she hadn't the slightest idea how to approach her part. 'It's so alien to me,' she said. 'I never know how to approach the classics.' I told her that, in my experience, it's common for actors to feel this way. The reason is simple. Most actors approach the classics incorrectly. Meaning they don't stick to working the way you've been taught here at the Studio. Let me ask you: What is the core tenet to our way of acting?"

"The reality of doing," says Trevor.

Bill nods. "And is the reality of doing the backbone of your acting only for certain projects?"

Trevor shakes his head. "It shouldn't matter if we're working on a soap opera, a play, or a Duncan Hines commercial. All good acting should be rooted in the reality of doing."

"Thank you," Bill says. "I couldn't have said it any better myself. And yet, for some reason, many actors throw the reality of doing under the bus when they start to work on the classics. Instead of treating their characters like living, breathing human beings who happen to live in a different era or place, they become seduced by the mannerisms and filigree of the milieu. By doing so, they cut off everything genuine, creative, and natural within themselves— the wellspring of their acting talent. Instead of creating living, breathing human beings, they concoct bloodless imitations of people, cardboard cutouts of stock renditions. Not characters, but caricatures in two dimensions, not three."

Bill pauses a moment before going on. "Fortunately, this is easy to fix. I mentioned two elements that affect the classics: period and style. Let's take them apart one at a time. We'll start with period, which is an easy notion to grasp. *'Period' refers to the era in which a piece takes place, an era which—for a variety of reasons—displays unique cultural values.* I'll give you an example.

"Here in America, nearly every decade of the twentieth century expressed itself differently than others. When we think of the 1920s, we think of massive leaps in consumerism, of jazz music, and of the repression caused by Prohibition, which led to a kind of society-wide subversion. When we think of the 1930s, we think of the Dust Bowl and the Great Depression. The 1940s were largely occupied by World War II. The 1950s were characterized by the Cold War, the space race, McCarthyism, and *Leave It to Beaver.* The 1960s had Vietnam, the Kennedy assassination, the civil rights movement, hippies, and the Summer of Love. The 1970s had disco, the Me Generation, oil and hostage crises, Nixon resigning the presidency. And so on.

"In each of these decades, the music was different and iconic, as was—to a large degree—the style of dress, the way people talked, the way they behaved, recreated, and so on. And since cultural values were very distinct, this would, of course, be reflected in any play or production that takes place within each time frame."

"That's one of the reasons TV shows like *Mad Men* are such big hits," says Melissa. "*Mad Men* leverages the period of the 1950s to highlight character traits and social issues we still recognize today."

Bill nods. "You make a good point. When performed well, period pieces always transcend their specific milieu to illuminate timeless and universal questions. It's one of the reasons we still perform *Hamlet, King Lear,* and *Macbeth* even though Shakespeare died four hundred years ago. The themes each play introduces will never die so long as human beings exist."

Bill spreads his hands. "I just ticked off some of the differences between decades in late-twentieth-century America. Now I want you to imagine period differences on a much larger scale, say, throughout the history of human civilization.

"Western drama begins with the Greeks, the plays of Aeschylus, Sophocles, Euripides, and others. The very word 'theater' comes from ancient Greek and means 'the place of seeing.' This gives us a clue as to how people of that day regarded our art form: they saw it as something holy. People regarded the theater as a portal through which to witness the truth about life. I would argue that mission remains the same even now, in modern times.

"Greek theater segued into that of the Romans even as Greek society was absorbed by the burgeoning Roman Empire. The theater of ancient Rome included plays by Plautus, Terence, and Seneca—all writers whose works are still performed today. As you might imagine, many of these plays are based on the Greek models of tragedy and comedy, and employ the same themes.

"Theater underwent a big change, however, during the Middle Ages. In that era, audiences went to see mystery and morality plays that were mostly blatant tutorials in the Christian ethic that controlled Europe for a thousand years between the fifth and the fifteenth centuries A.D. Plays were often performed in town squares and on pageant wagons that moved from settlement to settlement.

"Medieval drama gave way to the stock shows of commedia dell'arte, which, in turn, yielded to the much more expansive works of the Renaissance. During this period, the world was introduced to writers including Shakespeare, Christopher Marlowe, and Ben Jonson. If it helps, you can break the Renaissance down into subsets according to who ruled England at the time. For example, you have Elizabethan and Jacobean drama. Somewhat overlapping the latter, we have the Baroque, which swept through Europe and, in terms of drama, refers almost exclusively to works that derived from France.

"In 1660 or thereabouts, the Renaissance gave way to the Restoration in England. This was the period when Oliver Cromwell and the Puritans were overthrown, and Charles II was invited to resume his seat as King of England, Scotland, and Ireland. In a sense, this ushered in an era of wild partying in Great Britain. And naturally, with society free to laugh and dance and have fun once again, the theaters, which had been closed under Cromwell, reopened and became vehicles for comedy and bawdiness.

"The fervor faded soon enough. The morality pendulum eventually swung back toward repression during the era of Queen Victoria—the Victorian period is named after her. Theater of the day centered on burlesques and comic operas. Key writers were people like Oscar Wilde, who could be characterized as subversive of Victorian restraint.

"After sixty-five years or so, the Victorians yielded to the Edwardians—the time period of George Bernard Shaw and, in Norway, of Ibsen—and this ushers us into the twentieth century, whose playwrights worldwide include everyone from Luigi Pirandello to Bertolt Brecht, Jean Cocteau, Jean-Paul Sartre, Sean O'Casey, Eugene O'Neill, Federico García Lorca . . . at this point, the list of writers and the movements they represent practically explodes."

Tyrone has been writing furiously. Frustrated, he raises his hand. "Could we, ah, maybe slow down for a sec?"

Bill shrugs. "I could, but why bother? It's not my intention to deliver a primer on theater history. Instead I want to create a framework from which you can build your acting research. For now, can we simply acknowledge that 'period' refers to the era in which a piece takes place? And that each period represents different cultural values, which the characters you play must be aware of? Can we agree on that?"

The class nods.

"Good," Bill says. "As I said, the notion of 'period' is easily explained. What's less understood is the notion of 'style.' I have two ways I want you to think about this term.

"The first way is that every good writer has his or her own style. For instance, you can tell a Tennessee Williams play after hearing only five lines; his writing is that evocative. Or take Sam Shepard, whose plays brim with father/son embroilments and mythic figures from the American West. Or the plays of Wendy Wasserstein; she won a Pulitzer for *The Heidi Chronicles* because she so accurately nailed three decades of American life to the wall. Or August Wilson, whose Pittsburgh Cycle explores the African-American experience over the ten decades of the twentieth century and is characterized by his ample use of street language, magical realism, and musical elements such as jazz. I think you get the idea. A playwright's style derives from the way he or she uses language, the subject matter that dominates the work, and the values the playwright routinely celebrates or challenges.

"But the second way I want you to think about style is this: by style, we actually mean 'lifestyle.' I'm referring now, of course, to your characters. Each of them will behave in certain ways that are different from your normal modern behavior. Why? Because a character's lifestyle comes from the core system of values and beliefs upheld by his or her culture."

Melissa raises her hand. "Bill, can you give an example?"

"Sure. Whether we acknowledge it or not, modern Americans have a style that's unique unto us. For instance, our culture prizes democracy and individualism. This should come as no surprise. These values stem from the way our country was founded. In America, we believe that every person is equal to every other person, that everyone has the right to life, liberty, and the pursuit of happiness, and that no one is essentially better than anyone else. Whether or not we always live up to this creed can be argued, and rightly so. But that, at least, is the premise we all pay lip service to. And because of this notion that 'Everyone's equal,' our society tends to be very informal.

"For instance, in our country you might hear a cabdriver address a bank president by his first name and think nothing of it. In other parts of the world, that would simply never happen. Other countries have caste systems that must be recognized, hierarchies that must be upheld lest the whole social structure come tumbling down. Our code of informality is one reason why backyard barbecues have become the quintessential American social event."

The students, I notice, are writing furiously. Bill gives them a moment before going on.

"Keep in mind that most lifestyles have subsets that function as separate styles unto themselves. For instance, I just mentioned American culture, but that could be looked at as a bit general. We could easily break that heading down into smaller and much more specific groups. Consider people who serve in the U.S. armed forces—the army, the navy, and so on. They and their families live by a completely different code than, say, the club kids you find here in New York City, the ones who paint their fingernails black and pierce their noses and go to all-night rave parties. Or people who live in the Bible Belt. Or the Amish. They're a perfect example of lifestyle. Has anyone been to Pennsylvania and visited the Amish?"

A few people raise their hands.

"Consider the massive contradiction the Amish present," Bill says. "Here we are living in the twenty-first century, an era made marvelous by computers, cell phones, television, and other electronics. But the Amish reject these technologies in nearly all their forms. Instead of using cars, they ride in horse-drawn buggies. Instead of playing musical instruments, they only allow themselves to sing. Amish stoicism is even reflected in the way they dress. Clothing must be drab in color. Zippers can never be used. Men must wear suspenders and homespun shirts; they don't grow their beards until they've married, at which point they will shave only their upper lip. Women have a dress code, too; they must wear long skirts and aprons at all times and always keep their heads covered. If a member of the community should violate these rules, he or she will be expelled, with all connections to the family and people who raised that person cut forever.

"Why do the Amish do this?" Bill asks. "Every lifestyle has its own logic. An actor hoping to capture that style must research it, understand it, and—ultimately—empathize with it. The Amish believe that restricting contact with the outside world places stronger emphasis on a person's relationship with family and the church. They maintain their simple lifestyle because they believe this eliminates temptation and brings them closer to God."

Dom says, "So let me see if I've got this right. A play set in today's Amish country wouldn't be a period piece. But it would be a style play if all the characters are Amish."

"Exactly," Bill says. "Or, if you like, you can think of it this way: *Style can go without period, but a period cannot go without style.*"

"I get it," says Jon. "For instance, if a play takes place in Elizabethan England, that's a different period from ours and therefore the characters must have a different style. Elizabethans used a different form of English than we do today. They dressed differently than we do. They used different money. They ate different food. Their political system was a monarchy, with all the social differences that entails. And the technology they used will be four hundred years older than the technology we use today."

"Correct," says Bill. "Which brings me back to my story about the actor from Chicago. The point I was trying to make was this: When playing the classics, most actors treat their roles like museum pieces. In other words, they forget that their characters,

like characters in any play, are vital human beings. They're alive!
They feel! They want! They do! But most actors discard all this.
Instead they get hung up on aping what they feel are the mannerisms of a period or style without sticking to what we know the art
of acting truly is."

"Doing truthfully under imaginary circumstances," Joyce says.

Bill nods. "By the way, I blame this misconception largely on
the Brits. Now and then, I've heard people insist that British
actors should be praised for their mastery of the classics. If that's
true, I say they should also share in the blame when the classics
are played so miserably.

"The Brits sort of hijacked the classical canon early on. It's
understandable, really, since so many of the classics were written right there on their soil. Shakespeare came from England,
as did Christopher Marlowe, and William Wycherley. Great Irish
writers like Richard Sheridan, Oscar Wilde, and George Bernard
Shaw contributed to the legacy. These writers, in turn, gave rise
to the likes of Joe Orton, David Hare, John Osborne, Pinter, Shaf-
fer, Stoppard, and so on.

"And yet, too often, I've seen British actors and their emula-
tors here in America waste these great plays by using them as
vehicles for mellifluous recitation. They show off their beautiful
voices. They enunciate boldly in gorgeous declamations. Meanwhile there's not a spark of true life to be found anywhere in their
performances."

Bill shakes his head. "Sadly, I've sworn that I'll never see
another production by the Royal Shakespeare Company. I was in
London once with my family, and the RSC was presenting a play
by Philip Massinger called *A New Way to Pay Old Debts*. I was so
excited to see this piece! It's so rarely produced anymore. I told
my family, 'We have to see it! Even if it's a so-so production, at
least we'll have heard and seen the play.'

"It turned out to be one of the biggest mistakes I've ever made.

The production wasn't bad, it was awful. Wait. I take that back. It was beyond awful, it was ghastly!" Bill thinks for a second. "Actually, what's beyond ghastly?"

"Ouch," says Adam. "We get the point."

"I don't think you do," Bill moans.

The class laughs.

"What was so wrong with it?" Cheryl asks.

Bill claps a hand to his forehead. "The actors threw out everything we hold sacred about the art of acting. Truth. Proportion. The reality of doing. They ignored the fact that period behaviors aren't affectations, they were once someone's everyday lifestyle. And in place of these pivotal tenets of art, they SUB-stituted their mag-NIF-i-CENT VOYYYYSSIIIIS!" Bill rises from his chair, making wooden, superfluous gestures that conjure the worst stock player imaginable. "Don't you SEEEEEEEE?!" he booms. "I'm making this SOUND!!! And ISN'T it SIMply WOOOOON-DER-FULLLL TO HEEEEAAAAARR?!?!?"

The class cracks up, and Bill shrugs.

"For all their bluster, I couldn't even recommend the actors' vocal performances. They were all pushing too hard. And what got lost in the middle? Oh, nothing really. Just the play. As far as the reality of doing is concerned, well . . . the only thing those actors were really doing was singing, and poorly at that."

Bill looks at the class. "Of course this isn't true of all British acting. I consider myself privileged to have seen several productions at the National. These were excellent examples of brave and marvelous works, the kind that we aspire to here. But the atrocity I spoke of highlights a temptation that seems present in too many actors: the tendency to indicate a period or style's behavior rather than climbing down into the heart of that behavior and building a truthful performance from there."

Donna says, "So how do we start the process?"

"Good question," Bill says. "I'll show you."

▌▌▌▌

"Let's suppose you're cast in a play that takes place during the Baroque period, specifically at the court of Versailles during the reign of Louis XIV. Many actors would feel intimidated by this era's grandiosity. They would stare at the lavish tableau of lace and wigs and walking sticks with all the hopelessness of a child tasked to memorize every detail in a complex painting.

"What's all this fuss about snuffboxes? they might ask. Why do people use such heightened speech? How can I let myself into this world? What's my point of entry?"

Bill shrugs. "With so many details to consider, it's easy to feel overwhelmed. So I recommend a different approach. Whenever you're challenged to produce behavior that's altered from your normal mode, don't start with the details. That's a bit like building a house from the doorknobs out. Instead begin by researching the period.

"We must ask ourselves: What was France like during the reign of Louis XIV? What was its form of government? What was the nation's economy like? How did the common people fare? What were the culture's dominant forces? What did people hope to achieve? Knowing the answers to basic questions like these will ground us in the day-to-day values a character might have espoused.

"For instance," Bill says, "France was a monarchy during the seventeenth century, and a Catholic nation. For centuries, her people had subscribed to 'the divine right of kings.' This belief held that a monarch was empowered to rule by the will of God, and no one—not his people, the aristocracy, nor any other estate of the realm—could second-guess his authority.

"But as old as this belief was, it had begun to show signs of strain. Louis's father died of tuberculosis when Louis was only four and a half years old. Shortly before passing, Louis XIII broke with custom and, instead of naming his wife, Queen Anne, as regent, convened a council to rule on his son's behalf. Anne, however, had this decree annulled. She transferred the power of regency to Cardinal Mazarin, an Italian priest who essentially ruled France by her side while Louis was a child."

Ray shakes his head. "I'm sorry, Bill, I'm losing you. How is this relevant to acting?"

Bill looks at him. "We're establishing the political groundwork for the era. Imagine you're a citizen of France. Your king has died, leaving only a child, a toddler, to rule the country. Worse yet, the queen, who's an Austrian, has dismissed the late king's wishes and transferred power to herself and an Italian cleric. What do you suppose the average French citizen thought of that arrangement?"

"I bet they weren't happy," Vanessa quips. "Imagine if the U.S. president died and his wife, a Russian, staged a coup and decided to share power with North Korea."

"That's a perfect recipe for social disorder," Jon says.

"And that's exactly what happened," says Bill. "A civil war broke out after Mazarin established a tax to maintain funding for the Thirty Years' War. Louis was only ten years old."

"The Fronde," says Reg.

Bill nods. "Conditions in Paris got so dangerous that Louis had to be smuggled out of the city along with his mother. Living in exile left a big impression on the young king. He learned firsthand the perils of letting your power be usurped. But the war eventually ended, and Louis was back on the throne in his early twenties. So what do you think he did?"

"He centralized the government under his absolute authority," Reg says. "Call it a backlash against the Fronde. From that point forward, he refused to tolerate any dissent against his rule. In keeping with this policy, he moved the French court out of Paris and set it in Versailles, which became like a weird hotel."

"Why would he do that?" Ray asks.

Reg turns to him. "Louis saw the sprawling estate as the ideal golden cage in which to keep his aristocracy The palace at Versailles had something like three hundred fifty bedrooms, and Louis decreed that every member of his ruling class had to keep at least one family member in residence there at all times."

Bill smiles, impressed. "And why would he do such a thing?"

"Simple," says Reg. "It kept the nobility under his thumb. Since his dukes were never at home, they could never develop enough regional power to plot against the monarchy."

"Exactly," says Bill. "But did Louis stop there?"

"Oh no," Reg says. "No, that was just the beginning. He decreed that, while at Versailles, his courtiers had to maintain an entourage and dress for court each day. Which meant they had to spend massive amounts of money on wigs, fans, clothes, whalebone corsets, jeweled snuffboxes, you name it. As if that weren't hard enough, Louis's tastes reportedly changed at the drop of a hat. So Versailles became sort of a cross between a psychotic hotel and a dictator's surreal fashion show. One day Louis might wake up and say, 'I hate that jacket, I like this kind instead.' So everyone scrambled to buy the new jacket in order to stay in the king's favor. Most of the courtiers' garments were so elaborate, they could cost an entire year's income from the family holdings. But that was also part of the plan. Louis knew that noblemen who were constantly forced to spend money on *vêtements* and *accoutrements* could never raise enough money to finance a *coup d'état*."

Reg stops. Everyone's staring at him.

"I dig French history. Sue me."

"Everything he's saying is true," Bill says. "I once saw a picture of a doublet from this period. This garment featured four hundred yards of ribbon arranged in shockingly tiny loops. The work was all done by hand, of course. Machined clothing hadn't been invented yet."

Bill scratches his chin. "Now do you see why I chose Versailles to talk about period and styles? The setting demanded that court-iers subscribe to elaborate codes of behavior. Men, for instance, had to grow their right pinky fingernail quite long. Why? Because knocking on a door was considered rude. Instead, whenever a man presented himself at someone's chamber, he was expected to scratch his long fingernail very delicately on the door to let people know he had arrived."

"That's ridiculous," Ray says.

"Careful," Bill says. "Remember how I said that each life-style has its own logic? Versailles featured endless ceremonies designed to establish social hierarchy and keep people busy. Each morning, for instance, began with the king's *Levée*. A hundred men would crowd into the king's enormous bedchamber, which could really be likened to a small theater. I've read that Louis's bed was set on an enormous dais to raise it above everyone else in the room. This dais also positioned the bed so the first rays of sunlight fell through a set of massive windows and landed directly on the king. Coincidence? Of course not. Think of the signals that would send.

"The gentlemen present were *les valets de chambre*, members of the aristocracy whom Louis had hand-selected to help him rise and prepare for the day. One man might be charged with holding the king's chamber pot until he was finished using it. That man might pass the chamber pot to another man, whose job was to pass the pot to another man, and so on."

"I've heard," says Jon, "that it was considered a particular honor to hold the little silver bowl of cologne the king used instead of bathing."

"The king used perfume?" Ray says, and he snorts.

Reg nods. "Back then, people thought it was unhealthy to

bathe. Besides, what few toilets Versailles had belonged to the royal family. Imagine a building larger than a New York City apartment tower where everyone uses privy chambers that don't get cleaned very often. The smell in Versailles was—"

"I got it." Ray waves his hand.

"Bathing was indeed taboo," Bill says. "But body odors were considered unseemly, even as they are today. So nobles would spritz themselves with cologne to mask their funk. Louis would wiggle his fingers in his bowl of *eau de cologne* and *un valet de chambre* would hand him a towel. Another lord might collect the used towel and hand it off to another lord, and so on."

Ray shakes his head. "It sounds crazy."

Bill, clearly irritated, glances at Ray. "Look past appearances," he says. "Try to see the method to Louis's madness. Why would he want to have all of his courtiers fighting for the opportunity to hold his socks?"

"Because he was a dictator at heart," Reg says. "And like any dictator, he knew that the best way to stay in power was to keep the strata under him constantly shifting, with people trying to backstab one another, looking for the next foothold toward power. A person with access to the king could make small requests of him now and then. He'd be the first person in sight whenever the king felt generous and bestowed new titles or tracts of land. Fighting to hold the king's shoes while he dressed each morning was really . . . well, it was like an actor fighting to get seen for a part in a brilliant director's movie."

"Exactly," says Bill. "And I'm so glad you brought that up. *Even the strangest element of lifestyle in a period piece should boil down to an 'as if' which you, the actor, understand intimately, and therefore can play.* For instance, another ritual at Versailles was the way courtiers worked so hard to turn their calves forward when they bowed."

"I'm sorry," says Quid. "They turned their what?"

"Their calves," says Reg. "Remember how people dressed back then? Men wore hose, like tights, that showed off the musculature of their legs. A man's calf was considered a very handsome part of his body, the equivalent of today's six-pack abs."

"As it turns out," Bill says, "Louis XIV was especially fond of his calves. He showed them off whenever he could. And so, as in all dictatorships, the rank and file tended to follow whatever the boss did. Reg, would you mind . . . ?"

"My pleasure," says Reg.

Rising from his chair, he steps into the playing space and faces the group.

"Today," he says, "when we meet somebody new, we'll probably shake their hand. That would never happen in the court of Louis XIV. During the Baroque period, people bowed to one another, and the way a person bowed conveyed a lot about their personality and social status."

Placing one foot behind him, he turns it so the toes point away from him at a 45-degree angle. Flexing his calf for all he's worth, he bows low, sweeping his arms in grand fashion, stretching them out like wings.

"Did you see the way Reg moved his arms?" Bill says. With his hands, he copies Reg's rounded, expansive gestures. "This sort of theatricality was typical of the Baroque period, and it was inspired largely by the way people dressed. Men's clothing had lace dripping from every collar and cuff. Rounded movements therefore served a twofold purpose. First, they kept your sleeves from getting tangled—a very practical concern. Second, grand gestures showed off your finery. I've seen people with Rolex watches do the same thing whenever they check the time."

Bill moves his hand like a semaphore flag—a roundabout flourish of pure ostentation—before peering down his nose at the hands of his watch. The class cracks up.

"Women also moved in a way that stemmed from how they dressed. When sitting, they kept their feet together with knees spread wide to make a lap of their dress to accommodate socially approved handiwork such as needlepoint. Their deportment was different when standing, however. Remember that women wore whalebone corsets pulled ludicrously tight in order to achieve what was then considered the ideal feminine silhouette. Dresses were cut very high under the arms and featured bodices that were also tightly fitted. With all this constriction going on, where else could a woman's elbows go but out?"

Bill demonstrates, cupping his palms to his abdomen, one hand laid atop the other.

"Fashion accessories for both genders began to impart their own physical vocabularies," Bill says. "Men learned to trade subtle signals by the way they handled their walking sticks. In the same manner, women learned to convey various meanings by the way they handled their fans. And each of these rituals, like the physical act of bowing or any other custom in a style, is something the actor must practice as though it's an accent, a Physical Impediment, or any other facet of character we've covered so far," Bill says. "In other words, you must drill these behaviors until they become second nature. And the meaning of each gesture, as I mentioned, should be pinned to an 'as if.' Reg, what might your 'as if' be for the way you just bowed?"

"How well a courtier showed off his calves was a way of attracting the king's attention, and potentially his favor," Reg says. "Therefore, if I were acting in a Baroque play, my bow would be 'as if' I were submitting a job application, or auditioning for some great new show."

Bill smiles. "Will that help you execute the Action with a greater sense of truth?"

"Oh yeah," Reg says. "Once I make that connection, bowing

isn't some silly affectation; it's a tactic I'm using to get what I want."

Bill nods. "Once you've mastered the physical gesture, you're free to forget it, put your attention entirely on your partner, and go back to concentrating on the reality of doing."

He turns to the class. "As part of your research, I recommend that you steep yourself in the period's key artists. Go to a museum that features their paintings. View their sculptures. Notice the ideals they put forth in their work. Very often, these are the same ideals espoused by the people of that period. And, of course, you should listen to whatever music was popular in that day.

"For instance, no exploration of Versailles would be complete without your hearing the compositions of Jean-Baptiste Lully. Louis XIV considered himself a great dancer. He and Lully actually danced together in 1653. Less than a month later, Louis declared Lully his *compositeur de la musique instrumentale du Roi*. It was the beginning of a lifelong relationship wherein Lully and Louis laid the groundwork for what we now know as classical ballet. Lully wrote some thirty pieces, and advanced both his music and the dances that went with them to international fame. He also collaborated on musical comedies with the French actor and writer Jean-Baptiste Poquelin, known more widely as Molière.

"This reminds me," Bill says. "Here's one of the best pieces of advice I can give to any actor researching a period style. Whatever else you do, learn the dances! You can pick up a lot about a person's physicality and everyday deportment by understanding how he or she danced. In the Baroque period, for instance, the gavotte and the minuet offer bookends to the way people behaved in social settings. On one hand, you had the versatile, lively gavotte, descended from folk arts, a dance for the masses, with lots of lively leaping and stomping. On the other, you had ·

the delicate, toe-stepping minuet, as fragile as a Fabergé egg, an intimate dance designed predominantly for two people.

"I can't tell you the kind of impact this makes," Bill says, "learning a period dance, especially while wearing period costumes, and more important, period footwear. It changes the way your body moves. It's a little like being possessed by the age. The spirit enters your body, your bones, and something about it rubs off on you. It can't help but inform how you play your role."

Bill thinks for a moment. "Now do you see why period and style work can be so challenging? We have all these factors to consider and we've barely scratched the surface of what it takes to truly research a part in a Baroque play. The actor must internalize each of the customs I've mentioned, and so many more. They must mix and macerate inside him like a great big bubbling stew. It's a lot to take in, a lot to process, a lot to rehearse. And it all must take place separate from but in concert with everything else we've learned so far, the actor's art and craft."

Joyce raises her hand. "Bill, can you recommend any sources that will help us in our research?"

"Museums," says Bill. "And art collections. Music troves and costume libraries. Rent some quality period films and pick up some very good books that describe the social manners of various eras.

"One excellent book that springs to mind is a little-known volume called *The Polite World: A Guide to English Manners and Deportment from the Thirteenth to the Nineteenth Century,* by Joan Wildeblood. There are other books, but many of them contain too much information, and I want you to be wary of that. It's not a good idea for actors to become walking encyclopedias about a style. Too many facts can swamp your ability to stay out of your head and play a part well. You don't need to prepare a doctoral thesis, you simply have to understand what customs were present and why the culture adopted them. In my opinion, books like *The Polite World* do an excellent job of presenting information that's relevant and actable."

▊▊▊▊

Later, back in his office, Bill says, "I didn't get a chance to talk to them about language. Remind me to do that?"

"I will," I say. "But what will you tell them?"

"That language is a major component of period and style work," Bill says. "People in Shakespeare's day didn't speak the same way you and I are speaking right now. The language was richer, more evocative and poetic in its rhythm. It was written to be spoken aloud, unamplified by the many technologies you and I take for granted. It was also—and most actors miss this point—indicative of a person's social status. Even today, in England, you can tell a person's class by the way they speak. You might know what school they attended and which region they grew up in."

I nod. "I remember something you told us at Rutgers. As a general rule, the actor hoping to play in any kind of period or style piece must have mastery over his or her voice and speech."

"That's true," Bill says. He thinks for a moment. "I remember when I first got interested in language, period, and style plays. I was teaching at the Neighborhood Playhouse and I wanted to direct a wonderfully funny short piece by George Bernard Shaw called *The Inca of Perusalem*. So I took the play to Sandy and he thought about it some. Finally he said, 'Okay, you can do it. But just remember: When the audience leaves the theater after the show, they have to say to themselves, My God! Didn't those people speak beautifully?'"

I laugh. "Can students do that today? How do their voice and speech hold up?"

"For the most part?" Bill says. "Miserably. Most students who start at the Studio are lucky if they can get through a soap script. They're so used to speaking in the modern pedestrian manner, they don't have a prayer of handling anything more complicated. But you can't do Shakespeare with a contemporary regional American accent.

"I once knew Bob Prosky, a very accomplished actor who sent his sons to Rutgers, where I trained them. Bob made his living for two decades doing the classics, often at Arena Stage in Washington, D.C. He played King Lear, Willy Loman, roles of that calibre. Later, he turned to TV work to help put his sons through school; he ended up in the cast of the hit show *Hill Street Blues*.

"So here was an actor who'd handled some of the finest plays in the canon of our English language. Then he got hired to do the part of Shelly Levene in *Glengarry Glen Ross* in the original Broadway production. I went backstage to congratulate Bob on a fine performance. I asked him, 'What's it like to do Mamet?' He said, 'Boy! You think it's going to be easy, a play like this. A walk in the park, so to speak. But it's not! It makes all the demands that Shakespeare does, and then some.'"

I nod. "It goes back to what you said before: that every playwright has his or her own style. When I think of David's plays, I think of speed, interruptions, and vicious vocabulary. The characters talking over and around one another form a kind of psychic dance that shows how deeply committed they are to manipulating one another."

"That's because you're a writer yourself, and you also know how to listen," Bill says. "Whereas uninformed people would simply assume the playwright is parroting street speech and would miss the point entirely. Over the years, several productions of David's work have failed because the actors weren't up to the challenge his writing set forth. The producers hired actors who may have

been well-known entertainers but didn't have the kind of training in voice and speech that David's plays require. One of the
strengths of his plays is that they're as much fun to listen to as
they are to watch."

"So what do you do with a student who doesn't have sufficient
chops in voice and speech?"

Bill frowns. "We get them into classes as fast as we can and try
to build some competency."

"How do they take to that?"

"Well, by and large. Occasionally some very misguided actor
will say, 'Oh, I don't need training in voice and speech, I'm going
to be a film actor.' To which I say, 'Great. I assume, however, that,
even on film, you'll want to be understood?'

"Every actor must learn to command people's attention with
his or her voice. Ideally, when the actor speaks, everyone listening sits up and hangs on his every word. And no, film actors certainly aren't exempt. Look at Paul Newman. Blue eyes or no blue
eyes, he would not have been the movie star he was without his
trained voice and speech. Look at Harrison Ford; he has an excellent voice. Neither of these actors ever rammed his vocal elo-
quence down an audience's throat, like some British actors I've
seen. The quality of their voice and speech never called attention to itself, but it was always there. That's the ideal state for
an actor to reach with his instrument. The moment an audience
can't hear or understand you, you've lost them, and they'll hate
the production."

"So what now?" I ask.

"Now," Bill says, "we see how they deal with the scenes I've
assigned. Working with the classics will challenge these actors to
use every skill they've learned in their nearly two years of training."

"How do you think they'll do?"

"Who knows? We'll take it moment by moment."

TWELVE

PERIODS AND STYLES IN PRACTICE

"When you reread a classic, you do not see more in the book than you did before; you see more in *you* than there was before."

—CLIFTON FADIMAN

"Great literature is simply language charged with meaning to the utmost possible degree."

—EZRA POUND

Jon and Cheryl are struggling with the first scene from George Bernard Shaw's one-act play *Overruled*. They work at the table, where things started well enough; for the first few lines, they were really listening to each other, really allowing themselves to affect and be affected by the other person. But one missed moment followed another; they fell into indication, and their interaction devolved into a kind of cheap and cynical imitation of BBC mannerisms. Soon after that, Bill halted the work.

"Who am I kidding?" Jon moans. "I've never done Shaw before."

"So what?" Bill says. "Martin Scorsese once directed a film adaptation of Edith Wharton's *The Age of Innocence*. He'd never dived into the classics before. During an interview, he was asked what it felt like. Scorsese said that, on one hand, it was like nothing he'd ever done before. On the other hand, it was like everything he'd done before. Do you see what he meant?"

Jon frowns. "I should stop focusing on what I don't understand and start working from what I know?"

"Exactly. Tell me what's going on in this piece."

"My character's name is Gregory Lunn. I'm a married man and I've just been on a cruise, which my wife didn't attend. While at sea, I met a young woman who's beautiful, witty, and kind, so I made love to her."

"Right," Bill says. "But keep in mind that 'making love' back then did not mean what the phrase implies today. Though, to keep the stakes high, you should play it as if you've had a sexual affair with her."

Jon nods. "I'm head over heels for this woman. But then I find out that she's married, too, and that offends my personal code. See, I thought she was a widow, and widows are okay to sleep with because—"

Bill waves a hand. "You're getting way ahead of yourself. What do you come into this room to do?"

Jon looks at Cheryl. "I want to profess my undying love for her. So that's what I should prepare for."

"That's right. And what happens once you get through the door?"

"I put my entire attention on her and improvise moment to moment."

"You see?" Bill says. "You're not so far out of your league after all. So here you are, trying to profess your undying love. And what happens?"

"Like I said, I find out she's not a widow at all. She's married!"

"And why is this important?"

"My mother, on her deathbed, made me promise that I would never have sex or conduct an affair with a married woman. It's a terrible burden for me right now. I've found the love of my life." He gestures toward Cheryl. "But it's impossible for me to pursue her."

"You understand that well enough," Bill says. "So what keeps tripping you up?"

Jon sighs and waves his script. "It's these endless speeches. Shaw wrote all this text for me to say. I wish he wasn't so long-winded. I feel like I'm being run over by the language."

Bill claps a hand to his forehead. "You're right. You were. You're missing what George Bernard Shaw was all about! You have to create the same need in yourself that Shaw possessed: a need that was so powerful it *demanded* that all of those words be said.

"When Laurette Taylor did the first production of *The Glass Menagerie* by Tennessee Williams, she felt that some of his more poetic lines were repetitive and redundant. She went to Williams with her script and asked if some of her lines could be cut. Williams gave her this sharp look and said, Oh no, Ms. Taylor. I *need* every one of those. So she went off on her own and discovered her own reasons for saying those lines. And that's when the writing began to work the way Williams had intended it to.

"Shaw was a man who had passionate opinions about everything under the sun, which he constantly expressed in the street, as an early member of the Fabian Society, and as a critic of art, music, and drama. He talked about why he was such a militant vegetarian. He talked about his politics. He was such a gifted speaker that his public appearances sold out faster than today's rock concerts. People would travel miles to be spellbound by his voice and his wit. Shaw was a literary genius during an era when literary figures were the equivalent of today's movie stars. That's hard for us to imagine today, but imagine it we must. This was a man who never saw any reason to curtail the expression of a single one of his opinions.

"Very often in his plays, the characters become embroiled in intense debates. They go on and on, rigorously defending their Points of View; you see this yourself in your own part. You have this speech about married women having a board in front of their chests that says TRESPASSERS WILL BE PROSECUTED. The only way that you're going to make that speech work—or any of these speeches—is *by finding within yourself an emotional necessity that demands and propels the text*. Let me ask you this, Jon: Have you ever found yourself talk-talk-talking nonstop about something? It's as if you can't help it; no matter what, the words just leap from your mouth?"

Jon thinks about it. "That's happened, sure. When I'm really excited or passionate about something."

"Bingo," Bill says. "This dynamic where passion drives speech is an element essential to playing Shaw."

Jon considers this. "So the technique is to find something I'm passionate about and associate that with the play's long arguments."

Bill nods. "You should paraphrase those long blocks of text exactly as you did with Spoon Rivers. In fact, you'd better. Delivered cold, all Shavian pieces sound preachy and lecture-like. But when you couple true passion with the impulse to speak, your text—no matter how long it is—will transmit as Shaw intended it: like your character is using every fiber of his being to defend his outlook on life.

"Here's something else to consider. Shaw maintained very deep and countercultural notions about sex. He was an avowed celibate because, as a young man, he had an affair with a woman who was a friend of his mother's. This woman was jealous and hysterical. She followed him everywhere and even broke into his room searching for evidence that he was seeing someone else. He found this predicament ghastly. Once he extricated himself from it, he swore off sex for good and all. By his own admission, he never consummated his marriage. But his wife was a wonderful intellectual companion, and Shaw carried on countless flirtations with intelligent women, many of whom were married. He found these relationships quite satisfactory."

"He was a prude," Jon says.

"Not at all," Bill says. "He simply believed that the most erotic organ human beings possess is their brain. Shaw loved to *talk* to women! In his opinion, talk was better than sex."

Jon gets excited. He waves his script. "You know? I have a whole speech about that!"

"Of course you do," Bill says. "Did you read the preface Shaw wrote for this play? He discusses the notion of theatrical limitations. He says that we can no more present actual fornication onstage than we can have Macbeth actually kill Duncan. Therefore, what better way to represent a character's libido than by letting him talk, talk, talk!"

Jon nods. "I have this line: 'As long as I have a want, I have a reason for living. Satisfaction is death.' Now I get it. I'm saying I adore this woman so much, I'd rather make conversation with her for eternity than consummate and kill the moment."

Cheryl gets excited. "And I have a line: 'When one feels in danger, one talks endlessly to stave it off.' The danger I feel is the danger of falling in love with this man, so that's why I keep speaking."

"Exactly," Bill says. "And speaking and speaking and speaking. The more impassioned your characters get, the longer their speeches will be. That also adds to the comedy, if you approach it the right way. And woe betide any production that dismisses this quality. You know, early in his career, Shaw had great difficulty finding actors to be in his plays. At that time, British theater was dominated by the commercial theaters of the West End, which produced drawing room comedies where characters lounged around the stage composing witticisms to amuse one another. Shaw couldn't use these actors at all. He ended up seeking out actors who had done a great deal of classical work, whose voices and speech could command an audience's attention and make them listen to every word they had to say.

"Even then, he ran into trouble. There's a famous story about how Ralph Richardson once played Captain Bluntschli in a revival of *Arms and the Man*. Richardson was a trained classical actor, with exceptional command of his voice and speech. In the first scene of the play, he bursts through Raina Petkoff's bedroom window, having just climbed up her drainpipe, fleeing enemy soldiers. His first lines explain why he might have to kill Raina. He talks about what it's like being a soldier. How some soldiers are different from others. Why he, for instance, carries chocolate instead of pistol cartridges. And so on. Richardson played all this while panting. He acted exactly like a man who had just physically exerted himself climbing up a drainpipe.

"Well, one night, Shaw came to see the play. Afterwards he gave Richardson a note. What you're doing is very good acting, he said. It's a very good performance for Ralph Richardson. Unfortunately, it's not so good for George Shaw.

"Do you see what he meant? Richardson's realism was weighing down the moments. My plays won't stand lengthy pauses, Shaw said. They won't respond to subtext. I write knockabout farces that have to go like the wind in order for them to succeed. *In order to play Shaw well—and Shakespeare, too, for that matter—you must act on the line.* This is very different from acting, say, in film or television, where acting happens between the lines.

"To be in a Shaw play, you have to understand what Shaw meant his plays to be," Bill says. "That's the only way to catch the style of his pieces. And of course I'll repeat what I've already said several times this year: You can't handle Shaw—or any of the classics, for that matter—using your modern, pedestrian speech. That's like trying to lift an elephant with a car jack—it can't be done. You need a stronger instrument, the oratorical equivalent of a forklift. And that means you have to train yourself. I recommend that you read poetry aloud each day. Take classes in singing, voice, and speech. Develop the breath control of a professional horn player. Most of you probably go to a gym to develop your bodies? Would that you valued your voice and diction enough to put them through similar training."

"I hear what you're saying about horn players," Cheryl says. "When doing this material, I find myself running out of breath a lot."

"Part of that is because you're not yet grounded in what you're saying," Bill says. "If you know what point you're trying to convey and work to make your partner see the logic—really understand it in every detail—your words will ride on the flow of your breath, the same way they do when you tell your friends about that crazy adventure you had last weekend. Do you ever get winded when telling that kind of story?"

Cheryl grins. "I don't."

"Because you're in your own element," Bill says. "You absolutely believe in what you're saying and you insist on getting your point across for the listener's benefit. Apply that same motivation to Shaw and you'll start to see some improvement."

Cheryl says, "What about costumes? Should we try to work with them?"

"Yes," Bill says. "You should approximate the fashions of the day as best you can. People of Shaw's time dressed more formally than people do today. Anything you can wear to give yourself a sense of the period will be helpful; that includes changing your hairstyle. In your case, Cheryl, the use of corsets had declined by 1912, but women of breeding still possessed unerringly upright posture. Very expensive dresses still dripped with ornamentation, but you don't have to worry about that for your rehearsals. Get practical. Find a long skirt or dress. Do some research on shirt-waists and take plenty of hints from films such as *My Fair Lady*, *The Winslow Boy*, *A Room with a View*, and *Titanic*, and pretty much any episode of *Downton Abbey*."

Bill turns to Jon. "You could learn a lot from the same sources. The key to men's clothing of this period is the sack coat, which is cut much longer than suit jackets you and I wear today. Don't fret about finding an actual sack coat, though. A shirt, tie, and jacket will give you the same basic silhouette. A waistcoat will also help; you can use a suit vest for this, and the higher the buttons extend, the better. Ideally, if you have a tuxedo, you can wear that. It should work perfectly."

"That won't be a problem," Jon says. "My day job's in catering."

Bill nods and turns to the class. "In a professional production, these elements would be handled by your costumer. But take this piece of advice: If you're cast in a period piece, visit the costume shop before rehearsals begin. Women should ask for a corset and fan if those pieces apply. Men should get a swagger stick, a cloak, a hat, or reasonable facsimiles thereof. But regardless of gender, ask for a pair of period shoes and start moving in them right away."

"Why shoes?" Quid asks.

"Our culture has grown addicted to sneakers and loafers," Bill says. "As a result, our posture suffers. Even a good pair of modern shoes won't help you find the authentic carriage of someone from a different era. Don't wait until your first dress rehearsal to explore how your character stands and walks. Physicality is such a major cornerstone of character work, you should work with it from the beginning; it's a foundation for your role."

∎∎∎∎

William Wycherley's *The Country Wife* debuted in 1675. The comedy's intersecting plots concern a renowned rake with the apt name of Horner who returns to London from France declaring that syphilis has rendered him impotent. This is a ruse. Horner's real ambition is to seduce as many women as he can. Convinced they have nothing to fear from a eunuch, men grant Horner unfettered access to their daughters and wives. At which point, Horner makes good on his mission.

Enter Margery, a seemingly simple, pretty girl whose husband is the decrepit and cantankerous Mr. Pinchwife. Pinchwife found Margery in the country and married her hoping that her naïveté would prevent her from having affairs. Sadly for him, young Margery's lack of experience only inflames her budding libido. Instead of disdaining affairs, she wonders, Why shouldn't I have one? Or more than one, for that matter. Driven by her urges, Margery tears through the societal mores of seventeenth-century England while, hilariously, forcing her husband, Pinchwife, into fits of high anxiety.

To protect his investment, Pinchwife locks Margery in her room. She complains so much that he eventually lets her out of the house. But Pinchwife, always on the lookout for rakes, insists that she disguise herself in men's clothes, the better to conceal her womanly charms. While masquerading, Margery gives her husband the slip and meets Horner, who sees through her disguise and sets about seducing her.

When Pinchwife discovers the affair, he doesn't take it well. Incensed, he hauls Margery to a table, where he forces her to sit and write a letter to Horner, which he dictates:

> *Sir, though I suffer'd last night your nauseous, loath'd kisses and embraces, yet I would not have you presume that you shall ever repeat them. . . . I am out of your hands [in order] that you may forever more cease to pursue her who hates and detests you as much as she loves her Husband and her Honour.*

Margery attempts to doctor Pinchwife's language, but he discovers her deception and threatens to stab out her eyes with his penknife. So she concocts a new plan. While Pinchwife runs to fetch sealing wax, she writes a second letter to Horner—this one is a love letter. Pinchwife returns, reviews the first letter, and finds it satisfactory. He never suspects that the innocent little dope who is his wife will switch papers before sealing the second letter under his very nose.

When Bill assigned this famous scene to Trevor and Amber, he said: "In many ways, this is a cynical play. By the end of it, the bad guys stay bad, the innocents are no longer innocent, and Horner, the rake, has gotten away with cuckolding half the men in London. To get a grip on that kind of sentiment, you should know what England was going through during this period.

"We call this era the Restoration because the English monarchy returned to power after ten years' parliamentary rule by the Roundheads and Oliver Cromwell. Cromwell helped bring about the beheading of King Charles I. He later became lord protector of England, Scotland, and Ireland, but his new world order collapsed when he died and his son, Richard Cromwell, showed himself a weak leader. The Royalists returned to power and asked Charles's son to be their new king, Charles II.

"Charles II had lived in exile during the interregnum. When the English Civil War started to turn against the royals, loyal supporters had dressed Charles as a woman and smuggled him out of the country; he was sixteen years old at the time. It took fifteen years for the Royalists to regain power. By that point, Charles had grown into a handsome, lazy, womanizing cynic. Nonetheless, he was a shrewd man, and very much a political animal. He accepted a throne with limited powers. He allowed Parliament to choose which plotters would be punished for overthrowing and executing his father. As a perfect nod toward the mood of the era, Oliver Cromwell's corpse was exhumed and hanged as a traitor before authorities decapitated it and posted the head on a spike above Westminster Abbey."

Bill pauses to think. "Sometimes I equate the mood of the Restoration with that of the Roaring Twenties. Imagine what it was like when the long, brutal campaigns of World War I had ended. Repression lifted throughout the West and all hell broke loose in a kind of giant party. In both eras, sexual mores very quickly evolved. Charles II was a libertine who later acknowledged twelve illegitimate children by seven mistresses.

"By the way, the poster child for the Restoration's hedonism had to be the Earl of Rochester, the extraordinary poet. Charles and Rochester used to go whoring together but Charles, being the king, never carried any money. On one occasion I read about, Rochester finished his outing first and exited the brothel. He left Charles there to explain that he was, in fact, the king; evidently, no one believed him. A great book that will help you get a feel for this period is Graham Greene's *Lord Rochester's Monkey*.

"But to really understand the Restoration's cynicism, consider the era's three great disasters. You can read all about these in the *Diary of Samuel Pepys*. London was a city of about four hundred thousand people back then. They say that between seventy thousand and one hundred thousand succumbed to the Great Plague of 1665. Imagine what it would be like if a quarter of the population of New York City suddenly took sick and died. In all likelihood, the actual number was probably higher than that; during the outbreak's zenith, officials became so inundated, they simply abandoned their record keeping.

"No one knew what caused the plague. Whenever someone contracted it, the authorities sealed the victim and his or her whole family inside their house and painted a big red cross on the door and posted a guard out front so no one came in or got out. The infected would lower baskets out their windows so people could give them food. And every night, people threw bodies out their windows. Porters would come around, pick up the corpses, and cart them away to mass burial sites. People fled London in droves but found no succor in the countryside. The citizens of nearby towns would stand outside their settlements holding pitchforks, allowing no one in. Religious leaders preached that the Day of Reckoning had come. All order broke down. And that's when the next disaster struck.

"The Great Fire of London started in a bakery on Pudding Lane off Eastcheap in early September, 1666. It grew for three days and eventually obliterated most of the city. Again, it's impossible to know how many people perished; the heat of the blaze likely cremated anyone caught in its grip. But we know that fully seven-eighths of the city's inhabitants were rendered homeless. By any measure, the destruction was catastrophic.

"Disaster number three. The following June, in 1667, the Dutch delivered what, to this day, remains England's greatest naval defeat. With no money left for their upkeep, Charles left his heaviest warships docked at Chatham. The Dutch ships simply sailed up the River Medway, with those aboard destroying whatever they pleased. They burned three of England's greatest ships and towed the royal flagship, which was named after Charles, back to Holland as a trophy. This led to yet another Anglo-Dutch war, which eventually spread to consume colonies in the Caribbean."

Bill turns to Trevor. "So what's in all this that can help your acting?"

"Society is breaking down," Trevor says. "There's no such thing as law and order anymore. That can lead to desperation, which can be food for comedy."

"It can if you have a clear idea for your character," Bill says. "What are you working with?"

"The script says Pinchwife is in his fifties," Trevor says. "But I think the older I make him, the more he'll contrast with his very young wife, and the funnier he'll be. He's also so cantankerous, he threatens to kill Margery's pet squirrel."

"These are details," Bill says. "I'm interested in something more holistic. Do you have a concept for your part?"

Trevor pauses. "I'm not quite sure what you mean."

"I once had two students play the Pinchwifes as dogs. He was an old bulldog, lumbering, growling. A menace, you see what I mean? But slow. This worked in part because the actor looked like a bulldog. On the other hand, the actor playing Margery was a poodle. She pranced around like a show dog, lithe and high-pitched, always posing. Using these templates helped the actors create specific behaviors that highlighted the contradictions between them. The result was hysterical.

"I had another student play Pinchwife like a rooster. Each of his manic ejaculations came out like a cockle-doodle-doo! Another student played Pinchwife like a Model T Ford."

Trevor blinks. "A Model T?"

Bill nods. "He made the character so decrepit that, whenever he got excited, it was like his motor was cranking up." In his chair, Bill's eyes go suddenly wide. His body begins to quiver then tremble, until, finally, he's shaking full out and a line from the play bursts forth from his lips. "Force you! Changeling!"

The class laughs. Amber frowns. "Isn't that a bit theatrical?"

Bill shrugs. "What's wrong with being theatrical in the theater? And what better venue to apply broad behavior than the classics? Frankly, it's this notion of having a clear idea for your character that actors often miss when playing the classics. And that's a shame. I mentioned playing Pinchwife like a rooster. If that's what you choose, that becomes the framework in which you build your performance. All your Actions, all your lines, every component of your performance can find a home within the concept. If your idea is sound, it will serve as a worthy vessel for everything the playwright intended your role to be, and everything your creativity makes it. In rare instances such as these, your take on the author's brilliant writing creates something more than the sum of its parts. You may even capture some things the author did not intend, yet which nonetheless lurk within the character he or she wrote. When this happens, you've achieved the pinnacle of the actor's art and craft: a synthesis between word and deed, writer and actor, that creates a living character."

"You're encouraging us to take on outlandish behaviors," says Trevor. "I guess I'm concerned. If my behavior is so outlandish, can it still be taken as truthful?"

"It can if you stick to the reality of doing," Bill says. "Pinchwife is a comically anxious character, but make no mistake: his anxiety is real. *The Country Wife* is farce, which I define as the intense pursuit of a ridiculous objective. So the technique is this: Devise a simple, specific concept for your character. This provides the platform on which you create behavior that's normally off the charts.

"I once had a student, Richard Gang, whom I directed in *The Rivals,* another Restoration comedy. Richard came up with a great idea: His character lost his train of thought whenever he got angry. Whenever he saw his son, he'd get sputtering mad. Apoplectic! He'd point his finger and launch a tirade, but his anger would render him speechless." Bill's face turns livid; enraged, he points at Trevor and says: "You . . . you . . ." He can't find the right word, but suddenly he barks: "Arf! Arf! *Dog!*"

The class howls.

"You see how it's all the reality of doing? Richard *really* got angry. He *really* lost track of what he was saying. *Really* hunted for the right word. *Really* went with the first sounds that popped in his mind. Which *really* led him back to the word he'd intended to say in the first place. So there you have it. No idea is too crazy if the actor can make it work, and he did." Bill turns to Trevor. "So tell me. In this scene, what does Pinchwife do to his wife?"

Trevor looks at Amber. "I Interrogate Her a lot. I Command Her to do things. I Threaten Her. I Lie to Her in order to manipulate her. Often, in asides to the audience, I Celebrate My Genius."

"Exactly," Bill says. "And do you see how lucky you are? We've already discussed how Actions are universal across cultures and eras. In other words, there's no difference between Interrogating Somebody back then and Interrogating Somebody now. So your Actions won't change one bit. Whatever character element you choose will simply inform *how* you play those Actions." Bill thinks for a moment. "Will it help you to break this scene into Beats?"

"We're way ahead of you," Trevor says. "We've broken it down into four, and we've named them using lines from the play. The first Beat is How Was't, Baggage? In this Beat, I drill Margery with questions to get to the bottom of how completely Horner has violated her. I balance everything she says against my inner truthometer and determine that she can still be saved so long as she never sees Horner again.

"This leads us to the second Beat: I'll Have You Write a Letter to Your Lover. This is where I dictate the letter to Horner. Margery protests, but I Hound Her until she complies."

"Correct," says Bill. "You'll need some props at this point. A pen—a plume would really be best—plus a little bottle you can use as an inkwell. You'll also need paper, sealing wax, and the penknife you use to threaten her. Make sure it's something that isn't really sharp, please."

Amber nods. "The next Beat is I Will Not Send It. This Beat is really my monologue. My husband leaves to get sealing wax and I talk aloud about why I don't want to write a bad letter to Mr. Horner. Which leads me to concoct my scheme: I'll write a second letter expressing my true feelings and somehow switch one for the other before my husband can find out.

"The fourth and final Beat is Where's the Wax and Seal? My husband returns. He examines the first letter and finds it exactly as he dictated it. Satisfied, he goes to seal the letter, but I intervene. I say, 'Lord do you think me so errant a fool, I cannot seal a letter, I will do't, so I will.' Quickly, I switch letters, seal the second one, and give it to him.'"

"And Pinchwife leaves none the wiser." Bill nods. "I'm curious. Your husband asks about your exploits with Horner. He makes you repeat the story over and over again, hoping you'll slip up in the recounting. Why are you so frank and honest in your answers? Wouldn't it be easier for you to lie about your rendezvous?"

"That's not the kind of woman I am," Amber says. "What makes this scene really fun for me is that I have a different type of intelligence from my husband's. He's one of those people who are so smart, they're dumb; I'm one of those people who are so dumb, they're smart. Or 'simple' is really a much better word. Why shouldn't I be honest about what's happened to me? I found it exciting! It made me feel great! I'm going to play Margery sort of like a hippie: a simple, blithe spirit who can't really fathom how anyone could be as mean as Pinchwife."

"That could work," Bill admits. "I've also seen actors make Margery more conniving. Knowing how old and jealous her husband is, she feeds him horribly graphic details about her rendezvous hoping he'll have a heart attack and die."

"I thought about that," says Amber. "It just didn't sync with my take on the script. My instincts tell me the third Beat comes from a more honest place. I'm not scheming, I'm trying to improvise my way out of the situation. Like: 'My husband wants me to lie to Mr. Horner but I don't want to lie to him, so what's the answer? Aha! I'll write another letter! But what will I say? Let's try a few lines.' For me, that spontaneity of ideas and the way I respond to them holds the key to Margery's innocent brilliance."

"Good," says Bill. "Let's see if it works. Can you put it on its feet for next time?"

Trevor and Amber nod, but Amber has one more question. "Bill, in our rehearsals, I've followed the reality of doing and tried to really write out the lines my husband dictates to me. It's not working. It slows down our rhythm too much. I haven't even started using a real quill, which will probably slow things down even more. What should I do?"

"Do you remember how I suggested you play sleep last year?" Bill says. "Obviously, you can't really go to sleep onstage. But you could give yourself a sleeplike activity to play."

Amber nods. "I thought that's what you might say. Writing the actual words isn't so important as making sure I understand everything he wants me to say. Or using the proper language of love when composing the second letter."

"Correct," Bill says. "So give yourself a substitute Action when you write, one that will help you move the scene along but still gives you an activity to concentrate on. Also, note how your lines help you. For instance, you say 'So' a lot. What can you do with that?"

"I say that word to announce I've written the end of a sentence," Amber says. "Whenever I say it, I'll dip my pen in the inkwell to refresh it. That will give the illusion that the writing is rolling along."

"Very nice," Bill says. "As far as your costumes go, long skirts were the order of the day for women. You could certainly use a corset, though I've seen this played where, alone, in the privacy of your chambers, you're simply wearing a dressing gown. After all, it's not like your husband allows you to go outside." He turns to Trevor. "Men of the Restoration wore the equivalent of our Cuban heels. See if you can find a pair of shoes that gives you an inch and a half of lift. Get some tights and roll up your pants to the knees to show off your calves. If you have a bathrobe, take the tie off it and use the robe, because it almost perfectly mimics the cut of a period frock coat. You're lucky the Studio's located in the Garment District. Look around the shops in our neighborhood. Buy a cheap felt hat and get a plume to put on it. Get something to wear as a cloak as well. Experiment with how it feels to move in this getup and build that into your performance."

▪▪▪▪

After a few adjustments, *The Country Wife* turns out to be hysterically funny.

Trevor's tall, skinny frame looks positively skeletal in the costume he's put together. He has found a frazzled period wig that keeps sliding off the top of his skull whenever he gets angry; this happens frequently. His Pinchwife is preposterous: a petty, preening pout of a man, bipolar in his mood shifts. One moment, moon-eyed, flashing his underdeveloped calves, he stares at Margery, hoping she'll pay attention to him. The next, he erupts with a fury that makes him hop up and down like a child, or a flea.

In Trevor's capable hands, Pinchwife has become a stutterer. The angrier he gets, the more impaired his speech becomes. This would be funny enough in itself, but each time he stammers, Amber does a double take that spirals the comedy further and further out of control. Her simple, innocent Margery has all the girlish enthusiasm of a kid who's just come from the circus.

"'He put the tip of his tongue between my lips!'" she swoons. "'And so musl'd me! And I said, I'd bite it!'"

Her meaning is so clear, so lascivious, Pinchwife clutches his chest and nearly collapses. Margery reacts as though she's amazed, which wrenches more laughter out of the audience.

Trevor has also found an interesting take on Pinchwife's asides; he uses them to reveal his inner vision of himself. When speaking to the audience, his stutter vanishes. He draws himself up to his full height and squares his shoulders in a manly posture. His manner becomes debonair, cunning, and eloquent, like that of a master criminal. But the moment he returns to confronting his wife, his body slumps and his stutter resumes.

This sudden devolution makes a clear and poignant point: Pinchwife is a legend in his own mind. To him, his scheme to dictate the letter is a stroke of brilliance rivaling the invention of, say, the wheel, or possibly indoor plumbing. To the rest of the world, however, he's nothing but an old geezer with eyes too big for his plate. His interior and exterior worlds stand diametrically opposed to each other.

"Very nice," Bill says when they finish.

Trevor and Amber beam. Bill rarely offers higher words of praise.

"This probably reveals my ignorance," Amber says. "I didn't know the classics could be so much fun!"

Now it's Bill's turn to beam.

THIRTEEN

ACTING IN FILM AND TV

"Theater or film? I often compare the two media to love-making. In theater, onstage, one goes through the entire experience: curtain up, foreplay, excitement, then finally an orgasmic release, curtain down. In film, there's action, foreplay, excitement, and just before you reach the glorious moment of release, the director yells, 'Cut! Let's do this scene again.'"

—ELI WALLACH

"What you learn in the theater, you sell to film."

—SIR RALPH RICHARDSON

One day, toward the beginning of spring, Melissa raises her hand and says, "Bill, I just got a call from my agent. I have an audition the end of this week for a TV show, but I've never acted on camera before."

"Didn't we talk about this last year?" Bill says.

"A little," says Trevor. "Toward the end, but only for a few moments."

"We should spend some time on it," Bill says. "These days, working in film and TV is practically a matter of financial survival. Marlon Brando once said that modern audiences would make a pauper of any actor who dedicated his life to Shakespeare.

Sadly, I fear he was right. The theater may be the most artistically rewarding environment for actors, but it's hard to make a living at it these days. You could work fifty-two weeks a year and still earn barely enough to keep you over the poverty line. Film and TV work rarely challenge an actor's artistic aspirations, but they pay a lot more. You'll need to be facile in these mediums if you want to stay in the business."

Melissa nods. "I want to be one of those actors who bring quality to whatever venue they're working in. So how do I adapt my acting technique to work in front of a camera?"

"The ultimate answer is that you don't have to do much," Bill says. "I was at a luncheon once and someone asked Diane Keaton what she thought the difference was between acting for stage and acting for film. She laughed and said, 'I don't do anything different. Film or stage, it's all the same to me. Acting is acting.' Robert Duvall said the same thing, and you'll hear this from other great actors as well.

"The first adjustment you need to make is one of expectation," Bill says. "The actor's level of control over a finished product varies greatly between mediums. In theater, obviously, the actor connects directly to a living audience. It can be a bit like walking a tightrope without a net. If you stumble and fall, there's nothing below to catch you. We sometimes take that for granted in here, but you won't when you start working in film and TV.

"Few other artistic disciplines are as ephemeral as theater. If an author or a painter or a recording artist isn't happy with what she produces, she can churn out another draft, paint over a landscape, or lay down a few more tracks. But theater exists in the now. This is what Antonin Artaud meant when he said that all words, once spoken, are dead; they function only at the moment they are uttered. He also said that the theater is the only place in the world where a gesture, once made, can never be made the same way again.

"You can't say the same for film or TV acting," Bill says. "In these media, the actor's job is slightly different. Onstage, an actor lives through a whole life in two or three hours. In front of a camera, he lives through tiny moments, most of which last only five to ten seconds. It's challenging work in its own right, but, of course, at the end of the day, for any number of reasons, every moment an actor creates could end up coiled on the cutting room floor."

"That sounds pretty grim," Dom says.

Bill shrugs. "It's the nature of that art form; don't let it discourage you. Think of it this way: The better the moments you create, the more likely they are to stay in the picture."

"I think I understand what you're saying," Melissa says. "But I'm still not clear on what I should do differently when acting in front of a camera."

"Again, very little," Bill says. "And for a simple reason. Your training hasn't been in stage acting or TV acting or film acting, it's been in *acting*. Period. *In other words, truth is always the truth, and truthful acting is truthful acting.* That's one of the reasons this studio has such a fine record of producing actors who work in all mediums. You've trained yourselves to a point where you simply can't help but be truthful. The actor who's properly trained in this manner can easily make the transition to film and television. The opposite isn't necessarily true. It's like learning to drive in a car with a clutch. Once you do that, you can drive any car. But if you learn to drive in a car with an automatic shift, you'll face a massive learning curve. So working on film won't necessitate any major change. You'll just have to make some simple adjustments to help the camera see you."

"Such as?" Amber says. Her pen stands poised.

"You will have to consider the proportions of your performance," Bill says. "Bill Hurt once said that actors should put the truth in the space where they find themselves. What did he mean by that? In a physical sense, he was pointing out that, onstage, the actor projects to an entire house, whereas on film, she can be more intimate. She need only project to the camera, which may be only several inches away. So a moment that demands an actor's physical gesture onstage can often be done through the actor's eyes on film.

"This notion of proportion should also be applied to the actor's voice," Bill says. "When you're acting onstage, you have to make yourself heard; that's a job requirement. Not so when you're working in film or TV. In front of a camera, you should never strain to be heard; let the microphone do all the work.

"I had a student a few years back who was cast in a film with Michelle Pfeiffer. Right before shooting began, the director gathered the principal cast members and had them read the screenplay at a long table. I was curious to know how Michelle Pfeiffer worked at the table, so I asked my student, 'What was she like?' My student said, 'Honestly? I have no idea. I was sitting pretty close to her, but I couldn't hear a word she said.'"

Donna nods. "She never lifted her voice."

"She didn't have to," Bill says. "By that point in her career, I bet she'd done so many films, she must have known that anything theatrical looks awful in front of a camera.

"I had another graduate of the Studio, Harold Perrineau, whose principal teacher was one of my associates, Barbara Marchant. Harold once worked with Sir Anthony Hopkins in a movie called *The Edge*. Harold was still starting out back then, but Hopkins, he said, was very kind to him. Sometimes after a take, he'd call Harold aside and say, 'Don't act so much, it's okay, you don't have to act so much.' Harold said this was very helpful. It was a lesson in proportion, you see? It made Harold realize you don't have to put so much into what you're doing. The camera will pick up whatever you offer and amplify it immensely.

"You should start thinking about the camera like it's a great eye that sees only the truth about you. If you're pushing a moment, the camera will notice. If you're tense, the camera will notice that, too. It's one of the reasons that actors gifted in musical theater sometimes come across as flashy and garrulous on film. Broad gestures and a grandiose presence might work in a big house where most of the audience sits fifty feet away in the upper balcony. On camera, it can be the kiss of death.

"Imagine how uncomfortable you'd be sitting on a crowded bus next to someone with really extroverted intonations and gestures. Now imagine sitting in a dark movie theater and seeing that extroverted person's face splashed fifty feet high on a screen."

Bill stiffens his face to a rictus and waves his arms to indicate that he's filling a massive frame. The class laughs.

"Enough said," Bill says. "Proportion your truth to fit the space you're playing in.

"Here's another adjustment: In film and TV, you have to get used to working alone. This can be jarring for actors who relish the collaborative process. In theater, we have the luxury of exploring a play over several weeks with the director, other members of the cast, possibly even the writer. You probably won't have this experience when working in front of a camera. In film and television, you almost never rehearse.

"Part of the reason is the need to stay on track with production," Bill says. "In almost any film or TV production, there's a lot of money on the line. Directors get hired to stay within budget. To do this, they have to cast their parts well and shoot most scenes very quickly. In TV especially, it's not uncommon to shoot ten pages a day, a very demanding schedule.

"I had a student once who booked an Under 5 on one of the *Law & Order* shows. The show wanted this actor to go out kayaking in New York Harbor. The production team set their cameras up on a nearby wharf. The scene involved floating a Styrofoam cooler down the waterway so the actor could bump into it with his kayak, haul the cooler out of the water, and open it. Turns out there was a dead baby inside. This scene introduced the episode.

"Well, the weather turned bad on the day of the shoot. It was windy, there was a storm moving in. The harbor was choppy, which made it very hard to control the kayaks, let alone maneuver one so it bumped into the cooler on cue.

"The producers decided to push ahead. They had no latitude to reschedule. It took the actor a couple of hours to get the shot the production team wanted, but he finally nailed it—the bump, the lines, the cooler getting hauled from the water. My student said he was never so happy to hear the word 'Cut!'

"Neither, apparently, was the production team. From the wharf someone shouted, 'Okay, guys! Great job! See ya!' Then everyone—the director, stage managers, grips, boom guys, cameramen, makeup folks—they all jumped into their trucks and took off, leaving my student in his kayak holding a Styrofoam cooler as the storm slammed in and it started to rain."

The class laughs. Bill raises his eyebrows.

"You see what I mean? Television shoots can be a grind house where actors are often considered the least essential part of the production. But here's another, more complimentary reason why you won't get much by way of collaboration:

"Another graduate of the Studio, Yul Vazquez, once got hired to work on a Steven Soderbergh film. He was so excited. Here he was working with Soderbergh, a great director! On the day of his shot, Yul arrived on set and met his scene partner. Mr. Soderbergh came over and introduced himself. 'Okay, nice to meet you,' he said. 'Can you show me what you're going to do?'

"The actors started to run through the scene. Soderbergh watched and nodded and said, 'Okay, that's great. Let me just move you over here a bit . . . under this light—there. You're okay with that? Great. Okay. Where's the camera?'

"Soderbergh often shoots with a camera on his shoulder. So an assistant handed Soderbergh the camera and Soderbergh said, 'Let's do a take. Action.'

"The actors did the scene and Soderbergh said, 'All right! That was really great. Thanks.' He handed the camera back to the assistant and said, 'What's next?'"

Dom looks incredulous. "And that was it?"

Bill grins. "That was it. But listen: A couple years later, Yul got hired to work with Steven Spielberg on *War of the Worlds,* starring Tom Cruise. Again, he was so excited. Spielberg! The master of film himself! Again, Yul arrived on set. He met Spielberg, who introduced himself and was very courteous. 'Okay,' Mr. Spielberg said. 'Let's have you start right over there, okay? I want you to walk down this street, see? Right down this street. When you get to that corner, make a right, okay? Let's give it a try. And . . . action! And . . . cut! That was great. Hey, thanks.'"

The class laughs. Bill spreads his hands.

"Were these directors being disrespectful of their actors? Hardly. *They respected them enough to leave them alone so they could do their jobs.* I sometimes hear actors say they want more input from their directors. For the most part, I think that's a big mistake. If you get hired to do a job, you should assume it's because the director liked your work in some other project, or he or she liked your audition tape. You should think of yourself as a professional who's been engaged to render a service, no different from a mechanic hired to fix somebody's muffler or an accountant hired to prepare someone's taxes. Only your job is to create moments of human behavior."

"I get it," Dom says. "If you hire a good dentist, you don't coach him on the proper way to scrape plaque."

Bill cocks his head. "Exactly," he says. "You work alone in film and TV, because you were hired to solve a problem. So that's what you should show up on set prepared to do. Dustin Hoffman once said that the best thing any director can do for an actor is leave him alone. By leaving an actor alone, the director is saying, You're the expert. Now show me how you would play this moment."

Vanessa says, "Bill, I've heard that a lot of TV and film directors don't have the first clue about how to work with actors. Do you agree?"

"Very often, yes," Bill says. "And it makes sense when you think about it. A lot of directors were educated at film schools where they were taught lighting techniques, camera angles, and cinematic storytelling. That makes them experts in shooting a film, not in how best to communicate with actors.

"I often work with the National Film School of Denmark, which is one of the best film schools in Europe. Every time I go to Copenhagen, I meet a fresh crop of directors. Many approach me and admit that they don't know a thing about acting. To them, it's such a mysterious thing. They want to know more about the art form so they can work more productively with actors for the betterment of their projects. I always let them audit my classes so they can see for themselves what the work entails.

"But you know what? In the end, I tell these directors the same thing: No matter how well you come to understand the actor's process, the best thing you can do is leave him or her alone. *Trained actors will always come to work prepared, will always be spontaneous, will always come up with great ideas to put in front of the camera.* Therefore, the less you say, the better. If it's absolutely necessary, give them a little nudge here and there. Then stand back and watch what they do. Keeping your distance will more than likely produce the best results."

Adam says, "Let me get this straight. You're saying that good film and TV actors work out their performances in advance. At home, they take their scripts apart, break them down, and make choices. That way, they come to the set with their homework already done. And this allows them to put their attention on their partner, leave themselves alone, and work moment to moment, letting the improvisation take them for a ride."

"Now that sounds really familiar," Donna quips.

"Does it?" Bill sighs. "I was hoping you'd say that."

The class laughs. Bill thinks.

"Another adjustment you'll probably have to make deals with pace," he says finally.

"What do you mean by that?" asks Quid.

"Stage actors learn to pick up their cues. It's part of our training: to act on the line and to keep the text moving, always moving. But film and TV don't stress this dynamic. In fact, they often discourage it.

"I remember seeing an interview with Frank Langella right after he did the movie version of *Frost/Nixon,* directed by Ron Howard. It was 2008. Langella had already enjoyed many years as a star of Broadway, TV, film—you name the medium, he'd worked in it. He's a genuine actor's actor, but he'd never been asked to carry a film before in the same way he was being asked to carry one here. He called it a great learning experience. At one point, they filmed the first take of a scene. Ron Howard approached him and said, 'You know, Frank, that was great. But you could have taken ten times the amount of time you did. There's no need to rush.'"

"He was trying to give the actor permission to relax and really live through the moments," says Trevor.

Bill nods. "Claude Debussy once defined music as the space between notes. Great film acting is the same, I think. It relies on what happens between the words, not on them. *In front of a camera, more than ever, the actor must never push. He must really leave himself alone and let things happen.*"

"I understand that," Vanessa says. "But I've worked on a few films, and I find it tough to stay focused when somebody's pushing a boom mike under my chin."

Bill raises his eyebrows and nods. "Film sets can be very tumultuous places. You have all these people running around doing their jobs, the caterers, grips, the sound folks, the cameraman, directors, assistant directors, maybe a studio head pops by."

Jon says, "So, Bill, isn't it true that acting for film and TV requires a great deal of concentration?"

"What," Bill says, "you don't need to concentrate onstage? Your work so far has required no concentration at all?"

The class laughs. Bill grins.

"No, it's true," he says. "There's a certain type of focus you have to have. My son shot a film with Ben Affleck once. He said the crew spent all day on one long, elaborate crane shot that would catch the characters one at a time as they entered a party and follow each of them for a bit before picking up another character, then another, while a crowd moved back and forth between them. The way he described it, it seemed more like dance choreography than a scene in a film. But film actors handle these challenges all the time.

"There's also the Hurry Up and Wait syndrome. Working in TV and film may seem glamorous, but it can also be tiring, very tedious. You might find yourself shooting on location, living in a trailer or a hotel room, away from your family, faced with a lot of downtime. You might spend days waiting around while the technical crew arranges the lights just so. And yes, in such a distracting environment, it's more important than ever that actors stay focused—but not too focused."

"What do you mean?" asks Melissa.

"I'm thinking of something I once heard Sir Anthony Hopkins say. He has no use for concentration; the moment he tries to concentrate on something, it makes him tense. And there's no place for tension in what I do, he said. But if you notice, his attention is never on himself, it's always on something else. So the actor is always involved. Always present. For him, this seems natural.

"Then there was Richard Boone," Bill says. "He studied at the Neighborhood Playhouse long before I did, but I knew him when he was starring in *Have Gun—Will Travel,* a wildly popular TV Western. He told me one time that whenever he was standing around waiting for the director to call action, he'd open his hand and place his entire attention on the lines crisscrossing his palm."

Bill demonstrates. As he studies his palm, his face grows quiet and interesting. His body relaxes at once.

"You see?" Bill says finally. "He gave himself a little activity. Something to break all the concentration he'd invested in his homework. Because really, at that point, just prior to shooting, if your homework's there, it's there. If it isn't, there's nothing you can do about it."

"Bill, not every director runs a noisy set," says Reg. "I have a friend who worked on a Clint Eastwood film. He told me the set was completely silent, no commotion, no noise, no people running around."

"I've heard this, too," Bill says. "Evidently Eastwood's crew have been together for a long time. They know exactly what they're doing and go about their jobs very quietly. And while they're working, Eastwood might amble over to the actors. 'You know,' he might say, 'while we're fiddling with these lights, why don't you run the scene for yourselves? Don't mind us, just do it for yourselves.'"

Reg laughs. "That's exactly what my friend said! So the actors did the scene and Eastwood said, 'Oh, that was very good! Yes, thanks very much, we'll use that.' Evidently, he had the camera running the whole time. And that was it, that was the shoot!"

Bill nods. "I'm willing to bet that, being an actor himself, having been on countless film sets, Clint Eastwood knows a lot about the conditions under which actors work best. So he puts them in a position where they don't think they're acting and, as it happens, he films what occurs. That's a great way to get tremendous results.

"I read that director David O. Russell uses similar techniques. When he shot *Silver Linings Playbook*, for instance, he sometimes withheld lines from his actors. Instead he had them improvise a situation and, right in the middle of the action, he'd throw them their lines from off camera. Were the actors' performances spontaneous? Of course! They had no idea what words would come out of their mouths next. You could practically see that on their faces."

Bill turns to the class. "We've often discussed how spontaneity is the secret sauce of acting. It's practically the cornerstone I built this school upon. Spontaneity is never more important than when you work in film. As I mentioned, the camera sees everything. If you're not alive and completely in the moment, if you appear to be withheld at all, the camera will only amplify how uncomfortable you look. This is one reason why most people wince each time a politician appears on TV."

The class laughs, but Bill is serious.

"Consider Marlon Brando," he says. "In later years, people accused him of being a lazy actor because he wrote out his lines for *The Godfather* and placed them all over the set. He jotted one line on the blotter of his desk, pinned another one to the lampshade, hung another one on the ceiling. When the camera rolled, Brando didn't know what to say next, so he'd search for the line and read it. But you see, that wasn't Brando being lazy; he could certainly have learned those lines. He was striving for something altogether different: the kind of indelible spontaneity a person has when he really and truly has no idea what he's going to say next. Our technique is built on the reality of doing. Well, the camera would catch Brando's eyes darting about or a subtle twist of his head while he really and truly searched for the next words to say. Was it effective? I suppose. He won an Academy Award for that role."

"Bill, what about continuity?" Cheryl asks.

"That's something you have to keep in mind, of course," Bill says.

"I'm not sure what you're referring to," Ray says.

"Films are put together like puzzles," Bill says. "Think of each shot as a piece that fits somewhere into the final schema. But the pieces are rarely shot in chronological order, and this provides an additional challenge to the actor. Suppose your character has an arc that spans the length of the film—a scene in the beginning, another scene toward the middle, then another scene toward the end. You might shoot your final scene on your first day of work. Then your first scene. Then the middle. In essence, you might be forced to live your character's evolution backward.

"It's very challenging for an actor to ground himself in where his character is at the moment a scene takes place. You have to keep track of how your character's grown. You must ask yourself: What does my character know in this scene? What do I *not* know? What has happened to me? What do I want? And of course, in the end, you must always remember that *film is not an actor's medium.*"

"What are you saying?" says Mimi. "Some of the most memorable performances I've ever seen were on film."

"I'm sure," Bill says. "But those performances aren't solely the actor's work. Very often, they have a lot to do with the mechanics of filmmaking. How the film was edited, for instance. The camera angles employed, the lighting, the music, the Foley artists. Even the lines should be considered suspect, since, many times, actors get called back in to redub lost dialogue or to alter it in an ADR session.

"The point I'm trying to make," Bill says, "is that the actor's contribution is just one piece of a very large puzzle. So what can he or she hope to contribute? The answer should be obvious, I hope. The core of acting never changes. It's always about what goes on between you and another person, regardless of whether that person is an ape, an evil genie released from a bottle, or a magical talking robot car. You can fill in those blanks however you like. The possibilities are endless, as are the possible expressions of story, which have existed since the beginning of time. So, too, have the many ways people behave toward one another in different situations, and this is the actor's province."

"What you said about the many pieces to the puzzle," Joyce says. "It reminded me of something Ingrid Bergman once said about acting on film: Doing nothing is better than acting badly or wrong. In essence, she was saying that it's better for an actor to do too little on film, since 'There will always be the violins to give your character the right mood.'"

Bill chuckles. "I read that, too," he says. "Evidently, the script to *Casablanca* was rewritten so many times that Bergman didn't know what she should play in her big close-up at Rick's Café. Was she in love with Humphrey Bogart or with Paul Henreid? The script wasn't locked at the time she was shooting, so she decided to make her face a blank slate and let the sound track tell the story when they dubbed it in later. I'm not sure if I'd recommend that approach in all cases, but it certainly highlights something important about film as an art form. The camera loves secrets. It thrives on subtlety. Craft your performance accordingly."

Bill takes in the class. "Full-time students here at the Studio work in front of a camera for sixteen weeks. If you're not full-time, you can always take the class separately, and I urge you to do so. It will clarify how to implement a lot of the adjustments I'm talking about. There are other ways to explore this, of course. These days good video cameras are everywhere, and they cost very little. The best piece of advice I can give you is to pick one up. Get together with some of your pals and start to fool around with it. Give yourselves scenes and experiment with how to craft a performance that best fits inside a lens. You'll discover very quickly how to adapt your training. But more than that, you'll demystify what is, to many actors, a needlessly arcane subject.

"It should also go without saying," Bill adds, "that you should see as many performances by accomplished theater artists as possible. There's no better education for actors than to sit in front of the best practitioners of our craft and watch them create something living and unique before your very eyes. The actor who can master that process onstage will find that he or she has very little issue working in film or television."

FOURTEEN

COMMENCEMENT:
THE SERIOUS ACTOR BUSINESS

"Keep working. Never be 'available.' . . . Keep playing in theater or TV, anywhere, as often as you can. Eventually, if you're any good, somebody will see you."

—HUMPHREY BOGART

"'Get out of show business.' It's the best advice I ever got, because I'm so stubborn that if someone would tell me that, I would stay in it to the bitter end."

—WALTER MATTHAU

The final day of class has arrived. The actors turn in their chairs and kibitz with one another, laughing, though some have tears in their eyes. In their faces, I can see the immensity of this moment, the startled release that comes when a hard-fought battle ends suddenly—and better, perhaps, than expected. After such a long haul, the absence of struggle opens a kind of pocket in the psyche, a space that, sometime soon, will start to fill again with something new.

For now, however, a sunny yet bittersweet expectation hangs in the air of Bill's studio. Its presence reminds me of my own commencement from Rutgers some seventeen years back. A curious mix of emotions. You feel proud of and humbled by everything you've accomplished, but there's also an element of feeling like a kid on Christmas morning, waiting, almost unbearably excited to open your boxes and see what they hold for your life, your career, your future.

Bill enters and the small talk fades at once. He takes his seat, pushes his roll book aside, and smiles at the class.

"It's time to leave the Studio and set out on your own," he says. "Congratulations. You've all worked hard and grown a lot. You deserve to celebrate, and I hope that you will."

"Just try and stop me," Amber says.

The class bursts out laughing. Bill grins.

"I wouldn't dream of it," he says. "But before you go, I must deliver some sobering news. Forgive me if this dampens the mood, but I would be remiss in my duty as your teacher if I didn't do this." Bill's grin fades as he looks at each student in turn. "You should know that the odds will be dead set against you the moment you walk out that door. The acting profession has always been overcrowded. The last time I checked, only two and a half percent of actors get work, while the other ninety-seven and half percent—the overwhelming majority—do not. Tallulah Bankhead once called this one of the theater's greatest ironies: that the only person who can count on steady work is the night watchman."

Bill shakes his head. "You're a talented class and I've greatly enjoyed working with you. I wish I could predict that you'll all make a living at your craft or—dare I say it?—someday watch as the industry beats a path to your door. But I can't do that. There are too many factors at work: the vagaries of art, the business, and life itself. The only thing I can tell you with absolute certainty is this." Leaning forward, his eyes flashing bright, Bill says: "If you do not commit to this life in the arts—as crazy and wacky and strange as it is—it won't be art's fault that you never succeed. It will be yours."

The students, I notice, are not put off by Bill's directness. Most appear to welcome it. Heads have begun to nod in agreement.

"I once had a student whom I taught and directed at Rutgers," Bill says. "She was a wonderful actor, a gifted comedienne. Every night she got up onstage, she brought the house down. I don't say this very often at all, but she was someone I felt could have been a star; she had that kind of talent.

"After graduation, we put on a showcase, which a lot of agents and managers attended. Almost all of them were interested in working with this actor. Clearly, they saw what I had seen: this artist had immense talent, magnificent potential. The actor was starting to see that, too. But right about then, she panicked.

"She had taken out lots of student loans to finance her under-graduate and graduate education, and she was worried about how she was going to pay her bills. So she went and got a job managing one of those stores where everything in the place is under ten dol-lars. You know the kind I'm talking about? A closeout store where they buy up surplus alarm clocks, wooden hangers, knickknacks, that sort of thing. 'I need to pay off these loans,' she said. 'I *have* to pay off these loans!' And that was that."

Donna frowns. "What do you mean?"

Bill shrugs. "She worked a few acting jobs, but she never went on to have a career. How could she? Her focus was everywhere else." He frowns and shakes his head. "I still count it as one of the saddest moments in all my years of teaching.

"Sandy once told me that he felt his real job was to help art-ists make a living. I feel that responsibility, too. I told this actor she had something special, that she should follow her bliss and take the same leap of faith she always took so ably in her work. 'Everything will work itself out,' I told her. 'You don't know how right now, and that's scary, of course. But you're not supposed to know such things. That's part of the bargain we make with life, with art, with our careers. Get out there and see where your talent leads,' I said. But she wouldn't hear me. 'No, no,' she said. 'I *have* to pay back these loans, don't you see? My God, just look at these *bills!*' So that's the life she committed to. And that's the life she got in the end."

The room has grown awfully silent. Again, Bill shakes his head.

"You know what I hope you'll tell yourselves in days to come, when things look bleak? 'Thank heavens I wasn't born a poet!' T. S. Eliot was the greatest poet of his generation, but he had a day job up until he died. Or you could say, 'Huzzah! At least I'm not a modern dancer!' Can you imagine earning a hundred fifty dollars a week for the ten years your body's in peak physical shape? Most modern dancers have narrower career windows than professional athletes, and they get paid a scintilla the amount. With that in mind, you should thank your lucky stars. Acting, at least, is a profession you can grow in and improve upon as long as you're alive. As you get older, you start to play older parts, but nobody puts you in mothballs."

Bill thinks a moment before going on. "I want you to hear me when I say this," he says. "Actors struggle and that's a fact. They struggled when I was teaching in the 1960s and '70s, they struggled when I taught them through the '80s and the '90s. They're struggling more than ever right now. Unless you're incredibly fortunate, you should gird yourself for a long campaign. To do anything less would be foolish.

"It didn't have to be like this. I remember when Tyrone Guthrie touched off a movement to build great regional theaters here in America. If you don't know him, Guthrie was the founding artistic director for the Stratford Festival in Canada back in the 1950s. It was such a success that he ran an open solicitation in the *New York Times*. Which cities, Guthrie asked, would be willing to host a theater with a resident acting company? One that can produce the classics without the commercial pressures of Broadway? One where culture comes first and profits second? Who would like to take part in a venture like that?

"Minneapolis responded with such enthusiasm that the Guthrie Theater was founded in 1963. It was the start of something daring and new. That same year, Stuart Vaughan founded Seattle Rep. One year after that, we got Actors Theatre of Louisville down in Kentucky. Then St. Louis Repertory and Syracuse Stage. Then Steppenwolf. The Pittsburgh Public Theater. The American Repertory Theater in Boston. And on and on.

"It was such an ambitious time!" Bill says. "With so many theaters cropping up, we hoped that our country would finally come to accept, if not embrace, the arts. We hoped that actors would suddenly find havens where they could work in repertoire, hone their skills, and elevate theater to the cultural force it's become in Europe.

"What an accomplishment that would have been! Recently, Suzanne and I were in Paris, where we got acquainted with the Théâtre du Soleil. Mark my words: The members of that company aren't careerists in the usual sense. They work together, eat together, live together—they're an ensemble in the truest meaning of that word. These players maintain a relationship to our craft that dates back to antiquity, to the troupes of the commedia dell'arte, medieval pageant wagons, even the Greeks. They are voices from the past projected forward to summon the future. They are artists such as our world has always craved: artists for the sake of art, servants of the depthless and indomitable human spirit that's imbued our species since the dawn of time."

Bill spreads his hands. "You know, it wouldn't surprise me if, one day, scientists were to discover a gene for theater. How else can we explain how the actor's art and craft has surfaced across the world, and in every culture throughout history? How else do we explain why every human society has developed its own form of theater? A place where people meet as strangers. We take our seats, the lights go down, and we let them—because we sense we have nothing to fear from the darkness. Something inside us recognizes those fading lights for what they are: a rite of passage marking the moment when, together, we enter a writer's dream to learn something new about ourselves.

"In Bali, actors made this journey using elaborate masks carved from crocodile wood. In China, opera troupes were called Disciples of the Pear Garden; they sang and danced and played their roles for one dynasty of emperors after another. The Japanese developed Noh, Kabuki, and Bunraku. In Africa, Yoruba practitioners used tribal masquerades to summon ancestors and spirits.

"Now do you see why I got so excited about the Guthrie and all the theaters that followed? It was the excitement parents feel when their child begins to walk and talk, the passion of watching something you love step up to claim its place in the world. When regional theaters began to proliferate, I dared to dream that we actors would finally be afforded our rightful place in society: representatives of an ancient tradition which all humanity claims as its heritage. But it didn't turn out that way."

Bill shakes his head. "Yes, we got a lot of regional theaters, and yes, many of the venues I mentioned are still around. But nearly all of them struggle. Each year, it gets harder and harder for them to stay open. Each year, pundits rail about how money is wasted on the arts.

"I'm not naïve. America has always been a capitalist country, but these days I see it becoming more capitalist almost with each passing hour, and I think it's a tragedy. When President Eisenhower left office, he famously warned us to beware the proliferation of a military-industrial complex. That message carried deep ramifications for society, but it rang practically as a death knell for the arts."

"How so, Bill?" Jon asks.

"These days, people are raised to believe that, in order to be successful in America, you have to make a lot of money. But art and money do not always an equation make. Money can screw with an artist's head and soul, and this is one reason why you must work for the love of the work itself. *You must make your art because to do any less would be a fate worse than death.* Your body might live on without art, but it would do so without spirit, without love or grace or longing or any of the innumerable qualities that make us human."

"But we have to eat," says Donna. "We have to pay rent and we have to buy clothes. I agree with everything you're saying, but you can't take the need for money out of society, and therefore you can't take the need for money out of art."   .

"Please understand," Bill says. "I have nothing whatsoever against money. On a practical level, I'm trying to warn you: If money is why you became an actor, you're probably in for a nasty surprise. To you, I would say: Quit acting now. Go back to school and become a lawyer, a banker, or an accountant. Fields such as those are more likely to reward you financially than the arts ever will."

Trevor shakes his head. "It can't be all that bad out there. There's got to be some kind of happy medium, right?"

"There is," Bill says. "But I think you arrive at it by contemplating what success as an actor really means to you, and pursuing the goals of your craft rather than working to fill up your bank account.

"Success as an actor comes from knowing what Paul Sorvino once told me. We were talking about the issues he faced as a professional actor and Paul said, 'There's show business and there's the serious actor business. If you don't know which you're in, you're bound to get very confused.'

"Years ago, I trained an actor who became very successful on a certain soap opera. I saw her interviewed later on. She was very proud of her work on the show, which is great. She makes her living as an actor. That's an accomplishment to be proud of. But she's not doing O'Neill. She's not doing Shakespeare or Shaw. She basically plays herself, day in and day out.

"Maybe some of you will have careers like that. If soap opera work is the extent of your ambition, then may you find your bliss. But many of you will crave more. You'll hunt down scripts by excellent writers and commit to playing in them regardless of what you're being paid or where you perform. And why? Because you are actors. You were born to steep yourself in life, to search for the things that puzzle, confound, and intrigue you the most, find meanings for them, and add them to your understanding of the world."

Bill raises his eyebrows. "Paychecks and opportunities come and go. The only people who stay in the acting business are the ones who fall head over heels in love with the work, the ones who are junkies for doing things truthfully under imaginary circumstances, addicts for creating a living, breathing character out of nothing but the playwright's words, their imagination, and their experience of life. To people like this, creativity is more vital than breathing. They eat, sleep, and dream about filling moments with truthful, idiosyncratic behavior. So that's what they pursue in their lives—not wealth or fame or superficial trappings like that. They live to be artists. Sandy Meisner once said that every human being has a certain number of biological drives. The drive to seek food, water, and shelter. The drive to procreate. But it's as if the artist has one more biological drive: the drive to make art."

Mimi says, "I remember reading an interview with Philip Seymour Hoffman right after he won the Oscar for *Capote*. The interviewer said, Well, you're a big star now, how does it feel? Isn't it wonderful? But Hoffman confessed that he'd never imagined himself doing films. He'd dreamed of a simple life in the theater—riding his bicycle to a Sunday matinee, doing a show, then riding home to his family."

Bill nods. "Sounds like his dream of success was clear: a life where he got to practice the craft he loves. Or, to quote from Stanislavsky, a life where you 'love art in yourself and not yourself in art.' Would any true actor want more?"

Bill turns to the class. "Paul Sorvino knew the truth of it, all right. He knew you'd be a fool to measure your worth as an artist by the number of parts you book. Because the truth is, ours is a curious business that doesn't always value what you've learned here at the Studio.

"I once had a student who graduated from Rutgers, a great actor. She was living in Los Angeles and her agent called with an appointment for a TV show. She got the script and worked on it, did all her homework, planned things out. She did her audition and the show's producers fell in love with her. They called her agent and said, 'We want to take her out to dinner tomorrow night and talk about the show!'

"So the actor went and met everyone—the writers, directors, the show runner. Everyone was so effusive. 'Our show shoots on location,' they said. 'Do you want a house with a swimming pool? We can get you one of those. Do you need a car? No problem. We'll have the studio get you one.'

"My student said she was overwhelmed. Here was her wildest dream come true. She told me she practically floated home.

"But the next morning, these same effusive people called her agent and apologized. 'The producers and I just spoke,' the agent said. 'They're sorry, but they think they made a big mistake.' My student was stunned. 'What?' she said. 'What happened?' The agent said, 'Well, the man who called me said it was lovely to meet you. But once they did, they realized you're not like the part they're casting at all.'"

For a moment, the room is silent.

"They don't trust acting," Tyrone says.

Bill shakes his head. "Not in this case, they didn't. Not in a lot of cases. Very often, film and television producers know nothing about acting, so they can't conceive that someone could do what my student did: bring all of her training and talent to bear on a role and play it as well as she did. They feel safer casting someone who *is* the part."

Joyce says, "But that's so limiting. Michael Caine tells this story about a director who needs to fill the role of a butcher. Someone says he should get a real butcher so it'll look authentic when he cuts meat. But the director says, If I hire a good actor, I'll get a real butcher. Whereas if I hire a real butcher, the moment I put a camera on him, the man will go stiff and the acting will be horrible."

"I couldn't agree more," Bill says. "But this kind of mentality exists in our industry, and there's really nothing you can do about it. Which is all the more reason you should never let the business appraise you. Know your own worth in your heart and your art, and you'll always be a success."

Cheryl has a question. "Bill, can you give us any advice for breaking into the business?"

"I was at a theater conference once where Olympia Dukakis also sat on the panel," Bill says. "Olympia's a respected artist and a generous person. Countless young actors have sought her advice over the years. On this panel, she said she's been asked that same question thousands of times. 'How do you get an agent? How do you become successful?' As if there's some magic pill or a formula, she said, and she laughed.

"She said what most young actors don't realize is that, for every real success she's had, there were hundreds of disasters, awful mishaps where she fell flat on her face. And you've got to be willing to go through that if you want to get anywhere—both in the business and in life."

Bill looks at Cheryl. "Your focus should never be on how to make money. How to get an agent. How to cause a splash. That will come in its own good time provided you put your focus on your work. Rather, the questions you must always ask yourself are these: How can I make this scene better? How can I attack this acting problem from a different direction? How can I gain a deeper perspective on this character? What does this moment mean to me? What's the most interesting way I can play it?

"Do this and you'll stand a very good chance of something really happening in your career, and for all the right reasons: because you're a consummate artist. Because you're on a nonstop quest to master your chosen craft. So get out there," Bill says. "Audition. Be seen. Build your résumé, build your confidence, and take the words of Steve Martin to heart. I once saw him interviewed on *Charlie Rose*. Charlie asked, What's the key to success in show business? Steve Martin didn't miss a beat. He said, You have to be so good, so good they can't possibly not hire you."

Cheryl nods and smiles. "Okay."

Joyce raises her hand. "Bill, I've been in the business awhile, but I still don't feel like I've carved out precisely the place I want. Can you talk about that?"

Bill shrugs. "Maybe the place you want isn't the place the business wants you to have."

"I'm not sure what you mean by that."

"A student graduated from Rutgers and went to L.A., where he started booking jobs very fast. Let's call him Paul. He was a big guy. He reminds me of Reg, a portly fellow, character actor. Paul was very talented, but he ended up being unhappy, so he quit the business and moved back to his hometown.

"A few years later, I bumped into Richard Robichaux, a wonderful actor from Paul's graduating class. I knew they were friends, so I asked Richard what happened. 'Why did Paul leave the business?' I said. 'He was doing so well.' Richard shrugged and said, 'Oh, it's pretty clear to me, really. He didn't want to wear the dress.'"

A moment of silence.

Adam shrugs. "I'll bite. What the hell does that mean?"

"It means you have to know what you're selling," Bill says. "Did you ever see Girl Scouts selling cookies door to door? Have you noticed how they always wear the Girl Scout dress when they do? That's a very big part of making a sale. The cookies are delicious, but wearing that dress, it seals the deal. If you don't wear the dress, you won't sell many cookies."

"The problem with Paul . . . ," Bill says. "He was a character actor, but he desperately wanted to be a leading man, which was never going to happen. When he walked in a casting director's office or stepped in front of a camera, people didn't see Cary Grant, they saw this big lug."

"So that's what they wanted him to be," Joyce says. "I get it."

Bill frowns. "You know what the real shame of it is? At its core, show business is the business of storytelling. And stories present an infinite range of mythologies. There's a place for everyone in the canon—actors of all types, shapes, colors, sizes, and temperaments. Paul was a big lug, but like I said, there's plenty of parts for big lugs—good parts, too—and a million actors dying to fill them. But Paul wouldn't do what the industry wanted, so . . ."

"He sold no cookies," says Trevor.

Bill nods. He turns to Joyce. "You asked me how to carve out the place you want in the business. Here's the best way I know how: Discover yourself and accept yourself. Revel in who you are, but know how people tend to see you and work within that tranche. Don't try playing against it. Accept the parts that come your way until such time as you can choose your own roles. And if that time never comes, well, at least you've enjoyed a great career."

Mimi says, "Bill, I've been in the business awhile, too, and one thing I still have trouble dealing with is the lifestyle. What can you say about that?"

"An actor's life is full of vicissitudes and peculiarities. You might go years without working, especially in the beginning. You might find yourself living between checks, robbing from Peter to pay Paul, or traveling to distant towns where you don't know any-one, and nobody knows you. Playing to empty houses. Showcas-ing in church basements. You might get tired of subletting your apartment. Having a friend or a boarding center care for your cat while you're gone. Running from one audition to the next. Wait-ing around on a film set. Learning your lines while other people are out attending parties, going on vacations, taking trips to dif-ferent parts of the world. I've often said that being an actor is like being in love with a whore. You might put yourself out there again and again and get absolutely nothing in return.

"The actor's lifestyle is very distinct, no matter which level your career is at. I've seen this wear on actors I consider immensely talented. It's probably the primary reason so many leave the busi-ness and take up other pursuits."

"That happened to my friend," Quid says. "He got married. He and his wife wanted kids. They had two, and then . . ." He shrugs.

Bill shrugs back. "In the words of my very talented student, Richard Robichaux, 'The business can be awful for family life.' Richard and his wife wanted a family, so they moved to Austin, where he opened his own studio. Now he has his cake and eats it, too. Richard's a charismatic actor and he successfully auditions for major film roles. Having worked with several of his students, I know that they find him a truly exciting teacher."

Reg raises his hand. "Bill, can you talk about teaching? I've thought now and then about trying it. I bet you have kind of a rare perspective, since you've taught acting both at the Studio and in academia."

Bill nods. "Be warned: Colleges and universities can be highly competitive places where internecine struggles destroy good theater. Academics and artists don't always mix so well. I was on a panel in London once and there was an academic in attendance who'd published something like seventy books on theater. Recently he'd written a critique of Sandy's book. Total hogwash. His whole angle was to single out a few lines Sandy had written about Particularizations and object to the phrasing.

"I found his focus infuriatingly narrow. With all his so-called intelligence, this man had either completely missed or willingly ignored everything Sandy Meisner was about—his intent, his spirit, the art and the ethic to which he'd devoted his entire life. This academic's critique had no bearing on art whatsoever. He was nitpicking, pure and simple. But that's how some intellectual luminaries make a living and a name for themselves. As far as I'm concerned, their antics amount to little more than head games, and head games play no part in my conception of art."

"It's like you told us when we explored period work," Melissa says. "Actors might do a lot of research, but we never get granular for the sake of granularity. We only conduct research to inform our overall performances."

"Precisely," Bill says. "An actor's goal is never to sound smart or to become an encyclopedia. It's to figure out why your character makes certain choices so you can build your performance. For the actor, everything goes back to the reality of doing." Bill pauses for a moment. "I want to be clear on this point: There are still some excellent college and university theater programs out there. You'll know it if you're lucky enough to work with a good one." He snorts. "You'll also know it if you work with one that isn't."

The class laughs.

Reg raises his hand again. "I get your take on academia. But what about private schools and studios?"

"Again: beware," Bill says. "There's plenty of bad teachers out there—actually, atrocious ones. These days almost anyone can read a book about acting and hang out his shingle. These so-called teachers have no reputation and may never have worked in our profession. They want to teach because they think it'll be more fun than working in a bank or going back to law school or something. They often have absolutely no sensitivity to or any interest in art. They never go to the theater. They consider themselves experts, but they don't understand the most basic elements of the work. To people like this, teaching is just an enterprise, and better than that: an enterprise where they can set themselves up as gurus. Some people find this very attractive.

"I once had a student who came to me very confused. She'd taken another so-called Meisner class where her teacher led her through first-year exercises that bore a vague resemblance to our own. The actors practiced Repetition, then came to the door and knocked and improvised their way through a scene. But this teacher told his class they must never express their Points of View.

"It keeps you from putting your total focus on the other person, he told them. Pay no attention to your Point of View, he said. It's worthless."

Adam cringes. "That's crazy. How could that possibly help an actor?"

"It can't," Bill says. "In fact, it would ruin him. Take away an actor's Point of View and what does he have? Nothing! But here was this person pontificating, engendering a new breed of poorly trained actors, some of whom probably went out and taught more actors, and so on. And people wonder why there are so many terrible actors out there."

Bill rolls his eyes. "For anyone with feelings of inadequacy, the sense of power that teaching might grant can be very dangerous. He becomes the kind of teacher that sits people down and says, 'Ha! I'll teach you something, all right. Let's start with this: You're all shit!' Teachers like that tear people down because it makes them feel better about their own utter lack of talent." Bill fixes the class with a pointed look. "Again, I should clarify. Sometimes tearing an actor down is precisely what he or she needs to grow. But a real teacher will then commit to the hard work. A real teacher will make sure to build that actor up again before their time together is through."

Bill looks at Reg. "If you plan to teach, I urge you to see it as both an honor and an immense responsibility. If possible, you should apprentice yourself to a master teacher. Your students will come to you with their dreams. This is a tremendous act of trust that must be met with the same truth and honesty our art has always demanded."

"I understand," Reg says.

"Good," Bill says. "Would that more people did." He looks at the class. "I'll leave you with this. The great playwright Anton Chekhov had a great piece of advice for those who seek to become artists. He said, 'You must once and for all give up being worried about successes and failures. Don't let that concern you. It's your duty to go on working steadily day by day, quite steadily, to be prepared for mistakes, which are inevitable, and for failures.'

"We use the word 'graduation' to refer to the time when you're ready to leave the nest. But there's another word I prefer: 'commencement.' By now, I bet you know why."

Dom nods. "This isn't the end of anything. It's just another moment."

"That's right. So get out there now, and get on with it all. The beauty of your art awaits."

AFTERWORD

S. I. Hayakawa was a semanticist. Semantics is the study of how language influences thought and action. This, coincidentally, is the title of his most famous book, *Language in Thought and Action*. I discovered the book as a young writer and found it fascinating. I still find it so.

As a gag-writer slash dramatist, the central idea of semantics and its implementation have paid my rent for close to fifty years. Here it is: People speak not to express what they mean but to get what they want.

The dramatic application of this idea first became clear to me at the Neighborhood Playhouse, in classes taught by Sanford Meisner, Bill Esper, and others. In its ultimate reduction, dialogue is just gibberish: Its meaning (to the audience) comes—and comes only—from the intention of the actor.

Or, in the words of Bill Esper, "Until you've pinned down an acting object that has a real and deep meaning for you, your speech won't produce any acting. Instead you'll just be reciting the lines."

I have spent my working life endeavoring to quantify the mystical (drama and acting) sufficiently to explain a vision to the actors and the audience. As has Bill Esper, who started me down that road in 1967.

—*David Mamet*

ACKNOWLEDGMENTS

First, I must again offer my profound thanks to the late Sanford Meisner, who taught me to act, direct, and teach.

I must also thank my wonderful children, Michael and Shannon, who, as their careers unfolded, taught me about the rapidly changing demands that our profession places upon young and talented artists.

In addition, I must include all the teachers at the New York Studio. First and foremost, of course, is my wife, Suzanne, who combines a strong technical understanding of Meisner's work with a deep understanding of the imagination and personalities of talented actors. Also, I must acknowledge the important contributions of Terry Knickerbocker, Barbara Marchant, Bruce McCarty, David Newer, Joel Rooks, Deb Jackel, Nancy Mayans, Bill Bowers, Per Brahe, Patricia Fletcher, Judith Grodowitz, Jules Helm, David Kaplan, David and Linda Laundra, Eric Loscheider, Ted Morin, Joseph Pisapia, Anne Waxman, and the late Meir Ribalow.

Of course, we cannot leave out the fabulous, hard-working office staff, led by Laith Nakli, without whom we would not have a William Esper Studio. Thank you to Jared Szafman, Angela Atwood, Eddie Wong, and Quincy Beard.

My thanks also to our astute editor, Diana Secker Tesdell, and our agent, Martha Kaplan.

And finally I must thank all the talented students who through all the years kept the faith and in the end taught me as much as I taught them.

—*William Esper*

Thanks, as always, to Martha Kaplan, ever the steady hand at a bucking tiller.

To Diana Secker Tesdell for making countless astute observations, including the fact that most people don't blush as often as I seem to think they do.

To everyone at Anchor for contributions seen and unseen.

To Bill's students at the Studio, who, over the years, have graciously allowed me to play the role of Fly on the Wall.

To my own students and colleagues, who continue to enrich my craft as both actor and writer.

To Laith, Jared, Angela, Eddie, and Quincy, for always being so helpful.

To Suzanne, Michael, and Shannon Esper, for priceless input and boundless enthusiasm.

And finally, to Jessica and Ethan, who make everything worthwhile.

—*Damon DiMarco*

ALSO BY WILLIAM ESPER
AND DAMON DIMARCO

THE ACTOR'S ART AND CRAFT
William Esper Teaches the Meisner Technique

William Esper, one of the leading acting teachers of our time, explains and extends Sanford Meisner's legendary technique, offering a clear, concrete, step-by-step approach to becoming a truly creative actor. Esper worked closely with Meisner for seventeen years and has spent decades developing his famous program for actors' training. The result is a rigorous system of exercises that builds a solid foundation of acting skills from the ground up, and is flexible enough to be applied to any challenge an actor faces, from soap operas to Shakespeare. Co-writer Damon DiMarco, a former student of Esper's, spent over a year observing his mentor teaching first-year acting students. In this book he recreates that experience for us, allowing us to see how the progression of exercises works in practice. *The Actor's Art and Craft* vividly demonstrates that good training does not constrain actors' instincts—it frees them to create characters with truthful and compelling inner lives.

Performing Arts

ANCHOR BOOKS
Available wherever books are sold.
www.randomhouse.com